STRATEGIC SPORT MARKETING

4

5

STRATEGIC SPORT MARKETING

David Shilbury,
Shayne Quick
& Hans Westerbeek

ALLEN&UNWIN

I dedicate this book to my unforgettable father,
Wim Westerbeek (31 January 1936 to 3 June 1997).
His love of life will continue to inspire me:

Hans Michel Westerbeek

First published in 1998 by
Allen & Unwin
83 Alexander Street
Crows Nest NSW 2065
Australia
Phone: (61 2) 8425 0100
Fax: (61 2) 9906 2218
E-mail: info @ allenandunwin.com
Web: www. allenandunwin.com

National Library of Australia
Cataloguing-in-Publication entry:

Shilbury, David, 1958– .
   Strategic sport marketing.

   Bibliography.
   ISBN 1 86448 461 6.

   1. Sports—Marketing. 2. Sports sponsorship. 3. Sports—
   Economic aspects. I. Westerbeek, Hans, 1965– . II. Quick,
   Shayne P. (Shayne Pearce). III. Title.

796.0681

Set in 10/12pt Garamond by DOCUPRO, Sydney
Printed by South Wind Productions, Singapore

10 9 8 7 6 5 4 3

Contents

Preface

The face of sport has changed radically over the last 25 years. What was once just a local Saturday afternoon activity for both participants and spectators, now takes place on any night of the week, and can be intrastate or interstate, with the fan experience live or mediated. In increasing numbers supporters are demonstrating their allegiance to sport via the merchandise they buy, the literature they read and the television they watch. Sport in the 1990s is a multifaceted, multimedia industry, with growing appeal to an ever-increasing number of stakeholders and supporters. What was once a clearly defined, stable activity is now a highly complex, constantly changing industry. This is the environment in which the current generation of sport marketing practitioners must operate.

The sport experience can present a host of problematic consumer preferences for the sport marketer to target—this is compounded by the fact that sport no longer faces competition merely from within its own ranks. With decreasing amounts of leisure time, and discretionary income being judiciously allocated, sport now has to compete for the consumer dollar with a vast array of both sport and non-sport activities. The various branches of the arts, the increasing proclivity toward short-term tourist activities and the growth of passive recreation all provide viable alternatives to the sport experience for the modern consumer. Sport is now just one component, albeit a very important one, of the entertainment milieu.

Given this cluttered environment, sport attracts consumers not through serendipity, but rather through carefully structured planning, creativity and perseverance. Successful sport marketing is the implementation of clearly defined strategies which are rooted in both perspiration and inspiration. The notion 'if we build it they will come' is no longer appropriate. Planning processes are now required that view sport not merely as an athletic endeavour, but as an activity in which multiple individuals and groups can engage.

There is little doubt that sport is changing both on and off the field. While athletes have become fitter, stronger and faster to cope with the demands of the modern game, the management of sport has, at the same time, become a highly professional endeavour. To facilitate this process, and enhance the expertise of those charged with its effective management, education and training is now a vital component of the sport environment. Increasingly both the sport industry and educational institutions have realised that sport can no longer be managed by individuals or groups who do not come equipped with certain skills.

It is important to recognise the range of skills required to manage the modern sporting organisation when preparing the educational framework for future sports managers. The growth in sport marketing teaching and practice is accompanied by a growth in sport management education generally. Sport marketing remains a popular area of study, viewed as exciting and attractive to the next generation of sport managers. The challenge of preparing graduates and practitioners for the rigours of sport management lies in balancing the emotion and tribal character of sport with the need for an objective application of business principles. Modern management of sport is more than just a response to traditional actions or present realities. It encompasses a vision for the future and the strategies and implementations required for bringing about that vision. This vision is based on a well-rounded curriculum cognisant of the need to integrate sport industry knowledge with the fundamentals of management, marketing, accounting and finance, and other business studies. Texts such as this one play an important part in assisting in this process. They are constructed by individuals and groups who understand the sport experience and what it means to play, spectate and officiate, and who understand the meaning of management. In many instances they have moved beyond sport and have appropriated from other fields of endeavour those theories and strategies which, when used appropriately, result in a successful sport experience for all concerned.

The ability to translate theory into effective strategic practice is the result of management education programs that utilise business practice to comprehend contemporary sport while simultaneously remaining cognisant of what sport means to the end consumer or fan. The modern consumer is discerning and needs to be treated as such. This text, through the provision of theory and example, will result in future generations of sport marketers having the skills critical to the successful promotion of their sport.

Strategic Sport Marketing is unique from two perspectives. It is the first sport marketing text to truly integrate international examples. Case studies, sportviews and examples from a myriad of national and international sports and events have been used to reinforce theoretical positions and key points. From Australian Rules Football to European Soccer, from the Sydney Kings to the Chicago Bulls, a concerted effort has been made to include as many popular sports and events as possible.

While this is important, more significant is the fact that there has been a conscious decision to place the text within a framework of strategic decision making. The three major components of the text underscores this commitment. Part I of *Strategic Sport Marketing* concentrates on identifying market opportunities. This section focuses on the consumer and the way in which information can be gathered, collated and utilised in order to establish an effective marketing management process. Part II delves into determining the best strategies to use when dealing with a particular component of the sport experience. Included in this section is the recognition that sporting organisations provide a service. Subsequently, *Strategic Sport Marketing* develops in some detail the theoretical and practical significance of marketing the sport service. Finally, Part III establishes mechanisms for the ongoing evaluation, adjustment and maintenance of the strategic marketing process. Collectively, the three sections provide a seamless comprehension of the integration of consumer, activity and process.

Strategic Sport Marketing is aimed at senior undergraduates and entry-level graduate sport marketing students. It is also a useful resource for the practitioner engaged in sport marketing. While the case studies provide obvious examples of how the text can be used, we hope that this text will be used by sport marketing teachers and practitioners not only to stimulate the thought processes, but to engage with and improve the sport experience for the benefit of all concerned. Finally, it is hoped that the utility of this text will result in calls for ongoing literary contributions to the field of sport management.

DAVID SHILBURY
SHAYNE QUICK
HANS WESTERBEEK

About the authors

David Shilbury is an Associate Professor and Coordinator of the Sport Management Program in the Bowater School of Management and Marketing at Deakin University. In 1990, he was responsible for the implementation of the first business-based programs in sport management in Australia, establishing the Bachelor of Commerce (Sport Management) and the Master of Sport Management. Prior to commencing at Deakin University, David worked for the Australian Cricket Board in Perth, the City of Stirling and the Western Australian Golf Association. He was a member of the Victorian Sports Council in 1995 and has been a member of the Australian Football League Tribunal since 1992. He is also the Foundation President of the Sport Management Association of Australia and New Zealand.

David has been published widely in various journals and has presented papers at conferences in Australia, New Zealand, USA and Europe. He received a Diploma of Teaching and a BAppSc (Recreation) from Edith Cowan University in 1976 and 1984 respectively, a MSc (Sport Management) from the University of Massachusetts/Amherst in 1989, and PhD from Monash University in 1995.

David's principal research interests lie in the areas of strategy, marketing and organisational effectiveness in sporting organisations.

Shayne Quick is a lecturer in Sport Management at the University of Technology, Sydney, and is course director of the Sport Management Program. He has taught undergraduate and graduate subjects in sport management and marketing at universities in both Australia and North America, and has been a consultant for the Sydney Kings, Sydney Swans, IMG, Western Bulldogs, Houston Rockets and the Australian Rugby Union.

Shayne is the founding Vice-President of the Sport Management Association of Australia and New Zealand, and the regional representative for Global

Sport Management News. He obtained a MA from the University of Western Ontario, Canada, and a PhD from The Ohio State University, USA.

Shayne's research has focused on the management of professional sporting organisations in Australia, sport and consumer behaviour, and sport globalisation. He has published widely on these topics and presented papers at domestic and international forums.

Hans Westerbeek is a lecturer in Sport Management in the Bowater School of Management and Marketing at Deakin University, teaching Sport Marketing and Facility Management at both a graduate and undergraduate level. Prior to his appointment at Deakin University in 1994, Hans worked at the University of Groningen's Sport Management Institute in the Netherlands. He was also a founding member and secretary of the European Association for Sport Management and the Sport Management Association of Australia and New Zealand.

Hans has published in the *European Journal of Sport Management* and in conference proceedings of the Sport Management Association of Australia and New Zealand and the European Association for Sport Management. He has also presented papers in Australia, New Zealand and Europe. Hans is currently enrolled in a PhD at Deakin University. He received his BA (PhysEd) and MSc (Human Movement) from the University of Groningen and earned his MBA from Deakin University in 1997.

Hans' principal areas of research are sport marketing, services management, and marketing and culture and their impact on service provision.

1

An overview of sport marketing

CHAPTER OBJECTIVES

After studying this chapter you should be able to:

1   Discuss the role of marketing in organisations.
2   Identify the marketing mix.
3   Describe the importance of marketing in sport organisations.
4   Describe the unique product features of sport and their impact on sport marketing.
5   Define sport marketing.

HEADLINE STORY

MORE GOALS—THAT'S THE LONG AND SHORT OF IT

A good soccer goalkeeper needs to be strong, athletic, brave and outspoken. Until now, being tall has not been a prerequisite . . . the world governing body, FIFA, announced that larger goals were destined to be introduced . . . The motivation is to increase the number of goals scored, a perennial talking point as soccer strives to remain the world's most popular sport ahead of the American-driven challenge of basketball. (Happell & Cockerill 1996, p. 26)

Soccer's dilemma is indicative of the challenges confronting sports in an increasingly competitive environment. Soccer has long remained unchallenged as the world's most globalised sport. This competitive advantage has been based on the high levels of participation and interest in so many countries throughout the world. More than 1 billion people watched the 1990 World Cup, and nearly 2 billion watched the Cup final in 1994 with more than 190 countries receiving television coverage of this event (Waldrop 1994). Gilbert (1995) noted that the 1994 World Cup raked in a profit of $60 million for the US organisers and a further $100 million for the World Soccer Federation (FIFA), the international governing body for soccer. Some of the world's largest advertisers lined up to sponsor the 1994 World Cup. Multinational organisations including Canon, Coca-Cola, Energizer, General Motors, Gillette, Mastercard, McDonald's and Philips were official sponsors of the 52-game event. With intensifying business relationships emerging between major sporting events and large corporations, the marketing function assumes a heightened level of importance. Soccer must develop a range of marketing strategies at all levels to ensure that it remains the world's most popular sport.

Soccer's need to maximise its entertainment value has produced a conflict between the game's traditions and the need to modify and adapt the game to compete in this globalised sportscape. This conflict depicts the heightened importance of sport marketing in positioning organisations to compete successfully, by attracting either spectators and television viewers or, alternatively, participants. In general, the larger professional sports in the past believed that sport would always remain an important leisure pursuit for the bulk of the population. This view has diminished the importance of the marketing function.

Although sport itself has remained popular, individual sports have had to strive to maintain market share as the forces of competition within the recreation and leisure industries have increased.

In the technological world of the 1990s, many other sports have emerged via the media to challenge soccer's position. Basketball, via the National Basketball Association (NBA) is one example, as are tennis and golf. Major changes to the competitive positions of a variety of sports have occurred as a consequence of the media's ability to show sporting competitions played in all parts of the world. Domestic competitions also have increased in familiarity through the media. For example, the former Victorian Football League (VFL) has expanded from a twelve-team state-based competition to become a sixteen-team national competition played in five states. Basketball also has capitalised on its increased exposure, creating the National Basketball League (NBL). Television has contributed to the emergence of new and restructured competitions. Changing environmental conditions have forced sport managers to develop marketing strategies for their sports, leading to the creation of sport-marketing departments and the employment of marketing specialists in sporting organisations.

The purpose of this book is to examine the role of marketing within the sport context. More specifically, it will consider the role of marketing from a strategic perspective, highlighting the ways in which marketing contributes to the growth and development of sports. Marketing assumes greater significance than other management functions in sporting organisations as it remains the principal means by which sports compete off the field. For instance, large firms such as BHP, Pepsi Co. and Pacific Dunlop have the option to pursue acquisition-type strategies to build market share, or to engage in product development or diversification. These strategies are generally not available to sporting organisations, whose principal responsibility is as a national governing body, such as the Australian Soccer Federation, Australian Softball Federation or Women's Cricket Australia. In the broader context of the sport industry, major manufacturing firms such as Nike, Adidas, Puma and Spalding are examples of large firms that do have the capacity to pursue acquisition-based strategies. In sport, each governing body is responsible for a specific code, and its charter is to develop and enhance that particular sport. Minor game modifications may occur, but sport-governing bodies rarely use strategies based on product diversification or acquisition. This is particularly evident for club-based sport systems.

Soccer's desire to make the game more attractive by increasing the number of goals scored is an example of a sport embarking on a market development strategy: creating new markets for existing products by making minor modifications to the product. The importance of marketing strategy in sport management is illustrated by soccer and is further discussed later in this chapter.

MARKETING DEFINED

Marketing, as defined by Kotler et al. (1994), is 'a social and managerial process by which individuals and groups obtain what they need and want through creating and exchanging products and value with others' (p. 5). The identification of consumer needs and wants is a critical aspect of the marketer's role. Marketing strategies must be based on known consumer needs.

In sport, it has been assumed that the original form of the game is naturally attractive and therefore satisfies consumer needs. An analysis of sporting organisations in Australia shows this to be an outdated view. Many sports have modified rules to make their games more attractive, and in the case of cricket one-day matches have become an important part of the range of product offerings. One-day international matches played throughout an Australian summer have more readily satisfied consumer need for compressed entertainment and a quick result. At junior levels, many sports have been significantly modified to satisfy the desire of young people to participate more easily in the game. Inherent in this change has been the recognition that juniors wish to develop game skills through *actual* participation, to have fun, and in general to be with their friends through the sport setting.

The sport marketer must identify what needs and wants are being satisfied through the *exchange* process. Kotler et al. (1994) identify the process of exchange 'as the act of obtaining a desired object from someone by offering something in return' (p. 7). What can be offered in return for the sport consumer's membership fees or entry fee may include social interaction, physical activity, an avenue for competition, health and fitness, as well as entertainment. Identifying the needs of various segments of population is the challenge inherent in the early phase of the marketing process. Obtaining this information will allow the sport product benefits to be communicated in such a way as to define the sport's positioning. For example, the product attributes of one-day cricket matches and five-day Test match cricket are different and likely to attract different segments of the market.

Having established the range of product attributes in relation to needs and wants, the sport marketer embarks on the challenge of effecting the exchange. Sporting organisations must develop a mix of marketing strategies to influence consumers to buy their products, via either attendance or participation. Combined, the four variables of product, price, promotion and place are known as the *marketing mix*.

DEFINING THE MARKETING MIX

Figure 1.1 depicts the four component strategies of the marketing mix, also known as the 4Ps of marketing. The 4Ps form the nucleus of this book, and each will be described in more detail in later chapters. Assael (1990) provides a brief description of each:

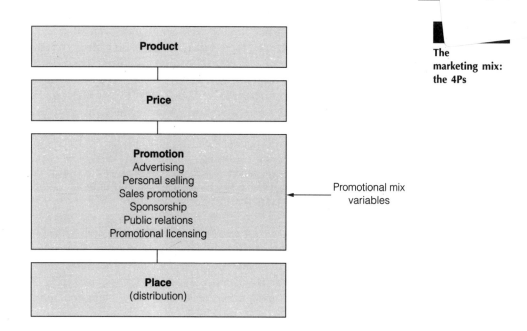

The marketing mix: the 4Ps

- *Product*—ensures that product characteristics provide benefits to the consumer (includes identifying the actual product).
- *Price*—ensures that the product is priced at a level that reflects consumer value.
- *Promotion*—communicates the product's ability to satisfy the customer through advertising, personal selling, sales promotions, sponsorship, public relations and promotional licensing.
- *Place*—distributes the product to the right place at the right time to allow ease of purchase.

In sport, the combination and implementation of these marketing mix variables change due to the unique characteristics of the sport product. These are described in the next section.

UNIQUE CHARACTERISTICS OF SPORT AND SPORT MARKETING

In 1980, Mullin identified, for the first time, a series of characteristics of the sport product that affect the marketing process. Mullin argued that sport had progressed from a form of institution that was simply 'administered' to a form of organisation that required 'managing'. In making this distinction, he noted that sport had reached a phase in its development where it was incumbent on the sport manager to be actively seeking ways to increase the revenue base of the organisation. Typically, the *administrator* is responsible for maintaining the status quo within the sporting organisation. The *manager*, on the other hand, is responsible for assessing and evaluating environmental trends likely to impact on the organisation's survival and, ultimately, its success. The modern sport *marketer* is charged with one simple responsibility: to increase the sources of revenue for the sport. The tools to achieve this will be discussed in later chapters.

Mullin (1985) identified five special characteristics of sport marketing. In examining these characteristics he noted:

> Almost every element of marketing requires significantly different approaches when the product being marketed is sport. Predictably, the critical differences lie in the unique aspects of the sport product, and the unusual market conditions facing sport marketers. (p. 106)

The five characteristics noted by Mullin are summarised in Table 1.1, with supporting examples. Interestingly, some of these characteristics reflect attributes associated with marketing *services*. Whether this was intentional is uncertain; clearly sport is a service product. Service-marketing implications for sport marketing will be further developed and integrated throughout this text.

Consumer involvement

Perhaps the most readily identifiable characteristic is the 'expertise' demonstrated by the sport consumer. On the one hand, this is a disadvantage, as every move made by the sport manager and coaching staff is critically examined and dissected. The 'armchair selector' syndrome is an issue within sport. It is, however, one reason why sport is so popular. The pervasiveness and universal nature of sport, and the ease with which the consumer identifies with the sport product, compensate for the intensity with which the consumer follows sport. Very few businesses in the world are viewed with such simplicity and such personal identification by the consumer.

Unpredictability

Like most service products, the consumer's interpretation and enjoyment of the sport product are open to considerable subjectivity. Participation in, and attendance at, sporting contests allows the consumer to gain varying forms of gratification. For example, some spectators may enjoy the closeness of the game, others the entertainment surrounding the game, and yet others the inherent strategies of the contest. This makes it difficult for the sport marketer to ensure a high probability of satisfaction and hence repeat attendance. The intangibility and subjective nature of sport spectating and sport attending clearly align sport with the service industry. No tangible product is taken from the sporting contest, as opposed, for example, to the purchase of a washing machine or similar good. These characteristics of the service experience will be further examined in Chapter 5.

TABLE 1.1

Unique
characteristics
of sport
marketing

Market for sport products and services
- Sport organisations simultaneously compete and cooperate.
- Partly due to the unpredictability of sport, and partly due to strong personal identification, sport consumers often consider themselves 'experts'.

Sport product
- Sport is invariably intangible and subjective.
- Sport is inconsistent and unpredictable.
- Marketing emphasis must be placed on product extensions rather than the core product.
- Sport is generally publicly consumed, and consumer satisfaction is invariably affected by social facilitation.
- Sport is both a consumer and an industrial product.
- Sport evokes powerful personal identification and emotional attachment.
- Sport has almost universal appeal and pervades all elements of life, i.e. geographically, demographically and socioculturally.

Price of sport
- The price of sport paid by the consumer is invariably quite small in comparison to the total cost.
- Indirect revenues (e.g. from television) are often greater than direct operating revenues (e.g. gate receipts).
- Sport programs have rarely been required to operate on a for-profit basis.
- Pricing is often decided by what the consumer will bear rather than by full cost recovery.

Promotion of sport
- Widespread exposure afforded to sport by the media has resulted in a low emphasis on sport marketing and, often, complacency.
- Due to the high visibility of sport, many businesses wish to associate with sport.

Sport distribution system
- Sports generally do not physically distribute their product. Most sport products are produced, delivered and consumed simultaneously at the one location. The exceptions are sporting goods and retail and broadcast sport.

Source: Adjusted from Mullin (1985).

Equally unpredictable is the actual sporting contest, which varies week by week. This heterogeneity is a feature of sport. It is the unpredicability of the result, and quality of the contest, that consumers find attractive. For the sport marketer this is problematic, as the quality of the contest cannot be guaranteed, no promises can be made in relation to the result, and no assurances can be given in respect of the performance of star players. Unlike consumer products, where consistency is a key feature of marketing strategies, sport cannot and does not display this attribute. The sport marketer therefore must avoid marketing strategies based solely on winning. As a consequence, the sport marketer must focus on developing product extensions rather than on the core product (i.e. the game itself). Product extensions include the facility, parking, merchandise, souvenirs, food and beverages—in general, anything that impacts on spectators' enjoyment of the event. In Chapters 5 and 13, we discuss the methods by which sport marketers can develop and improve the quality of product extensions.

Competition and cooperation

Another feature of the sportscape is the peculiar economy that dictates, in professional leagues at least, that clubs must both engage in fierce competition and at the same time cooperate. This is necessary to ensure that each club's contribution to the league enhances the strength of the league. An unusual blend of politics and competition emerges in sports leagues, often amplifying the importance of the public relations function, to be further explored in Chapter 11.

Sponsorship

Sponsorship of sport is also a unique feature of the sports economy. While not necessarily specific to sport, sponsorship has provided, and continues to provide, an opportunity for commercial advertising by corporations and businesses. Sponsorship represents the 'industrial' component of the sport product, and is manifest through commercial advertising its industrial aspect.

Publicity

Complacency in developing adequate marketing strategies has resulted from an almost unlimited amount of media exposure for sporting clubs, leagues and associations. Sport has traditionally been able to rely on publicity as its principal form of marketing and promotion. The disadvantage of relying on publicity is the amount of negative press that occurs during a season or major event. More recently, major leagues, clubs and associations have become more cognisant of the need to develop an effective public relations strategy to counter the issues that typically occur during a season or event. This book views the public relations function as a very important aspect of the promotional mix.

Distribution

The final characteristic relates to the distribution system used by sport. Like most service providers, sports participation and spectating revolve around specific facilities for specific sports. To attend a sporting contest, spectators must travel to the venue, usually a major facility within a city. The actual facility becomes an integrated component of the marketing function, as the sport product is produced, consumed and delivered at the same time at the same venue. Many facilities, such as the Melbourne Cricket Ground (MCG), Royal Melbourne Golf Club, Fenway Park in Boston and Wembley Stadium in London, have all developed an aura and mystique typically as a result of heroic performances on the ground over the years.

As a consequence of developments in television networks, the distribution system for sport has undergone radical change during the last decade. It is now possible to distribute a game to all parts of the country and the world via the networks. The recent introduction of pay-television to Australia will further enhance the distribution network for sport, as well as increase the number and levels of different sport competitions shown. In general, however, the televised sport product is different from the live event. The mix of benefits is slightly different in each mode of consumption.

Due to the relatively stable nature of distribution (i.e. one major stadium per sport per city) it is vitally important to locate teams and facilities so that they are able to compete effectively in the market. In Australia, product distribution has been the focus of intense debate during the last decade. This is particularly evident in the move to expand the Victorian Football League (VFL) to become the Australian Football League (AFL). In the early 1980s, the VFL was a twelve-team state-based competition primarily located in Melbourne. By 1991, the league had changed its name to the AFL, as it had relocated the South Melbourne Football Club to Sydney, and admitted the Brisbane Football Club and West Coast Football Club in 1987, followed by the Adelaide Crows in 1991. By 1995 a second team from Western Australia (Fremantle) had joined the competition, and a second team from South Australia (Port Adelaide) entered in 1997. Nine teams, however, remain in Melbourne, a city of 3.7 million people. While this is an example of a league reconfiguring its distribution, once established it should remain relatively stable.

A comparison between the United States and Australia illustrates how important location of the product is in terms of developing appropriate marketing strategies, particularly in view of the substantial population differences between the two countries. The United States, for example, has a population of approximately 250 million compared to Australia's 18.1 million. The US national competitions of basketball (National Basketball Association, NBA), football (National Football League, NFL), baseball (Major League Baseball, MLB) and ice hockey (National Hockey League, NHL) have evolved past the point of overcapacity in any one city. Significantly, the three major markets of New York, Los Angeles and Chicago (all with a population of 10–14 million) all host professional franchises. However, not one of these markets hosts more than two teams of any one code. The importance of marketing as a revenue-generating activity for the clubs is important in this issue of location. Overcapacity intensifies competition and reduces the available income for each of the teams located in any one common market.

IMPORTANCE OF MARKETING IN SPORT MANAGEMENT

As indicated earlier in this chapter, marketing plays a key role in the sporting organisation's overall planning efforts. This, however, has not always been

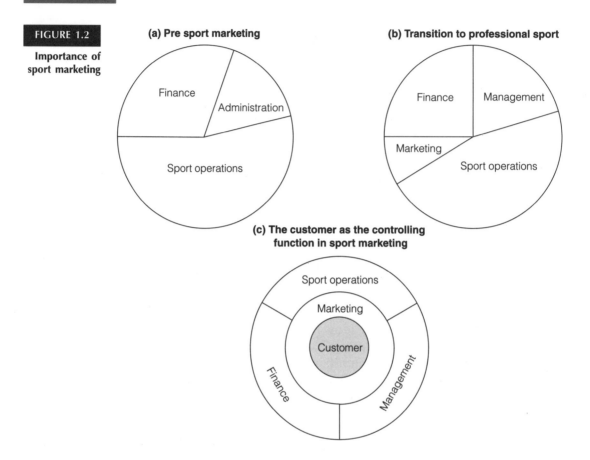

FIGURE 1.2

Importance of sport marketing

(a) Pre sport marketing

Finance

Administration

Sport operations

(b) Transition to professional sport

Finance   Management

Marketing

Sport operations

(c) The customer as the controlling function in sport marketing

Sport operations

Marketing

Customer

Finance

Management

the case. The professionalisation of sport during the last 20–30 years has raised the level of importance of the marketing function.

For much of sport history, volunteers have administered organisations in the true spirit of amateur participation. As sport systems founded on club-based models evolved from amateur to professional clubs, leagues and associations, there was a lengthy transition period between what is described as 'kitchen table' administration and professional management. In Australia, this was the period pre 1970. As Figure 1.2(a) illustrates, during this period of voluntary administration the marketing function was non-existent. The predominant tasks were to ensure the ongoing operation of the club, league or association. Administrators adopted a very narrow view of their organisation, preferring to concentrate on the internal operations of the club, league or association. Typically, administrators dealt with only half of the accounting and budgetary process: the allocation and control of expenditures. Even as sporting organisations began to professionalise, the administrator 'culture' lingered for some years.

Figure 1.2(b) displays the progressive movement away from administration to management of organisations. One of the manager's main tasks is to monitor environmental trends and plan for the organisation's ongoing growth. Sport was very reluctant to embrace proactive growth. The Australian Cricket Board's (ACB) dispute with Kerry Packer over television rights, and the players' push for improved remuneration and playing conditions in 1977, are an example of a major sport adopting narrow internal perspectives. The introduction of colour television was an example of a technological change ignored by the ACB. World Series Cricket (WSC) subsequently proved to be the catalyst that forced sporting organisations in Australia to embrace a greater range of business functions. This view is supported by Halbish (1995), noting that 'looking back traditional cricket had grown out of touch with the fast emerging professionalism of sport in Australia' (p. 3). By 1980, WSC and the ACB had reconciled their differences; however, from that point marketing was to become an important element of business activity in sport.

Initially, marketing activities were outsourced by a number of sports. The ACB, for example, granted marketing rights to a company known as PBL Marketing. Taylor (1984), managing director of PBL at the time, made the following observations about the status of marketing and sponsorship in sport following the reconciliation:

> Five years ago the Australian Cricket Board did not have a published program . . . Last year more than 300 000 copies of the ACB program were sold and this year almost 20 publications will be on sale. Work has also been put into merchandising . . . it has taken five years to develop 29 licensees, but this season we expect cricket merchandise to top $5 million in retail turnover and to start producing a satisfactory level of return. (p. 13)

Figure 1.2(c) demonstrates the importance that marketing has gained, despite a long period of resisting the need to promote and nurture new and fertile markets. For the first time, the identification and nurturing of new markets brought recognition that the customer is central to ongoing organisational survival. Sports had to find ways of generating revenue to sustain the increasing costs of professional competitions. One-day cricket is an example of modifying the product to increase market share for the sport. Together with sport operations (i.e. all that surrounds the management of fielding a team), marketing is a sporting organisation's principal ground for identifying and creating a competitive advantage. Normal acquisitional strategies associated with for-profit firms are not as readily applicable to sport. Internal growth strategies tend to be the major ground on which sport competes. These strategies will be further developed in the next chapter.

SPORT MARKETING DEFINED

The term *sport marketing* was first used in the United States by the *Advertising Age* in 1978. Since then it has been used to describe a variety of activities associated with sport promotion. Two distinct streams exist within the broad concept of sport marketing. The first form of sport marketing is marketing 'of' sport.

Marketing 'of' sport

This refers to the use of marketing mix variables to *communicate the benefits* of sport participation and spectatorship to potential consumers. Ultimately, the goal is to ensure the ongoing survival of the sport in rapidly changing environmental circumstances. It is this aspect of marketing that has only recently developed in sporting organisations. Survival largely depends on the principal purpose of the sporting organisation. National sporting organisations predominantly associated with elite-level professional sporting competitions will be striving to develop their marketing mix to ensure that the sport product is attractive as a form of live entertainment and live television. Sports-governing bodies will also be responsible for ensuring that participation in their sport remains healthy. Participants are the lifeblood for sports as they become the next generation of champions and spectators.

We do not make any notable distinctions in this book between marketing strategies specifically pursued for either *spectator* or *participant* sport. The theories posited are equally applicable regardless of the principal objective of the marketing strategy. Like all marketing strategies, when the objectives change, the actions or strategies used to achieve the objectives also change. The application of the marketing mix does not, although various components of the mix may assume more importance in the two different scenarios. For example, the outlets used to advertise a junior sporting competition would be different from those used to advertise a major sporting event. Students of sport marketing should adapt the concepts of sport marketing to either situation, because each is vital to the ongoing survival and financial well-being of individual sporting organisations.

Marketing 'through' sport

The second form of sport marketing is marketing 'through' sport. *Sponsorship* of sport by firms is an example. Large corporations use sport as a vehicle to promote and advertise their products, usually to specifically identifiable demographic markets known to follow a particular sport. Sports with significant television time are very attractive to firms seeking to promote their products through an association with sport. Developing *licensing* programs is another example of marketing through sport. Typically, major companies such as Tip Top (bread) or Coca-Cola pay for the right to use a sport logo to place on their products to stimulate sales.

Although the main emphasis of this book is on marketing 'of' sport, the role of corporate sponsorship and licensing in sport marketing will also be examined.

Definition

Given these perspectives, and information pertaining to marketing in general, the following definition of sport marketing is offered:

> Sport marketing is a social and managerial process by which the sport manager seeks to obtain what sporting organisations need and want through creating and exchanging products and value with others.

The exchange of value with others recognises the importance of the sport consumer. The many different types of sport consumer will be discussed in more detail in Part I of this book.

OVERVIEW OF THIS BOOK

The ability to recognise the needs and wants of consumers does not necessarily imply action. It is the action associated with the marketing process in sport that is the focus of this text. This is known as the *marketing management* process, which is described by Kotler et al. (1994) as 'the analysis, planning, implementing and control of programs designed to create, build and maintain beneficial exchanges with target buyers for the purpose of achieving organisational objectives' (p. 9).

Chapter 1 has defined marketing and sport marketing, as well as introducing the unique characteristics of sport and how they impinge on the marketing process. Hereafter this book is divided into three parts.

Part I examines how the sport marketer identifies marketing opportunities. Chapter 2 examines the place of marketing in the planning process and specifically reviews the strategic sport-marketing planning process. Chapters 3 and 4 concentrate on understanding the sport consumer, and marketing research, and the implications this information has for segmenting the sport marketplace.

Part II covers the strategy determination stage. It examines the marketing mix and the way in which the organisation is positioned in relation to target markets. Selection of the core marketing strategy is significant in this stage, and the contribution of the 4Ps—product, price, promotion and place—to strategy determination will be examined. Some of the issues specific to sport marketing contained in these chapters include sponsorship, public relations, television and its impact on sport marketing, and promotional licensing.

Finally, Part III returns to the important marketing management process of implementation and evaluation. This part comprises only one chapter, which examines how the sport marketer evaluates the success of marketing strategies and the coordinating function between the sport marketer and the rest of the organisation. Of interest to students in particular is a section on careers related to sport marketing.

REFERENCES

Assael, H. (1990). *Marketing: Principles and Strategies*, Dryden Press, Orlando, Fl.

Gilbert, N. (1995). 'Kickoff time for soccer', *Financial World*, 164 (4), pp. 78–85.

Halbish, G. (1995). 'Developing professional sporting leagues', Keynote address to the Sport Management and Marketing Conference, Sydney, August.

Happell, C. and Cockerill, M. (1996). 'More goals—that's the long and short of it', *The Age,* 4 January, p. 26.

Kotler, P., Chandler, P. C., Brown, L. and Adam, S. (1994). *Marketing: Australia and New Zealand*, 3rd edn, Prentice-Hall, Englewood Cliffs, NJ.

Mullin, B. (1980). 'Sport management: the nature and utility of the concept', *Arena Review*, 4 (3), pp. 1–11.

——(1985). 'Characteristics of sport marketing', in *Successful Sport Management*, eds G. Lewis and H. Appenzellar, Michie Co., Charlottesville, Va.

Taylor, L. (1984). 'The marketing and sponsorship of sport in Australia', *Sports Coach*, 8 (2), pp. 12–14.

Waldrop, J. (1994). 'The world's favourite sport', *American Demographics*, 16 (6), p. 4.

Identification of marketing opportunities

2

The strategic sport-marketing planning process

CHAPTER OUTLINE

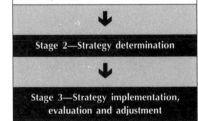

Stage 1—Identification of marketing opportunities

Step 1—Analyse external environment (forces, competition, publics)

Step 2—Analyse organisation (mission, objectives, SWOT)

Step 3—Examine market research and marketing information systems

Step 4—Determine marketing mission and objectives

⬇

Stage 2—Strategy determination

⬇

Stage 3—Strategy implementation, evaluation and adjustment

CHAPTER
OBJECTIVES
Chapter 2 identifies three stages comprising the strategic sport-marketing planning process. Within these stages, eight steps are isolated as constituting the marketing planning sequence for sporting organisations. Steps 1–4 are reviewed in this chapter, with the remaining steps covered in Parts II and III. In sporting organisations, the strategic sport-marketing planning process (SSMPP) assumes great significance because these organisations are often one-product entities, and therefore organisation-wide planning and marketing planning become the same process.

After studying this chapter you should be able to:

1   Understand the strategic sport-marketing planning process.
2   Recognise the role of strategic sport-marketing planning in sport.
3   Analyse the forces driving industry competition.
4   Conduct a SWOT analysis.
5   Recognise the principal strategies available in sport marketing.

HEADLINE
STORY

PLAYERS TO BENEFIT FROM TOUR EXPANSION

The better Australian golfers could soon be earning up to $600 000 on the Australasian circuit as the local tour expands to take in events from Europe, Asia and South Africa . . . The success of the trial marriage—which started with the $1.2 million Johnnie Walker Classic in Singapore—will almost certainly result in more co-sanctioned events, with South Africa the next target as a co-host. (Happell 1996, p. B7)

The Australasian Professional Golfers' Association (APGA) Tour's decision to establish a strategic alliance with other world golf tours is an example of the fine line that exists between organisation-wide strategic planning (planning concerned with the entire firm) and the strategic sport-marketing planning process. The objective of the APGA Tour is to ensure the ongoing survival of a tournament circuit allowing players to compete in a financially secure environment. This requires the Tour-organising body to attract star players such as Greg Norman, John Daly, Ernie Els, Nick Price and Nick Faldo, to ensure interest from the public, sponsors and media in tournament play. For many years, the APGA Tour has struggled because the bulk of the Tour is conducted in the off season for most of the world's northern-hemisphere professional players. The alliance between the Australasian, European and possibly South African tours provides the financial incentive to attract the world's premier players and build the individual strength and credibility of each tour. Rather than each individual tour conducting three different tournaments at three different locations, one large tournament is staged combining the financial forces and playing talents normally dissipated across the three events.

The purpose of strategic planning is to ensure an *ongoing fit* between the organisation and its competitive environment. The APGA Tour recognised that its fit with its competitive environment was diminishing. Its inability to attract star players and the timing of the golf season contributed to this disequilibrium. In essence, the APGA Tour had to find ways to rejuvenate tournament golf (its core product). The revitalisation of tournament golf will, in turn, restore the stability of the APGA Tour, which represents the professional golfers' interests in this region.

Given that marketing is primarily concerned with consumer needs, it is then the responsibility of a company to satisfy these needs. The APGA Tour, for example, must satisfy multiple needs:

- the players, who need tournament play with attractive financial rewards;
- the sponsors, who require star players to ensure that their financial investment in tournament golf attracts maximum exposure via the media;
- the paying public, who wish to see golf played at its optimum level.

Recognising and satisfying consumer needs ensures maximum market share, market development opportunities and growth. Kotler and Andreasen (1991) noted that, 'just as "customer centredness" is the advocated way of thinking about marketing, the strategic marketing planning process is the advocated way of doing marketing' (p. 68). In this book, the strategic marketing planning process is specific in its reference to sport and is labelled the *strategic sport-marketing planning process* (SSMPP). Figure 2.1 illustrates the SSMPP, which includes the following eight steps.

THE STRATEGIC SPORT-MARKETING PLANNING PROCESS

1 Analyse the external environment, the forces driving industry competition and the publics to be served.
2 Analyse the sporting organisation internally, to determine mission, goals and objectives, and to assess strengths, weaknesses, opportunities and threats.
3 Examine market intelligence data in relation to the existing product range.
4 Determine the specific marketing mission and objectives for the prescribed period of the plan.
5 Determine the core marketing strategy using marketing mix variables, identifying and selecting the desired competitive position in relation to an identified sustainable competitive advantage.
6 Establish tactics to achieve objectives, and formulate benchmarks to measure progress.
7 Implement and operationalise the planned strategies.
8 Measure the success of core strategies, and adjust strategies where necessary.

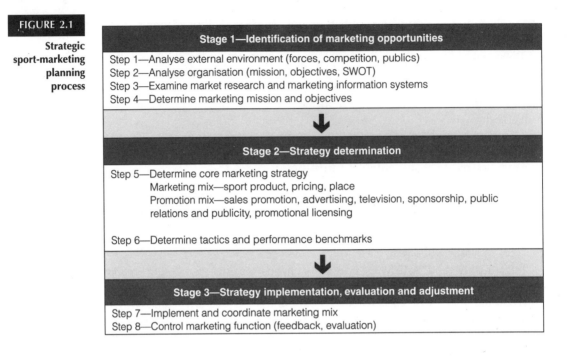

FIGURE 2.1

**Strategic
sport-marketing
planning
process**

This chapter examines Steps 1–4 of the SSMPP. Later chapters deal with individual aspects of the marketing mix variables, detailing the factors to consider in selecting a core marketing strategy. First we examine both the external and internal environments and the forces driving competition.

STEP 1: UNDERSTANDING THE ENVIRONMENT IN WHICH THE SPORT COMPETES

A marketing program is not delivered in isolation of the organisation-wide planning process. In normal circumstances, the marketing planning process must reflect the overall plans for the organisation. In sport, as indicated by the APGA Tour example, there is often little difference between organisation-wide planning and the marketing planning process. The APGA Tour's overall direction and success are based solely on its major product offering: tournament golf. Determining the difference between organisation-wide planning and marketing planning requires careful attention by sport marketers.

The first step of the SSMPP is equivalent to conducting an inventory. The data collected form the basis of decisions made later in the process.

External forces

Figure 2.2 shows the environmental factors requiring consideration, which are the forces that impact *indirectly* on an organisation. They include government

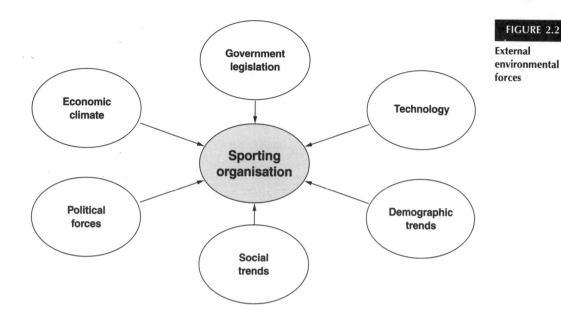

FIGURE 2.2

External
environmental
forces

legislation, economic climate, technology, political forces, and demographic and social trends. It is important for sporting organisations to monitor changes in each of these forces. For many years, sporting organisations neglected to examine these forces and the impact that a changing environment may have for their sport. The example of the Australian Cricket Board (ACB) cited in Chapter 1 indicates this neglect.

Industry competition

On a more *direct* level, sporting organisations need to monitor the industry in which they compete. Figure 2.3 incorporates an adapted version of Porter's (1980) *competitive forces model.* Porter described five forces that managers should review when examining competition and the attractiveness of an industry. These forces include:

1   the intensity of competition between existing firms within an industry;
2   the bargaining power of buyers;
3   the threat of substitute products;
4   the bargaining power of suppliers; and
5   the threat of new entrants.

The attractiveness of an industry is typically measured by profitability, which is not always the principal goal of non-profit and sporting organisations. Viability and winning games are important outcomes and become the primary measure of attractiveness for sporting organisations. In professional sports leagues, for example, the number and location of teams in respective markets

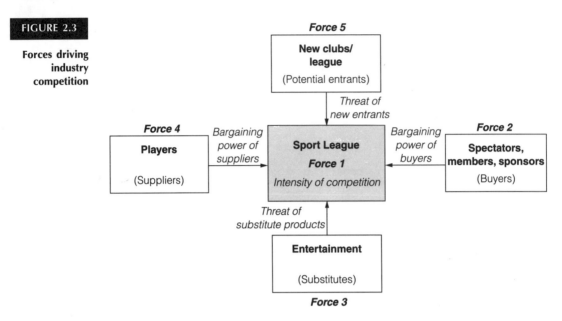

Source: Porter (1985, p. 5).

require the league to assess the attractiveness of a market in terms of viability. Other questions indicative of industry attractiveness may include: Is the economic base of a city or region large enough to sustain just one, or more than one, team? How many other professional sports already exist in this market? What other recreation and leisure pursuits are potentially competing for disposable income? A brief review of Porter's five forces follows.

Professional sport leagues for football will be used to illustrate the applicability of Porter's model. The model in this instance assumes that a professional sport league can be considered an industry, although this industry is subject to the broader market and competitive pressures of the entertainment and leisure sectors. The Australian Football League (AFL), for example, turns over in excess of $200 million, making it a large and significant economic entity.

Force 1: Intensity of competition
The first force is the intensity of competition within the industry. In the case of a sport league, the number of teams and their location are the first indicators of the intensity of competition. Obviously, nine AFL clubs based in Melbourne and ten professional rugby league clubs based in Sydney intensify competition in these markets. This competition is further heightened by the presence of other sporting codes seeking sponsor dollars, spectators and members. In both codes, despite the high number of teams in each market, exit barriers have remained very high. This highlights the peculiar economics associated with

sport leagues. Tradition, emotion and club loyalties often override the economic deficiencies experienced by some clubs, explaining why it has not been so easy to achieve a better geographical balance of teams competing in these national leagues.

Force 2: Bargaining power of buyers

The second force, the buyers or consumers of sport, are finite in relation to the number of teams located in one market—hence the intensity of competition to attract spectators, members and sponsors by clubs. Attendance, membership and sponsorship revenues are the main sources of income generated by sporting clubs. Typically, customers can force prices down, demand higher quality and play competitors off against each other. Too many teams located in one market exacerbates the leverage of consumers, although sport consumers in some sport leagues have less leverage in this regard, as club membership tends to be price standardised throughout a league and the cost of attendance common for all games. Most bargaining power lies with sponsors seeking to choose the best range of benefits from clubs. Sponsor bargaining power increases as the number of clubs based in a market increases.

Force 3: Threat of substitute products

Another major force comes from the substitutability of products, that is, other recreation and leisure activities offering similar benefits to those provided by participation in sport. It is this force which provides the greatest range of competitive forces for a sport league. Under the broad heading of 'entertainment' a variety of products have the potential to attract the consumer's money normally available for leisure pursuits. These may include other sports, the movies, videos and the theatre. A major determinant of the strength of these potential substitutes is the switching cost associated with each product. *Switching cost* refers to the cost of changing brands or products. If the cost is low, both financially and psychologically, then consumers are more likely to switch, and a product becomes susceptible to substitution. This of course has the potential to erode profits. A major advantage possessed by various sports is that brand loyalty (to the sport or club) is very high. Psychological association to a sport or club is often far more important than economic considerations. In part, this explains the fanatical support for some sports and clubs, such as for soccer clubs worldwide, and for AFL clubs in Australia.

Force 4: Bargaining power of suppliers

Suppliers can exert bargaining power on participants in an industry by raising or reducing the quality of purchased goods and services. In a sport league the major supply required to operate successfully is the players. No one source has exclusive control over player supply, and, with the exception of some sports like soccer, it no longer costs clubs to buy players. This is also the one area that the sport marketer has least control over in terms of product quality. The bargaining power of the players has the potential to erode industry profits via their salary demands, rather than via what it costs to procure players from specific suppliers. In their quest for the ultimate prize, a premiership or championship, clubs often accede to the demands of high-priced athletes, explaining why the sport economy is often regulated via the use of salary caps.

Force 5: Threat of new entrants

New clubs or a new rival league can reduce industry profits and specific market share for the existing clubs and/or league. The commencement of the Superleague competition in rugby league is an example of a rival league's entry. Superleague, owned by News Ltd, was established to form a breakaway league, enticing existing clubs and players in the Australian Rugby League's (ARL) New South Wales competition to defect to Superleague. In the process, contractual obligations of both players and clubs were displaced, ultimately creating serious divisions within the league. In attempting to overcome the barriers to entry, the structure and product offerings of the ARL competition were seriously threatened. The gravity of this threat largely depended on the barriers to entry. The major barrier in this case was provided by the established and recognised keeper of the code: the ARL through the New South Wales Rugby League competition. Access to a supply of talented players is usually a major barrier to entry.

Sportview 2.1 illustrates how the difficulties experienced by rugby league in 1995 and 1996 created an opportunity for the AFL. It exemplifies the importance of monitoring the external environment and how the forces driving industry competition are relevant.

SPORTVIEW 2.1

AFL GOES FOR THE GAP

Golden Opportunity: Australian Rules chiefs watch hungrily as rugby league strongholds weaken

'While both the traditional and rebel camps in the Australian rugby league power struggle continue to assure followers that the sport is not shooting itself between the bootlaces, rival code Australian Rules football is seeing an opportunity as priceless as it was unexpected. Until recently, the territorial ambition of the AFL stopped short of challenging rugby league's dominance as the major code in Sydney and Brisbane on a medium to long-term basis, but now the attitude at the AFL headquarters in Melbourne is distinctly predatory.

'The battle for control of rugby league in Australia, which began in February 1995, and the resultant split in traditional team and supporter bases have opened a gap in what seemed an impenetrable defence. Now the AFL is marshalling its forces to take every advantage should that ever-widening fissure become an open floodgate. AFL communications manager Tony Peek admits the rugby league power play has been monitored carefully in Melbourne.

"There is no doubt that many rugby league supporters are disillusioned with what has happened" he says. "And that alone means many must be susceptible to an alternative . . . Certainly, the message is coming through that the opportunity is there to further establish ourselves in Sydney and Brisbane."

'Since switching from the provincial title of the Victorian Football League to the more expansive Australian Football League in 1990, the code has coveted a major spectator market position in Sydney and Brisbane, with marginal return. But in 1995 the situation took a turn for the better. Apart from the rugby league turmoil—which may or may not have had the immediate effect of winning code converts—both Sydney and Brisbane AFL teams had marked upsurges. Crowds at Sydney's home ground, the Sydney Cricket Ground, were up by 63%, while Noble Stand Social Club arrangements saw packed functions after each game, where supporters mingled with players. An average attendance of 15,949 watched 11 Swans games at the SCG. The aggregate of 175,442 who saw the matches was a dramatic rise on the 107,947 (9,813) figure of the previous season.

'And the Brisbane Bears won notoriously parochial Queensland hearts for the first time in the club's existence. It remains to be seen whether any of those hearts make their permanent pride the Bears instead of the front-running Broncos, which has broken from the traditional Australian Rugby League competition. "Further improvement on-field from both Sydney and Brisbane is our number one priority," Peek says. He implies that Sydney in particular would be more affected by a winning Sydney Swans team than anything else.'

Source: Excerpt from Case (1996, pp. 92–3).

Publics

Examination of the external environment can be concluded by identifying the publics to which the sport is responsible. To an extent, some of these will have been identified from the competitive analysis conducted using the Porter framework. Kotler and Andreasen (1991) define a *public* as 'a distinct group of people, organisations, or both whose actual or potential needs must in some sense be served' (p. 89). The competitive forces model has already shown that diverse publics exist for a club competing in a professional league. Figure 2.4 illustrates the publics that may exist for a professional sport club.

Another group of publics exists within the organisation. This leads us to now consider Step 2 in the SSMPP.

STEP 2: UNDERSTANDING THE INTERNAL CAPABILITIES OF THE ORGANISATION

Sport managers gauge the significance of a sport's internal competencies on the basis of the opportunities and threats present in the sport's competitive

FIGURE 2.4

**Publics
impacting on a
professional
sport club**

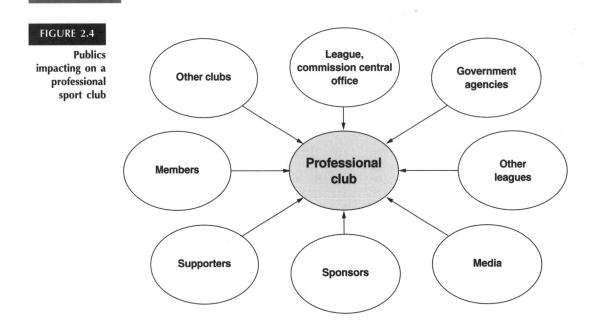

environment. For example, the introduction of colour television to Australia in 1974 represented an opportunity for sport. The ACB, as previously discussed, did not possess the internal capabilities at the time to capitalise on this development. Similarly, the globalisation of sporting competitions via the media has opened a window of opportunity for the APGA Tour.

SWOT analysis

An important foundation for understanding the internal capabilities of a sport is the ability of the sport manager or marketer to match *strengths and weaknesses* with industry *opportunities and threats*. The APGA Tour clearly identified the threat of being overrun by the larger and more powerful world golf tours. The choice to engage in an alliance is evidence of recognising an opportunity to share the production of tournament golf, rather than be forced out of it. Strengths, weaknesses, opportunities and threats (SWOT) analysis is a commonly accepted tool used by managers to assess the current capabilities of their organisations. In essence, it provides a structure for their analysis.

- *Strengths* are resources, skills or other advantages relative to competitors.
- *Weaknesses* are limitations or deficiencies in resources, skills and capabilities that inhibit a sport's effectiveness in relation to competitors.
- *Opportunities* are major favourable situations in a sport's environment.
- *Threats* are major unfavourable situations in a sport's environment.

Mission, objectives and goals

Having established the internal capabilities, it is necessary to ascertain the mission of the organisation, followed by a review of the organisation's principal goals and objectives. The *mission statement* provides direction for the sport, defining and clarifying its meaning and reason for existence. To be unambiguous, a mission statement should clearly answer 'What is our business?' For example, the Australian Sports Commission's mission statement is deceptively simple: 'To enrich the lives of all Australians through sport'. The key to defining a mission for a sporting organisation is to ensure that the mission statement is not so narrow that it limits its scope of operations nor simply a list of services provided.

In the context of sport, another factor impinges on formulating mission statements. Most sports are non-profit entities, and as such exist to achieve a common group of objectives by a relatively homogeneous group of people. Non-profits by definition exist to fight a cause. This cause becomes the *operating charter*, which is generally less flexible than the mission statement of a for-profit firm. If the cause ceases to exist, so too will the organisation. If profits cease to exist, the for-profit firm has the choice of redefining the business it wishes to be in and hence its range of product offerings. If, for instance, the APGA Tour's alliance with other world tours is not successful, the Australasian Tour could disappear and with it the APGA Tour. Defining the mission implicitly defines the broad goals to be pursued by an organisation.

Organisational *goals* refer to the broad aims that organisations strive to achieve. In sport, these may include ensuring financial viability, increasing participation, increasing the number of members, and increasing public interest in the sport. Examples of some broad goals are shown in Table 2.1 using the AFL's 1994 planning document.

Broad goals become the focus for devising more specific *objectives*. Goal 3, for example, is rather broad. How does the AFL wish to improve player and employee welfare, and in what areas? Organisational objectives provide the necessary detail to achieving goals. Objectives should be SMART, that is:

S—Specific
M—Measurable
A—Achievable
R—Realistic
T—Timebound.

For the AFL's Goal 3, for example, one of the objectives has been to lift minimum wages for rookie players, which contributes to enhancing player welfare. Rookie players may, for example, receive an increase in minimum payments of $5000 during a specific season. This can be measured as it becomes a league-wide standard in all clubs, and it is implemented during a specific time period.

TABLE 2.1 **AFL goals, 1994**	**Goal 1**	To ensure the financial viability of the competition by: ■ maximising the competition's net revenue generation ■ containing expenditure ■ improving the total debt to equity ratio.
	Goal 2	To achieve high levels of public interest and support throughout Australia, through both attendances at matches and audiences on television and radio.
	Goal 3	To enhance player (and other employee) welfare and incomes.
	Goal 4	To achieve growth in player participation rates at all levels and maintain the flow of talented players into the AFL.

Source: Adjusted from Australian Football League (1994, p. 10).

STEPS 3 AND 4: DETERMINING THE MARKETING MISSION AND OBJECTIVES

Steps 3 and 4 assume that the important phase of marketing research is concurrently being undertaken to ensure that decisions made in relation to marketing missions and objectives are based on a sound understanding of the marketplace. The marketing research conducted and marketing information systems used are discussed in detail in Chapters 3 and 4 and therefore will not be discussed here.

Marketing must devise its own specific plans complementary to the organisation's overall mission, goals and objectives. The purpose of the planning process is to establish a competitive advantage over rival firms. The mission of marketing is to develop a range of product offerings that reflect a firm's organisation-wide mission statement. These products may be in the form of goods or services or both, depending on the nature of the business. In sport, the product offerings tend to be limited, although they are clearly in the service domain. Inherent in the challenge confronting the sport marketer is designing this portfolio of product offerings to achieve a competitive advantage.

Competitive advantage

Porter (1985) describes *competitive advantage* as 'the way a firm can choose and implement a generic strategy to achieve and sustain a competitive advantage' (p. 26). This definition is specific to three generic strategies that he describes, which will be discussed later in this chapter.

The concept of competitive advantage, however, is broader than Porter's direct application to his theories. Implicit in this concept is the notion of *sustainability*. Without sustainability a competitive advantage becomes elusive. Coyne (1986, p. 55) posits three conditions that must be met for a firm to have achieved a sustainable competitive advantage:

■   Customers perceive a consistent difference in important attributes between the producer's products or services and those of competitors.
■   That difference is the direct consequence of a capability gap between the producer and competitors.
■   Both the difference in important attributes and the capability gap can be expected to endure over time.

The key to sustainability is *differentiation* among competitor products. Coyne further notes that:

> . . . for a producer to enjoy a competitive advantage in a product/market segment, the difference or differences between him and his competitors must be felt in the marketplace: that is, they must be reflected in some *product/delivery attribute* that is the *key buying criterion* for the market. (p. 55)

Each individual sport has its own unique set of product attributes, via the special nature of each sport. In this regard, some sports are inherently more appealing to some segments of the population. For many years sports believed that these unique features of their game would remain popular forever. In Australian sport, this was proven not to be the case. The traditional sports of cricket, Australian Rules football, netball and softball suddenly found that their competitive advantage was being eroded by changing attitudes towards leisure options. Increasing diversity of recreational and sporting opportunities saw these sports struggling in the late 1970s and early 1980s, and as a consequence they had to re-examine their key buying criterion and look to reposition themselves. One technique that these sports could have used to examine their range of product offerings is examined in the next section.

Product market expansion

Ansoff (1957) devised the *product/market expansion grid*, shown in Figure 2.5, to assist managers to balance their product offerings.

Market penetration
Market penetration (or concentration) refers to making more sales to existing customers without changing the product. Typically, this involves intensifying the advertising and promotions campaign to attract consumer attention. Often this strategy also involves a price reduction aimed to move consumers away from competitor products.

The New South Wales Rugby League (NSWRL) advertising and promotional campaign 'Simply the best' featuring Tina Turner is an example of a market penetration strategy in sport. Although there were some minor adjustments to the game in terms of a crackdown on excessive on-field violence during the 1980s, the game itself remained unchanged. The NSWRL was successful in increasing interest in the game, which translated into flourishing attendances and television viewership. The 'Simply the best' advertising campaign is

FIGURE 2.5

Product/market expansion grid

	Existing products	New products
Existing markets	1 Market penetration	3 Product development
New markets	2 Market development	4 Diversification

Source: Adjusted from Ansoff (1957).

considered to be one of the most sophisticated, inspiring, modern promotional campaigns seen in Australian sport, as will be shown when this campaign is examined in Chapter 8.

Market development

A *market development* strategy is a relatively inexpensive way of creating new markets for existing products. It typically involves few risks and requires only minor modification to the product. It depends on sound research indicating new segments of the population willing to buy the product.

Product development

A *product development* strategy involves offering a modified or new product to current markets.

Australian cricket's introduction of one-day cricket is an example of a sport that exhibits aspects of both market development and product development. One-day cricket can be considered to be the same product as four- and five-day cricket. Notably, the condensed version of the game has attracted a large following among women, which Test Match cricket previously did not. On the other hand, one-day cricket can be considered to be a modified form of the game and better described as a product development strategy by the ACB. The weakness in this view is that one-day cricket has obviously had the capacity to expand the market interested in cricket. The traditional form of the game was not creating this expansion.

Regardless of the final distinction, it raises an interesting dilemma in sport marketing: namely, the point at which the game has been modified to such an extent that in effect it is a new product offering. In one-day cricket, for example, the basic elements of the game are still apparent: batting, bowling and fielding. The condensed version of the game forces more action, but whether this constitutes a new or different product is debatable. This also illustrates the conflict that can exist between the 'purists' and those who prefer non-stop excitement in sport. This conflict is also central to soccer's dilemma regarding the number of goals, described in Chapter 1.

Another example of sports having to modify their range of product offerings has been seen in junior sports. For many years, juniors played the adult form of the game complete with all the rules and traditions associated with a particular sport. As research began to show that this was not providing a satisfactory sport environment for juniors, many sports have been modified to make them more attractive to juniors. In essence, sports have been modified to encourage more success in game elements, increasing the likelihood of juniors continuing to participate. Although sports initially did not see this as a marketing-related issue, this has now changed. The long-term fortunes of a sport, from both an elite performance and an ongoing interest and spectatorship perspective, are founded on the success of their junior programs. Market development and product development strategies therefore assume a heightened level of importance, with sports carefully considering their range of sport offerings for juniors in various age groups.

Product diversification

The final category of *product diversification* requires a firm to develop an entirely new product for a new market. This can be achieved internally through a strong research and development function or via the external acquisition of a new firm with a new range of product offerings. In terms of the core sport product, this strategy is not common in sport. Sporting organisations, in the main, do not seek to buy other sporting organisations, although it remains an option, as demonstrated by the Footscray Football Club.

In 1991 the Footscray Football Club purchased a half-share in the Melbourne Monarch's Baseball Club. This is an example of product diversification in sport, in this case developing or acquiring a new but related (in terms of sport) product. The objective was to provide Footscray club members and supporters with added value via the provision of another sport, as well as to attract new consumers to the club and associated facilities. Sportview 2.2 outlines the Footscray Football Club's marketing plans and planned acquisitions in more detail. By 1996, the Footscray Football Club was beginning to pay the price for its acquisition strategies earlier in the decade. The Melbourne Monarchs baseball franchise had become a drain on financial resources. The baseball business had not turned a profit since purchase and in 1996 was for sale for approximately $300 000. An ARL team had not been attracted to share Whitten Oval, nor had soccer materialised at the ground due to cricket's use of the facility.

FOOTSCRAY KICKS BACK

'There is a revolution going on in Melbourne which, if successful, will change the face of sport marketing in Australia. It is the product of recessionary times, creative thought and a survival instinct based on tough working class values. That it should spring from the Footscray Football Club, virtually dead and buried in late 1989, reinforces the fightback legend and continues the process of people power Footscray harnessed in those days of struggle.

'The bold plan could eventually see four national codes—Australian football, rugby league, soccer and baseball—all based at the Western Oval (now Whitten Oval), till recently the dilapidated home of the Footscray Bulldogs, in the heart of Melbourne's west. Because there is no precedent, the spin-offs—in terms of marketing, promotion, financial strength and long term viability—are incalculable.

'The Footscray plan, like most great ideas, is simple: make greater use of the playing surface, thereby attracting more supporters and more money while spreading the administrative costs across four codes. As a consequence of Footscray's 1989 fight for survival the club's charter has been to open the club to the community. A good example of that is the Care For Kids campaign. Players devote time to visiting children at school in an attempt to inspire better achievement. But all the goodwill in the world does not replace success on the field or money. Goodwill has a habit of dissipating; hence the need to lock in what has been an extraordinary outcome. That meant diversifying. To seek out other codes, it was necessary first to convince people the prospects were serious. That meant fixing up the facilities.

'With $800,000 in the kitty, it was time to put the masterplan into action. The method is to form a holding company, Wesports, which will have equal representation from four codes if the NSWRL decides to throw its lot in with the Dogs for an expanded competition. Joining up with the NSWRL would be a bonus for the Dogs if for no other reason than that it would maximise the use of the ground and reap extra revenue.

'Baseball has already been lured to the Western Oval. Whatever happens there Footscray is already in a position to capitalise on one of Australia's fastest growing sports—baseball. The club paid about $100,000 last year for a 50% stake in the Melbourne Monarchs, re-admitted into the Australian Baseball League in 1992. Despite being runners-up in the 1989 inaugural competition, the Monarchs ran into financial difficulties and were dropped from the league.

'Neither club president nor general manager are prepared to say the elaborate marketing structure is partly a defensive move to ensure the AFL does not step in again to cut the Dogs off at their knees. Clearly, it makes the threat more remote. But to escape it, Footscray must improve its performance on and off the field. The marketing strategies based on turning the Western Oval into the premier entertainment and leisure facility in the western suburbs must be successful.'

Source: Excerpts from McMinn (1992, pp. 46–8).

Sportview 2.2 illustrates the objectives of a product diversification strategy via acquisition. It also illustrates the pitfalls of such a strategy and why this type of strategy is not common in sport.

The product/market expansion grid provides a framework for the sport marketer to consider the balance of product offerings. This balance of product offerings should reflect the marketing mission, which in turn should mirror the overall mission, goals and objectives of the organisation.

Generic strategies

As indicated earlier, Porter (1985) describes three *generic strategies* that firms can use as an alternative framework to achieve competitive advantage:

- cost leadership,
- differentiation, and
- focus.

Both the *cost leadership* and *differentiation* strategies aim to seek a competitive advantage in a broad range of markets. The *focus* strategy aims to seek a competitive advantage by using either a cost leadership or differentiation strategy in a narrow or niche market segment.

Cost leadership is perhaps the simplest of the three options. The organisation's principal objective is to distribute its products to the widest possible market at a lower cost than competitors. Achieving lower cost may be the result of internal economies of scale, innovative technologies or lower distribution costs. In the end, it is the consumer who decides whether the cost differential is significant enough to warrant the purchase of one product over that of competitors.

Differentiation, on the other hand is typically more expensive. It involves an advantage based on distinctive product attributes. Products, for instance, may offer benefits that others do not, or it might be a new and innovative product not currently available. Again, differentiation is seeking to establish its product prominence in as wide a market as possible.

In sport, cost leadership strategies are difficult to achieve. In a sporting league, the clubs generally compete on equal terms in terms of cost. Standardised prices for attendance and membership reduce the significance of cost as a source of competitive advantage. For example, 1996 AFL club memberships cost $80 and ground entry to all matches was $12.50. Although there is league-wide price regulation, the restriction is the same for all competing clubs. As will be examined in Chapter 6, clubs and leagues cannot always achieve full cost recovery on ticket prices. If full cost recovery (in terms of covering event costs) were an objective, most sports would become too expensive for regular attendance.

Differentiation strategy provides scope for application in the sport setting. Although all the clubs in a league appear the same in terms of production, they do offer distinct brand images. These are of course the clubs themselves with their distinctive colours, heritage and traditions, with which supporters identify with a good degree of emotional intensity. On a macro level, each different sport is a differentiated product in its own right, all offering similar benefits to consumers. The choice for consumers, in terms of physical activity, competing or spectating, is which of the myriad of sports offer the best outlet to satisfy their needs and wants. This is equally applicable for juniors when choosing the sports in which they wish to participate. Some sports, such as cricket, golf, softball, swimming and netball, offer the challenge of special skill development without any excessive body contact. Football codes, basketball and wrestling offer a different range of skills to be mastered in the context of body contact sports. The challenge for the sport marketer is to accentuate the differentiated product benefits to potential participants, and this sometimes means changing the fundamental rules and traditions of a sport. Although this is obviously an option, sport managers and marketers need to carefully consider the impact of proposed changes before implementation.

SUMMARY

This chapter has introduced the SSMPP and reviewed the first four steps in this process. These four steps constitute the data collection and review phase of the planning process. Organisation-wide data are required to place into context the role that marketing strategy plays in ensuring that a sport creates a sustainable competitive advantage.

In the first instance, a sporting organisation needs to review the external environmental factors impinging on its existence. These factors are best described as the set of societal influences that encroach on all organisations, which include government legislation, economic environment, technology, political forces, and social and demographic trends.

A more direct form of analysis involves a review of industry characteristics specific to a sport. Porter's five-forces model provides sport managers with a structured framework to scan the competitive environment, and is the precursor to a review of the internal capabilities of a sporting organisation. SWOT analysis has been described in this chapter as a useful tool to assist with this internal examination.

Review of the external and internal environments is an important precursor to determining the best strategies to create a competitive advantage. In essence, marketing personnel are responsible for developing an array of product offerings that assist an organisation to achieve a competitive advantage. In predominantly single-product organisations such as sports, marketing's contribution to creating a competitive advantage is considerable.

Sport and marketing, in many ways, are still becoming accustomed to each other. For many years most sport administrators did not believe that the role of marketing was important. However, as the sport landscape became increasingly competitive, sport managers began to adjust their thinking. Most large sporting entities have now created marketing departments, and many smaller sporting organisations are beginning to employ marketing specialists to manage the contribution of marketing in the planning process. As indicated in Chapter 1, sporting organisations have been guilty of complacency in the past in relation to marketing and promoting their sport. This is clearly changing, as is exemplified by the case study at the end of this chapter.

This chapter has discussed the steps in the SSMPP and specifically outlined four of the eight steps shown in Figure 2.1. Part of Step 3 has purposely been left for the remaining two chapters in Part I of this book. Such is the significance of understanding the sport consumer, conducting market research and defining market segments. Part II of this book examines in detail the marketing mix variables that combine to form the nucleus of a core marketing strategy—a strategy based on the environmental scanning and data intelligence phase described in Steps 1–4 of the SSMPP in this chapter.

CRICKET CREATES ITS OWN PLAYING FIELD

CASE
STUDY

'Tradition has little to do with the Australian Cricket Board's bold game plan, which suits players and sponsors just fine. What is the Empire coming to? A cricket board talking about teams of eight players, games lasting only 90 minutes and a winter season on an Asian circuit . . . It's enough to make the gentlemen of Lord's choke on their watercress sandwiches. Maybe so, but the Australian Cricket Board's plans for what it calls a Super Eights competition might be just what the game needs to compete in the new world of pay television and its appetite for sporting "product".

'The board believes that in the new format, cricket can compete for time on the small screen with an afternoon at the football or an evening in the basketball stadium. What's more, Super Eights is expected to give international exposure to a growing band of young Australian players, and to extend the playing careers (and earning) of former cricketing heroes. Adding momentum to the move to take cricket to Australia's northern neighbours are some powerful influences within Asia. For example, governments are looking to sport as a means of promoting health and broadening lifestyle experiences in communities that have rapidly rising standards of living.

'As business sees new opportunity in the booming economies of Asia and the Indian subcontinent, so does sport. It is no coincidence that the world's highest paid cricketer is an Indian, Sachin Tendulkar who recently signed a five-year $US10 million sponsorship deal with the US based WorldTel Inc.

'Australian cricket is healthy, both financially and in terms of the depth of quality of its players. The game is administered by the Australian Cricket Board, based in Melbourne. The board turns over about $40 million a year and last year drew its biggest crowds since 1982. Chief executive, Graham Halbish, says that last season was the first $10 million season in gate terms. This followed a period when there was a school of thought, particularly during the 1980s, that Test match cricket was a dying art. "We never believed that, but it's nice to demonstrate that Test cricket is more than just a fading tradition". He says that more than ever, cricket is having to compete for players and spectators with other sports, and against the computer culture. "We feel we have to compete far more vigorously for market share, not just in terms of participants, but for our viewing audience".

'The ACB's main expenditure is on cricket development which Halbish says costs more than $8 million a year. Advertising and promotional expenditure is on top of that. The development programs are working so well that the great depth of cricketing talent being uncovered in Australia is, paradoxically, rapidly becoming one of the game's main problems. Some players regarded as being close to international standard, are battling to get a game even at state level. An example is Queensland's 20 year old, Andrew Symonds who hit a world record 16 sixes in an innings of 254 not out and scored 1438 runs in English county cricket last season.

'Former Australian captain Greg Chappell, now a sports business consultant, says cricket must change if it wants to avoid being "run over" by other sports. He draws attention to the contrast between opportunities in cricket and baseball. Chappell says: "If you are a parent of a promising young athlete or young sportsman who has an interest in pursuing sport as a career and cricket may be one of those sports, and you look at the last couple of intakes of the Commonwealth Bank cricket academy, you would find less than 1% have gone on to represent their country. You would have some reservations about your son committing himself to cricket and the academy, when there are other opportunities around these days".

'There are a surprising number of young Australians earning good money playing baseball in America at the lower levels. There are one or two higher profile guys, such as Dave Nilsson, who have reached the top level, but there would be between 20 and 40 young blokes earning in the hundreds of thousands of US dollars a year playing baseball. There wouldn't be as many cricketers in this country doing that, so if that continues to grow at the rate it's growing now, it's going to put enormous pressure on cricket. Some of the top 25 cricketers with the ACB are earning about $80,000 under the board's lower-end contracts.

'The ACB's plan to introduce a winter competition next year, involving a new format of eight players per side, and taking in Asian cities, is aimed at solving some of these problems as well as broadening the appeal of the game. Halbish says: "We worked tremendously hard to create depth in Australian cricket and we certainly do have a reservoir of talent that creates a problem of its own in giving it exposure . . . so I was very interested in putting to the board a proposal that would provide additional opportunities for our contract players off-season, to generate more income for them and perhaps to offset their desire to play in the UK".

'The Super Eights competition, as it will be promoted, will involve eight city based teams drawn from emerging talent as well as recently retired international players from South Africa, India, New Zealand and Australia. After a preliminary round of matches in cities in Queensland and the Northern Territory, the main competition will include venues in Singapore, Hong Kong,

Bangkok and Kuala Lumpur. Super Eight cricket is a compromise between the one-day concept and the more recent Hong Kong experiments with six-a-side matches, which turned into "slogathons". Eight-a-side cricket is designed to ensure running between wickets and fielding remain entertaining parts of the game.

'Australia which has an obligation to the International Cricket Council to assist with development of cricket in Asia, has received several recent approaches to do so. Halbish says: "We take that responsibility seriously and see, like any industry, some real potential for growth. If we can export some of our cricketers into those regions to coach and play, and help them promote and develop during the off-season, it is all to the good."

'Chappell, whose private consultancy has worked with the ACB on devising the Super Eights concept, regards the region to Australia's near north as having the most potential for development of cricket in the next 20 years. "Firstly, there are a couple of big players in the pay-TV market who are expanding in Asia and have sports channels that are desperate for product. You have governments in those areas that recognise that sport is going to be a very important part of their development and an important part of their health program for the future".

'He says the sums to be spent are large, particularly in a region with little sports culture. Chappell says cricket has an advantage over sports such as rugby league, rugby union and basketball, because physical stature is not critical. Height and bulk are not required. The other point to be aware of, Chappell says, is that 80% of the players and watchers of cricket in the world are in equatorial regions. "England and Australia have dominated cricket for so long, all of a sudden you look around and realise that as the Indian economy in particular, grows, the subcontinent has a real possibility of becoming the centre of cricket". For the first time, cricket will be part of the Common-wealth Games in 1998 in Kuala Lumpur. The son of the King of Malaysia, Tunku Peter Imran, as he is known in cricket, was educated in England, is president of Malaysian cricket and wants Malaysia to be a full member of the ICC by 2020.

'Chappell says that in Hong Kong, he met a member of China's sports ministry who had played cricket during four years of education in Australia, and now had a mission to include cricket as one of the new sports to be officially introduced to China. Some Japanese also are promoting cricket. "If you take Malaysia, Japan and China, and cricket can establish a foothold in those regions, the potential down the track is gi-bloody-normous", Chappell says.

'The Super Eights plan is attracting interest from potential new sponsors because of its strong Asian component. Halbish says the ACB will not go to the market place until it is satisfied it has got the product right and that should be very soon. Chappell, whose Sydney company, Greg Chappell Sports Mar-keting, has been negotiating for an involvement in the running of Super Eights, says sponsorship enquiries have come from "across the board" including some "very interesting areas". He says they include Australian businesses that have no interest in local sponsorships, but would consider sponsoring Super Eights in Asia for commercial reasons.

'New sponsorships will be needed to help fill the gap when the ACB's main sponsor, Benson & Hedges, exits early from its five-year contract next April, because of legislation barring tobacco advertising. Halbish says the ACB has been successful in finding a replacement sponsor to be announced soon, "but it's not tobacco money".

'A pay-TV agreement with Optus Vision for coverage of Sheffield Shield matches, and some Mercantile Mutual one-day games next summer, will bring in additional revenue, but it is "not significant". The Super Eight concept has been "very deliberately" packaged to appeal to television, Halbish says. "We think that pay might be more interested in it than free-to-air although we'll certainly be giving free-to-air a chance to bid".

'The ACB has had what Halbish describes as "some free advice" about franchising the Super Eight teams but has no idea whether the approaches were backed by genuine private bidders. "It's not a concept in which we are interested", he says. The "ownership" of the city-based teams is intended to reside with the domestic cricket associations of the countries involved.

'Halbish acknowledges that the more cricket develops successfully as a sport, and the more wealth it draws, the more likely it is to attract investment interest from the private sector. "But I suspect the reason they look to you is not because they love the game and want to be involved, it's because they see the opportunity to make money", he says. "What we have to ensure as an entity as Australian cricket in total, is that we stay a step ahead of that and organise, manage and promote the game well enough, so that all the people connected with the game are unified, and that the participants are being sufficiently well looked after not to want to look outside for a new master".

'"You don't ignore the prospect, but I think the best way of negating the likelihood of it (private ownership) occurring is by getting on with the job in the best possible fashion and letting people know that you are".'

Source: Reprinted from Massey (1995, pp. 87–9).

Questions

1   Describe the external environment in which the ACB exists.
2   Describe how the Super Eights fits within the SSMPP.
3   Identify the reasons for the ACB's introduction of the Super Eights.
4   Using the product/market expansion grid, describe how you would define the Super Eights product offering.
5   Identify the challenges confronting cricket in the next five years.

REFERENCES

Ansoff, H. I. (1957). 'Strategies for diversification', *Harvard Business Review*, September–October, pp. 113–24.

Australian Football League (1994). *AFL Strategic Plan 1994*, Melbourne.

Case, B. (1996). 'AFL goes for the gap', *The Bulletin*, 27 February, pp. 92–3.

Coyne, K. P. (1986). 'Sustainable competitive advantage—what it is, what it isn't', *Business Horizons*, January–February, pp. 54–61.

Happell, C. (1996). 'Players to benefit from tour expansion', *The Age*, 6 February, p. B7.

Kotler, P. and Andreasen, A. R. (1991). *Strategic Marketing for Nonprofit Organisations*, Prentice-Hall, Englewood Cliffs, NJ.

McMinn, I. (1992). 'Footscray kicks back', *The Bulletin*, 31 March, pp. 46–8.

Massey, M. (1995). 'Cricket creates its own playing field', *Business Review Weekly*, 20 November, pp. 87–9.

Porter, M. (1980). *Competitive Strategy*, Free Press, New York.

——(1985). *Competitive Advantage: Creating and Sustaining Superior Performance*, Free Press, New York.

3

Understanding the sport consumer

CHAPTER OUTLINE

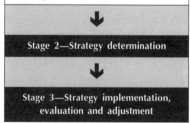

Stage 1—Identification of marketing opportunities

Step 1—Analyse external environment (forces, competition, **publics**)

Step 2—Analyse organisation (mission, objectives, SWOT)

Step 3—Examine market research and marketing information systems

Step 4—Determine marketing mission and objectives

⬇

Stage 2—Strategy determination

⬇

Stage 3—Strategy implementation, evaluation and adjustment

CHAPTER
OBJECTIVES

Chapter 3 is the first of two chapters relating to understanding the sport consumer and how marketing influences consumer purchase decisions. Specifically, the chapter explains the various predispositions that consumers have towards product purchase. It also examines the decision-making processes that consumers generally go through prior to purchase. Implications for the consumption of sport products are illustrated throughout the chapter.

After studying this chapter you should be able to:

1 Define consumer behaviour.
2 Identify the key components in the consumer behaviour process.
3 Describe the steps in consumer decision making.
4 Describe the levels of consumer behaviour.
5 Describe and discuss the key consumer characteristics.

HEADLINE
STORY

UNDERSTANDING CONSUMER BEHAVIOUR

. . . In the 12 months ending March 1995 44.3% of the Australian population attended a sporting event. The major attractions were,

Australian Rules Football	1,874,200
Horse Racing	1,701,100
Rugby League	1,462,100
Cricket	1,165,900
Basketball	691,600
Harness Racing	599,700
Soccer	558,800
Motor Sports	451,500
Tennis	431,700
Rugby Union	358,400
Netball	312,300

(Australian Bureau of Statistics 1996)

As the Australian Bureau of Statistics chart clearly illustrates, sport attendance and consumption of a wide range of sports are very important for a large percentage of the Australian public. Hence it is becoming increasingly important to ascertain *why* fans turn up to the game week in and week out. Is it for team loyalty, stadium preference, clashes between traditional rivals, star appeal or reasons we are yet to discern? Such is the dilemma facing sport marketing as we approach 2000. One thing, however, is unquestioned: the more we know and understand our consumers, the better prepared we are to deliver a satisfactory product or service.

There is nothing particularly mysterious about the manner in which the consumer's thought processes evolve. Basically, an individual realises that a need has arisen. They then seek out information that may lead to satisfying that need. The potential choices are evaluated, and the decision to purchase is made. After the consumption of the product or service, the consumer undergoes a post-purchase evaluation, which may result in a number of different behaviours.

Unfortunately, while sport marketers understand the process, we have very little understanding of how and at what level distinctive variables interact to impact on individual choice. These variables may be person specific, they may be psychological or they may be social. Furthermore, they may be internal or external to the product or service choice. While articulating the process may be simple, interpreting it is extremely complex. Stotlar (1993) refers to this as the 'Black Box Theory'. In this case, many variables enter (the black box), but only one emerges—consumption of a product. What is difficult to determine is what happens *inside* that black box.

A MODEL OF CONSUMER BEHAVIOUR

Mullin et al. (1993) suggest that models of consumer behaviour are a process rather than a prescriptive formula, and the model provided in Figure 3.1 is not an exception to that philosophy. To suggest that it is possible to construct a blueprint that is capable of determining behaviour is foolhardy, as the information sources for such models are both diverse and all inclusive.

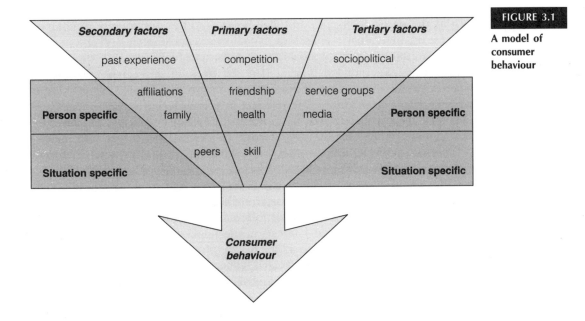

FIGURE 3.1

A model of consumer behaviour

The research on sport consumption is voluminous and in many instances emanates from disciplines beyond sport although, as recent works by Nowell (1995), Stotlar (1995), and Shoham and Kahle (1996) indicate, it is being given increasing attention in the sport-marketing literature. Disciplines such as psychology, sociology, communication and anthropology all have contributed to the understanding of consumer behaviour. Moreover, in many instances such work significantly predates current sport-marketing research. Stone (1955), Wise (1973), Lee and Zeiss (1980), and Ohle and Wise (1981) are representative of both the breadth and the depth in this area of scholarship. Not surprisingly, numerous factors have been regarded as determinants in influencing consumer behaviour. Furthermore, all factors both impact on, and are in turn impacted upon by, other variables to greater or lesser degree. Consequently, it may be argued that consumer behaviour is as much situation specific as it is person specific.

Nevertheless, certain factors are germane to all consumer decision-making processes, and the integration of such provides a framework for understanding the consumer behaviour process. Fundamentally, it may be argued that a model of consumer behaviour is invariably the product of what may be termed primary, secondary and tertiary factors. Figure 3.1 schematically represents the interaction of these factors.

Primary factors

Primary factors are those elements which are internal to the purchaser or consumer. It is the set of beliefs that an individual holds in relation to the impact that the use of a particular product or service will have on their life. These elements are the *intrinsic motivators* to consume. They include issues such as the desire for health and well-being, and the opportunity to compete and test an individual's skills and capabilities against a variety of opposing forces, to establish new friendships or to escape 'reality'.

For example, individuals may join the local fitness centre, or take up jogging, swimming, cycling or walking to improve the quality of their life in terms of *health and fitness*. The mindset in this instance is that a healthy, fit individual will be better able to perform life's daily functions. Similarly, the rock climber, surfer, martial arts student or even chess player may believe that personal development comes only when an individual tests their skill against another object or person.

The *social* aspect of sport has long been regarded as an important component of the consumer's decision-making process. Recent retirees ready to start the next phase of their lives join tennis, bowls, dance or fishing clubs to link with others of similar interests in the hope of starting new friendships. Similarly, joining the office sport team can provide entry into a new social group for a recent employee. This is especially so if the change in work situation is accompanied by a residential relocation.

Finally, the sailor, bushwalker, horserider, motorcyclist or even reader may pursue their activities as a form of *escapism*. An afternoon on the harbour or the highways may be the perfect rejuvenating tool for the harassed office worker. Similarly, the city dweller may be energised by a walk or horseride in the country. If the above are seen as too risky, expensive or time consuming, a browse through the local library, museum or art galley can provide a similar recuperative environment.

An important consideration in the pursuit of any of the preceding activities is an individual's *physical characteristics*. An individual weighing 65 kilograms may find contact or strength sports, especially those that do not have weight divisions, less enjoyable than sports or activities where lightness is an attribute. Likewise, potential consumers whose centre of gravity is closer to the ground may be at an advantage where balance is a prerequisite, such as in gymnastics and skating. Conversely, physically disadvantaged individuals may find particular sports and activities a challenge to be negotiated and overcome.

Secondary factors

Secondary factors are those elements that are *immediate influences* on the decision-making process. Having recognised that a need exists, the individual explores potential solutions to the problem via avenues perceived to provide quality input into the process. In this instance, each opinion held by the individual is weighted by their degree of respect for the source of the information.

Specifically, the most important secondary factor in the consumer behaviour model is the individual's prior exposure to the product or service. *Past experience* creates the evaluative mechanism on which future decisions to consume are based. Fans of the Collingwood Football Club, Arsenal, Auckland Warriors or Chicago Cubs continue to watch their teams play because of their past experiences as a fan of the particular club or code. If prior exposure had been less than satisfactory, the spectator would explore alternative avenues to fulfil their needs and expectations.

Family is an extremely influential secondary factor. In many instances children follow the same codes, clubs and practices as their parents and/or may be enthralled by, and wish to emulate, the feats of older sisters or brothers. If one family member plays golf, netball, soccer or volleyball, there is an increased possibility that children or siblings of the same gender (in gender-specific sports) will adopt that activity. Likewise, if parents are avid fans of the Australian Rugby League (ARL) or the Australian Football League (AFL), it would be a rare, even brave, family member who supported the opposing code. Even more significantly, a family divided by club loyalties—Carlton vs Collingwood, Manchester United vs Liverpool or Manly vs North Sydney—would feel less than harmonious whenever the teams met.

Peers also are an important secondary factor. The behaviour and choices of companions often stimulate an individual to act. If a particular group is heavily involved in the consumption of basketball through playing, watching and reading, the pressure to conform to the group is strong. An individual can either conform to the behaviour of the group or alternatively seek other groups whose interests are more in keeping with their own.

Other significant secondary factors may include *clubs* with which an individual is affiliated, *schools or universities* attended, or *ethnic groups* one is associated with. The values and beliefs of Scouts and Guides organisations, or the local Surf Lifesaving Club, will be incorporated into the individual's set of beliefs and impact on the decision-making process. Similarly, a private school that offers a variety of extracurricular sport activities, such as rowing, skiing and mountain climbing, offers very different possibilities from a state-funded, inner-urban high school that is cramped for space and resource poor. A new immigrant to Australia from North America could be expected initially to explore local basketball and baseball before sampling more indigenous offerings.

Geographical considerations are important. The sport offerings of country or coastal schools and universities can be very different from those of their city cousins. Furthermore, *climate* cannot be ignored. Differences in sport consumption between Darwin and Hobart would be expected to exist, based on climatic differences.

Finally, although many Australians believe that they live in an egalitarian society, differences based on *class*, predominantly linked to economic considerations, do exist. However, while individual wealth will enable the purchase of the equipment to undertake a particular sport or activity, membership may be restricted for a variety of reasons. It may be easier to join a local golf club than the Royal Sydney or Royal Melbourne, even though the same equipment will serve at all venues. Moreover, unless you are a prime minister, the wait to join the Royal Canberra Golf Club may be very long indeed.

Tertiary factors

Tertiary factors are those elements which are beyond the immediate sphere of influence and should be recognised for what they are. In most instances they are attempts to *modify* or *construct individual behaviour*, not just for the consumer's benefit, but for the benefit of the external group. Products, events and media provide information to the consumer in a manner that they believe will most likely encourage the consumer to buy. Occasionally, such groups may be at odds with each other.

An incident on a sporting field may be downplayed by the organisation concerned as it does not want adverse publicity, which could result in reduced attendance or a lessening of participation. Conversely, the *media* may play up the event. This is done in the belief that graphic pictures will sell additional newspapers or that television consumers will view other components of the host program or indeed other programming. In most cases, media sources suggest that they are engaging in responsible journalism by presenting the product in toto. Equally, the ongoing discussion associated with an incident may prove a boon to talkback radio and discussion-type sportshows.

Political, religious, cultural and service groups often use sport to place their organisation in a positive light or to piggyback on the popularity of a particular sport or activity. A local Rotary Club's support of a community fun run is conceptually not that different from the entry of various church groups into debate concerning the sporting use of religious holidays. In such instances, both groups are trying to establish a positive community profile. By linking themselves with sport and leisure they are endeavouring to position themselves as a similar product for consumption purposes.

Finally, an interesting trait on the part of our *political leaders* has been their willingness to be seen at a variety of sport events and to be photographed wearing a particular team's jersey or standing in the winner's circle with the victors. It is an attempt on the part of politicians to be seen as just like 'the person in the street'. In such instances, sport is being used as a fundamental link or lure to encourage the individual to consume a particular ideology. Along with Alan Bond's raising of the shroud on the controversial winged keel of *Australia II*, this nation's most enduring memory of the Australian 1983 America's Cup win is a champagne-soaked, gaudily dressed prime minister embracing a sport victory just like his fellow Australians.

THE CONSUMER DECISION-MAKING PROCESS

As previously mentioned, all the major steps in the decision-making process are influenced by various elements. Person-specific factors (whether they be situational or demographic), psychological influences and social forces all play a part in constructing the context from which the decision to purchase is made. Figure 3.2 illustrates the major steps in the decision-making process.

Given that sport consumption is not unique to any one of the above, the potential starting point for a specific decision-making process is almost indiscernible. However, the following five steps represent the major components in the way the consumption process unfolds. To exemplify this process, an individual's desire to elevate their energy levels will be used as an example.

Step 1: Problem recognition

Problem recognition is usually the result of the depletion of existing goods (. . . *I don't have the energy to do the things that I used to . . .*), change in motivation (. . . *I really wish running for the train in the morning wasn't so hard . . .*), change in reference groups or family situation (. . . *what with the new job and shifting into my own apartment I don't exercise anywhere near as much as I did when I was in university . . .*), and new information, which may be interpersonal or the result of mass communication (. . . *my friends*

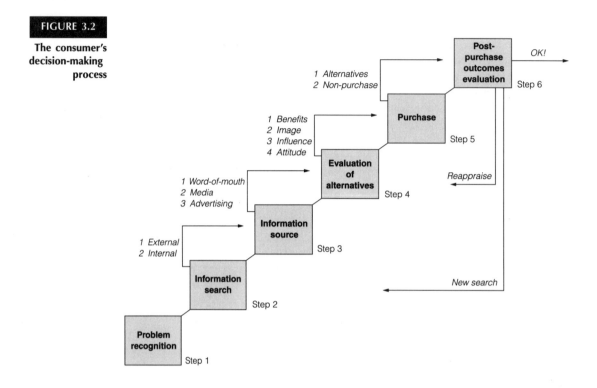

FIGURE 3.2

The consumer's
decision-making
process

*want me to join them in the upcoming event, and judging by the television
and newspaper advertising it will be a lot of fun . . .).*

Recognition of the problem will lead to the search for information needed
to make the decision.

Step 2: Information search

The information search can take either of two forms: a recall of stored
knowledge in the memory, or a seeking of additional information.

Some goods and services are purchased solely on the basis of an *internal*
search (recalled memory) and are usually related to habitual or routine
decision making. In this instance, the evaluation of alternatives is limited and
based on what is remembered (. . . *back to the local fitness centre. I suppose
I could resume swimming in the morning or try to make time for a run during
the day, but all of these are so intrusive on my busy schedule. I wonder if there
are any other fitness activities I could pursue that would be fun and not so
time demanding? . . .).*

With an *external* search the consumer is seeking information not contained
in the memory. The adoption of an external search is usually a response to
two factors: recognising that there is a risk involved in making the purchase
(price and negative consequences of poor choice), and believing that this

type of search will greatly increase the chances of making a correct choice (*. . . perhaps I could ride a bike to work — **or even skate!!**. . .*).

This leads to the consumer sourcing the information.

Step 3: Information source

A major source of information is via 'word-of-mouth' through family, friends and opinion leaders (*. . . my sister has a pair of Nike runners while my best friend has a pair of Saucony, and each says good things about their purchases. Moreover, one of Australia's leading athletes has endorsed the cross-training features of a third brand . . .*). Another source of information is through general media forms, which include magazine and newspaper articles, new product reviews and television coverage of events where the product is used (*. . . a number of brands/models got good reviews in a recent sport magazine . . .*). Finally, information can be obtained through promotion media, which include a myriad of forms of advertising (*. . . they really have a great Point Of Purchase display . . .*).

Once the consumer has the necessary information at hand, an evaluation of the alternatives occurs.

Step 4: Evaluation of alternatives

An evaluation of alternatives is conducted according to a set of criteria that may or may not include all of the following: product benefits, image and the degree of yielding to influence (*. . . if I purchase model X I will get style and durability and will not embarrass my family when I use it on the street . . .*). The evaluation of alternatives is also affected by the belief held about a certain product, the purchaser's attitude towards it and the intention to purchase (*. . . I really like model Y but it is far too expensive for me—model X will be a good buy . . .*).

Only after evaluation does the decision to purchase take place.

Step 5: Purchase

The decision to purchase a particular product or service can best be described as:

Choice = Intention + Unanticipated Circumstances

Having made the decision to purchase, consume or use, the individual proceeds with that intent in mind. However, at the last moment the individual may find that the store is out of stock, the stadium is full or the event has been postponed. In this case a decision has to be made whether to consume an alternative offering or to wait for the selected item to become available (*. . . the store just sold the last pair of model X and new stock won't be arriving until next week. I could buy model Z or I could even rethink the bike purchase . . .*).

Future product consumption is the result of post-purchase outcomes and evaluation.

Step 6: Post-purchase outcomes/evaluation

Invariably there are three major outcomes possible during this stage:

■ The consumer is entirely satisfied with the purchase and no further information is required (. . . *these new skates are great and my energy levels are really picking up . . .).*

■ The consumer is not entirely satisfied with the decision and may need to reappraise the alternatives gathered through the initial information search, or may indeed seek out new information (. . . *although the skates are fun I am still not feeling any more energetic than I previously did. I wonder what else I could do? . . .).*

■ The consumer is totally dissatisfied with the experience, may decide that the resolution to the initial problem may not be forthcoming from the sport/exercise experience, and may look outside this domain for satisfaction (. . . *I really need to relax more perhaps I'll take piano lessons . . .).*

Establishment of the process by which individuals arrive at the decision to purchase a particular product or service does not necessarily imply that each step in the process is always laboriously followed. Depending on the type and nature of the purchase, an individual may devote a significant amount of time and effort to the decision-making process, or conversely may make a snap or 'spur of the moment' decision. This latter state usually occurs when the adverse consequence of a poor choice is minimal or the purchase has become habitual behaviour. The amount of thought, and individual involvement, given to a decision to purchase vary considerably. While the purchase of new laces for basketball shoes requires little involvement, the purchase of the initial footwear is often the result of a far more protracted process. The cost of a club membership often has to be weighed against a series of competing forces for disposable income, yet an individual may make the decision to attend a game at the last moment. The membership (or shoes) is a high involvement purchase; the single game (or laces) is a low involvement purchase.

INVOLVEMENT IN THE DECISION-MAKING PROCESS

The *hierarchy-of-effects model* is a framework that has been used broadly to explain involvement in the decision-making process. Mullin et al. (1993) demonstrate how progression through the stages of involvement, from *cognitive* to *affective* to *behavioural*, can impact on consumer behaviour. This translates into the following course of action:

1   Information is obtained about a product or service.

2   An opinion or feeling regarding its use is formed.

3   A decision to accept or reject the offering is acted on.

For example, an individual may be watching television on a Sunday afternoon and see an Australian win the 500 Motorcycle Grand Prix in Malaysia. The viewer is now aware of product on offer. If the race is exciting, grabs the attention and demonstrates great skill, it may either add to the viewer's current feelings about motorcycle racing or even provide for a new perspective. The new perspective may lead to a greater likelihood to attend the Grand Prix when the Australian leg is held.

While such a model may be simplistic, it does provide one way of recognising how consumers arrive at a decision to purchase. Depending on how important the product or service is to the individual, the amount of time spent on the decision-making process may vary radically. This preoccupation exists along a high-to-low involvement continuum. Examples at every step in the process would readily blur into each other; so here we will examine just the ends of the continuum.

High involvement purchases

High involvement purchases make full and extended use of the decision-making process. Expensive, complex and high risk purchases fall into this category. In these instances the consumer will invariably undertake a thorough information search and carefully and selectively examine comparable services or products. The consumer may assess value for money, although cost may not be the major factor where special features, status or functionality is required. Finally, time will be allocated to the decision-making process, and the positives and negatives of the purchase weighed. Once a tentative decision to purchase has been made, affirmation may be sought from an expert in the field or from a significant other. Houses, motorcars and computers are obvious examples, but boats, golf clubs, snow skis or even club membership may fall into the same category.

Sport-marketing strategies aimed at consumers with high involvement in the decision-making process include pointing out .the specific or unique features of the offering, providing maximum technical or personal support for the service or product's use, and reinforcing the wisdom of the purchase choice. Advertising should be selective. It should target appropriate demo-graphic–psychographic market segments as well as affirm lifestyle and connote quality and excellence.

In 1996 Ford used the Australian Tennis Open and the Australian Rugby Union, while Goldmark used the Australian Women's Basketball Team (the Opals), to link their products with fans of tennis, rugby and women's basketball respectively. Likewise, Mitsubishi sponsored the National Basketball League (NBL) in an attempt to elevate awareness of its products in the minds of potential new car buyers.

However, it is not just products that use sport to reach potential clients.

Financial services, bank organisations and private health funds all use sport to promote their services, believing that purchase involvement is invariably linked to that with which the consumer has some familiarity. In the mid 1990s, QBE sponsored the Sydney Swans in an attempt to penetrate the AFL-saturated state of Victoria, and MBF sponsored Hawthorn.

Whether it is insurance or a new car, purchasers have a high involvement in the decision-making process. Sports selectively target and segment audiences for sponsors, and hence the connection between the sponsor's product and the sport creates a win-win situation.

Low involvement purchases

Evans and Berman (1987) define *low involvement* purchases as the decision-making process undertaken when the product or services to be consumed are socially or psychologically unimportant. In these instances information is acquired passively, the decision to act is made quickly, and the product is often evaluated before the purchase is made. Low involvement purchases, irrespective of item, usually follow the same pattern. The choice is usually routine or habitual; the level or prior experience with the product is high, as is the frequency of purchase; the pressure or time may be significant, but the consequences of poor choice are minimal. The purchase of a weekly sports magazine can be thought of as a low involvement decision.

In establishing a strategy aimed at consumers exhibiting low involvement in the purchase process, sport marketers need to provide repetitive advertising and information, encourage familiarity, offer a variety of inducements, create attention-grabbing point-of-purchase (POP) displays and, if possible, distribute in multiple outlets.

A number of companies use sport to saturate the whole market with their message as opposed to identifying a specific segment. Coca-Cola and the AFL, Kodak and the Olympics, and Optus with the ARL are examples. In such instances it is hoped that the purchase of their products will become habitual. Furthermore, in many instances athletes are used to promote basic everyday purchases. Andrew Gaze, Carl Lewis and Lisa Ondieki have each been spokespersons for Rexona; Michael Jordan has promoted Gatorade, Nike and McDonald's; and Lisa Curry and Trevor Hendy are synonymous with Uncle Toby's. In this instance, manufacturers believe that using athletes in marketing their products makes them stand out in a cluttered environment. Chapter 10 examines this concept at length.

THE CONSUMER'S PSYCHOLOGICAL SET

The consumer's *psychological set* is a combination of purchase importance, motivation, perceived risk, innovation, socioeconomic considerations and personality. These are all influenced by the positive, negative or neutral

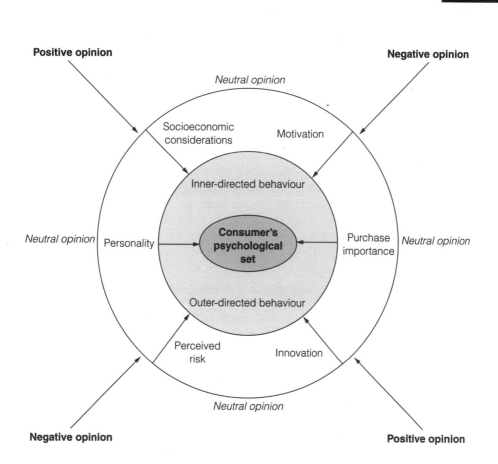

opinions the consumer has about issues and products. In combination, these factors create the impetus for purchase and consumption. One of the major functions of marketing is to create positive product attitudes on the part of consumers. Figure 3.3 illustrates the consumer's psychological set.

While motivation may be a compelling consumer force, it is perceived risk that leads to the greatest level of purchaser insecurity. Risk may relate to the inability of the product to perform as required or to possible injury to the user's health. Similarly, being seen using the product may cause embarrassment or may deflate the ego. Obviously, the greatest risk relates to price: the more expensive an item is, the greater the risk involved.

One of the more important psychological determinants is whether an individual is inner-directed (i.e. interested in satisfying their own needs) or outer-directed (i.e. influenced by the opinions of others). Mitchell (1984) established lifestyle characteristics based on the VALS (Values and Lifestyles) Research Program, which explored the psychographic differences between inner- and outer-directed individuals. Gunter and Furnham (1992) comment that a new VALS system was developed by SRI International in the late 1980s, in a response to an aging population, not a flawed methodology. The new system ensured that what was being examined was entrenched psychological stances rather than shifting values.

Inner-directed were defined as individuals active in outdoor life and sports; they enjoyed cultural events, reading, health food, the arts, travel and educational television. The key characteristics of this group were that they were impulsive, self-centred and oriented towards growth (both internal and external). Conversely, *outer-directed* individuals were seen to be stable and active in the pursuit of entertainment; they enjoyed sport on television rather than strenuous participation, reading newspapers and magazines, and fast food. The key characteristics of this group were that they were conventional, content, hardworking, ambitious and patriotic.

Renwick et al. (1991) argue that Australians tend to be more inner-directed and base their behaviour on that which is internal (i.e. preferences, feelings and expectations). This is a fundamental cultural difference between Australians and North Americans. Consequently, sport marketers must look beyond the core product and product extensions to discover those factors which allow them to capture and satisfy the consumer. Such factors may not be indigenous to the sport; they may be indigenous to the culture in which the activity is located.

This differentiation is important for the sport marketer given the propensity to adopt American styles of sport production for domestic products. The presentation of professional sport is a good example. Now more than ever the skills of highly paid athletes and coaches are on show, both at the stadium and at home on television. Moreover, this display of skill is usually augmented by mascots, cheerleaders, promotional contests, give-aways and other activities. All are designed to enhance entertainment and increase consumer satisfaction.

However, Renwick et al. (1991) argue that there are subtle but significant differences in the way Australians and North Americans respond to situations. While both are of similar extraction, look alike, have had similar pioneering experiences and speak a similar language, the historical development of the respective cultures has been unique. Furthermore, both cultures have encouraged the development of distinctive national identities, which has resulted in differences in values, priorities, attitudes, motivations and ways of interacting. Such differences have had a fundamental impact on the world of sport.

It could be argued that basketball in Australia disproves this notion of cultural nuance. However, the success of the Australian National Basketball League (NBL) in using the American model was the result of importing the US basketball package wholesale. In this instance, mascots, cheerleaders and entertainment were seen as a part of the total basketball experience, not just an add-on. Consequently, such extensions were accepted in Australia as a legitimate part of the sport product.

CONSUMER CHARACTERISTICS

Demographics

Demographics provides a statistical profile of a particular segment of a marketplace. Some of the more frequently recorded demographics include gender, age, marital status, household size and income, educational level and occupation. There may also be instances when information regarding an individual's religious or political affiliation, ethnicity and even class is required. Sportview 3.1 discusses the increasing financial contribution made to sport by the gay and lesbian market. Through the combination of these variables, sport marketers can pinpoint both expanding and declining markets.

PINK DOLLARS

SPORTVIEW
3.1

While diversity of consumer characteristics is already a well-understood concept, the volatility and fluidity of the behaviour patterns of many consumer groups need to be monitored carefully and constantly. The sport marketer must pay keen attention to the factors that impact on consumer characteristics and which motivate consumer behaviour. Moreover, there is a need to be alert to developments in the consumption patterns of specific groups, resulting from demographic and psychographic change.

In the June 1997 issue of *Inside Sport*, Douglas Booth and Colin Tatz discuss the concept of the 'pink dollar' and its impact on sport. The term 'pink dollar' in this context refers to 'the financial contribution made [to sport] by the gay and lesbian community' (Booth & Tatz 1997). Booth and Tatz provide evidence to suggest that there is in excess of 560 000 members of the gay and lesbian community involved actively in sport and leisure and, therefore, the group makes a sizeable contribution to the 'estimated 12 billion sport and leisure dollars generated by Australians each year' (Booth & Tatz 1997).

Both the demographics and psychographics of this group make it important and attractive to the sport industry. It is argued that households comprised of gay and lesbian couples have higher levels of income and education, and are predisposed towards a variety of forms of sport and entertainment. Booth and Tatz comment that the gay and lesbian community spends approximately 250% more on health and fitness related activities than their heterosexual counterparts.

Both Melbourne and Sydney are vying for the rights to hold the VI Gay Games in 2002 and it is easy to see why. In 1998 the Gay Games will be held in Amsterdam, the first time the Games will be held outside the United

States. During the first week of August, 12 500 sport and 2500 cultural participants will gather in Amsterdam to compete and participate in a wide range of activities, including track-and-field, chess, choir, storytelling and women and film. The size, economic power and diversity of the gay and lesbian community make it both a lucrative and popular target market.

Recent research (Quick 1994, 1995) suggests that the ratio of males to females attending sports as diverse as basketball and motorcycle racing has decreased over the last five years. Whereas males once outnumbered females at some sport events by four or five to one, it is now little more than two to one. The Australian Bureau of Statistics (1996) states that for the twelve months prior to 1995 the sports attendance rate of males was 51.5% compared with females at 37.4%. It appears that an increasing number of first-time consumers are women. All sport-marketing agencies would be well served to ascertain for themselves whether or not this is applicable to their sport.

Likewise, while the 15–24 years age bracket is the largest consumer group in terms of going to events, decline in sport attendance occurs thereafter. While the 25–44 age group is rather stable, there is a marked fall-away among the 45–54 age group. As this group is becoming an increasingly large segment of Western economies, strategies need to be implemented to ensure continued consumption of the product by this group at a level with which they are comfortable. Finally, there is an increasing need to concentrate on the family as a consuming unit and to develop market menus (family packages) that cater for their needs.

Lifestyle

Psychographics divides the market into segments or subgroups based on certain behaviours that relate to attitudes, lifestyles or values. Engel et al. (1985) suggest that an *AIO (attitudes, interests and opinions) inventory* is the appropriate psychographic research tool to determine consumer lifestyles. By asking consumers to respond to specific statements on AIOs, information may be gathered as to their hobbies, shopping habits, interests in fashion, food and media, and opinions on a variety of political, social, cultural or economic issues. Psychographics can be more important than demographics in the consumer decision-making process; however, they are often more difficult to quantify.

Observations from research (Quick 1994, 1995) with a psychographic dimension suggests that less than 5% of sport spectators travel from another entertainment venue (e.g. restaurant, bar or hotel) to the sport event. Consequently, sporting organisations should be aware of establishments, especially in the local vicinity, with which collaborative promotional efforts can be conducted.

Furthermore, while there is little doubt that television is a major source of event information for sport consumers, other media cannot be ignored. Specifically, when sport attenders are asked questions related to their magazine-reading habits, women's publications regularly fill three of the top five places. While sport-specific magazines usually rank number one, the increasing female acceptance of, and adherence to, many sports and recreational activities suggests that it is time for sport promoters to reallocate part of the advertising budget to women's magazines.

Personality

'Consumers tend to purchase products that most closely match their own [personality] or that strengthen an area they feel deficient in' (Hawkins et al. 1992, p. 307). In most cases personalities are individual, constant and enduring. They can change, *but* this is usually due to the impact of a major life event. The two most common approaches to understanding personality are individual learning theories and social learning theories, more commonly referred to as *trait vs state* theories of personality.

Individual learning theory argues that personality traits are usually formed in the early stages of an individual's development and remain relatively constant into and through adulthood. Reserved, quiet, shy, extroverted, relaxed or confident are examples of this type of personality. It is easy to see why certain individuals prefer the cinema to day/night cricket, bushwalking to basketball, or golf to aerobics, based on their individual personality characteristics.

Social learning theory argues that environment is an extremely important determinant of human behaviour. In such cases the personality of the individual may alter depending on the situation. An introvert in one instance can be an extrovert in the next, whereas an assertive, aggressive individual can very quickly become timid when faced with a particular fear or phobia. Bungy jumping is a good example of where bravado and confidence are absent in the moments before the leap.

In marketing sport and related activities it is necessary to cater for all personality types. For every fan who wishes to stand in the outer among 'like-minded supporters' and cheer themselves hoarse for their favourite team or athlete, there is another fan who wants to watch the action unfold while seated and in a less emotionally charged environment. For every consumer who wants the latest, brightest and most expensive athletic apparel, there is another who is more than comfortable in a nondescript tracksuit and functional footwear. It is important that the product fits the consumer's personality and vice-versa. An understanding of basic personality types ensures that as wide a range of consumers as possible is being catered for in the marketplace.

Environmental factors

In the latter half of the twentieth century environmental issues such as pollution in its various forms, rainforest destruction, overpopulation, urban sprawl, and the general degradation of land and ocean have been pushed to the forefront of public consciousness. However, while society's relationship to the physical environment is usually viewed from a negative perspective, judiciously utilised changes in technology have the potential to provide great benefits to the modern sport consumer.

Computer technologies and land management have allowed golf courses and resorts to exist side by side with rainforests and sensitive wetlands; sensible urban planning and council bylaws have allowed the establishment of new stadiums or facilities that are sympathetic to local architecture and demographics; and government legislation has been enacted to protect both the rights of individual consumers and the collective good. Although such cases have both supporters and detractors, as witnessed by the 1996 Melbourne Formula 1 Grand Prix, sport marketers and promoters must be diligent in their attempts to create the win-win environment. It is important that the views of all categories of consumers, whether long term, new, emerging or potential, be taken into account when sport promotion takes place.

SUMMARY

Understanding the sport consumer is not a simple task. The sport marketer not only needs to be aware of the primary, secondary and tertiary factors that impact on consumer decision making. They also need to comprehend both the process, and the level of involvement, by which the decision to purchase or consume is arrived at. Other important determinants that must be considered before establishing marketing strategies include the specific demographics and psychographics of the constituent group, along with germane environmental factors.

While comprehending the complexity of the sport consumer's decision-making process is one of the more intricate tasks facing the sport marketer, unquestionably it has become a critical part of marketing management strategy. Although it is not always possible to fully understand how this process takes place, assiduous attention to the unique characteristics of specific consumers, coupled with a broad awareness of how decisions are reached, will provide the sport marketer with a solid framework within which marketing strategies can be developed.

CASE
STUDY

WHERE HAVE ALL THE BALMAIN FANS GONE?

Until the mid 1990s Australian Rugby League (ARL) football had a firm foothold in many parts of Australia. The national competition had conducted a successful marketing campaign using Tina Turner, and both national and international expansion took place. Yet while the future success of the competition seemed assured, a number of the individual clubs faced uncertainty. One such club was the Balmain Tigers. This club once had a very successful association with the working class community in which it was located. However, Balmain's proximity to Sydney Harbour and the city itself have resulted in a gentrification of the suburb.

The decline of the once great club was attributed to the changing demographics of the area, and John Huxley's front page article in the *Sydney Morning Herald* (23 July 1994) 'Balmain boys don't cry over footie any more' did little to dispel the myth. Former rugby league club president George Stone suggested that 'the basketweavers—the new young professional class of people who have supplanted football's traditional working class support' were 'not interested in sport'. Balmain boss Keith Barnes displayed greater insight, suggesting that 'potential supporters may be switching sports'. By laying Balmain's plight at the feet of the suburb's young professionals who failed to be impressed by the 'club's tradition and [perceived] importance to the community', the club attempted to attribute decline to forces beyond its control.

Although this sporting organisation exhibited a lack of understanding of the consumer, it is not alone. It merely exemplified a serious flaw in the administration and marketing of a number of sports and recreational activities. With respect to entertainment, product marketing has long been surpassed by services marketing. Rather than merely informing the community of its existence, sporting organisations need to inform potential clients about the benefits to be had by consuming their products.

Having recognised the dilemma, it is up to organisations, like the various rugby league clubs, to undertake the necessary market research that will enable them to reconfigure their product with 'new consumers' in mind. Allowances have always been made for the 'traditions' of sport, and this has given it some leeway in a congested entertainment marketplace. However, the gap between sport and other activities has closed significantly, and in the 1990s sports need strategies that not only facilitate a quick response to change but may even anticipate it.

Questions

1   What was the flaw in George Stone's thinking?
2   Was the major factor influencing the consumer decision-making process primary, secondary or tertiary, or a combination? Why?
3   What were the major demographic and psychographic differences between past and present Balmain residents? Should this have resulted in declining attendances at Tigers' games? Why/why not?
4   The organisation exhibited a fundamental lack of understanding of the sport consumer. Explain how and why?
5   What real alternatives faced the Balmain Tigers' management?

REFERENCES

Australian Bureau of Statistics (1996). *Sports Attendance, March 1995,* Canberra.

Booth, D. and Tatz, C. (1997). 'Pink dollars', *Inside Sport,* June.

Engel, J. F., Blackwell, R. D. and Miniard, P. W. (1985). *Consumer Behavior,* Dryden Press, Hindsdale, Ill.

Evans, J. R. and Berman, B. (1987). *Marketing,* Macmillan, New York.

Gunter, B. and Furnham, A. (1992). *Consumer Profiles: an Introduction to Psychographics,* Routledge, New York.

Hawkins, D. I., Best, R. J. and Coney, K. A. (1992). *Consumer Behavior—Implications for Marketing Strategy,* Irwin, Boston, Mass.

Lee, B. A. and Zeiss, C. A. (1980). 'Behavioural commitment to the role of sport consumers: an exploratory analysis', *Sociology and Social Research,* 64 (3), 405–19.

Mitchell, A. (1984). 'Nine American lifestyles: values and societal change', *Futurist,* August, pp. 4–14.

Mullin, B., Hardy, S. and Sutton, W. A. (1993). *Sport Marketing,* Human Kinetics, Champaign, Ill.

Nowell, M. (1995). 'The women's golf market: an overview of spectators and participants', *Sport Marketing Quarterly,* 4 (2), pp. 39–41.

Ohle, M. A. and Wise, S. M. (1981). 'Football fan sees day in court', *National Law Journal,* 4 (11), p. 100.

Quick, S. (1994). *Fan Survey Report to IMG* (Australian Motorcycle Grand Prix), Unpublished technical report.

——(1995). *Fan Survey Report to the Sydney Kings,* Unpublished technical report.

Renwick, G. W., Smart, R. and Henderson, D. L. (1991). *A Fair Go for All: Australian/American Interactions,* Intercultural Press, Yarmouth, Maine.

Shoham, A. and Kahle, L. R. (1996). 'Spectators, viewers, readers: communication and consumption in sport marketing', *Sport Marketing Quarterly,* 5 (1), pp. 11–19.

Stone, G. P. (1955). 'American sports: play and dis-play', *Chicago Review,* 9, pp. 83–100.

Stotlar, D. K. (1993). *Successful Sport Marketing,* Brown & Benchmark, Dubuque, Iowa.

——(1995). 'Sports grill demographics and marketing implications', *Sport Marketing Quarterly,* 3 (3), pp. 9–16.

Wise, G. L. (1973). 'The business of major league baseball as a spectator sport', *Ohio State University Bulletin of Business Research,* 48 (10), pp. 1–3, 6–7.

4

Market research, strategies and information systems

CHAPTER OUTLINE

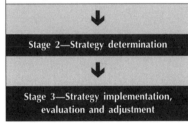

Stage 1—Identification of marketing opportunities

Step 1—Analyse external environment (forces, competition, publics)

Step 2—Analyse organisation (mission, objectives, SWOT)

Step 3—Examine market research and marketing information systems

Step 4—Determine marketing mission and objectives

⬇

Stage 2—Strategy determination

⬇

Stage 3—Strategy implementation, evaluation and adjustment

CHAPTER
OBJECTIVES

Chapter 4 examines the relationship between information systems and marketing strategies. The marketing information system (MIS) is described as necessary to store, organise, analyse and disseminate data useful in decision making. The chapter also establishes the link between information systems and market research. This link is crucial in organising data to understand the various market segments for sport products.

After studying this chapter you should be able to:

1   Create a basic marketing information system.
2   Discern the variety of sources for a marketing information system.
3   Articulate the components of small-scale market research.
4   Comprehend the market segmentation process.
5   Establish strategies for market segmentation selection.

**HEADLINE
STORY**

AFL CLUB MEMBERSHIPS ON THE RISE

. . . Between 1992 and 1996 memberships of the Sydney Swans increased more than three-fold, from 3,020 to 9,525. Essendon Football Club had the highest membership numbers of Melbourne based clubs with 24,324 members. St Kilda had the biggest membership jump in 1996 as their membership escalated from 8,870 to 14,375. However when compared to interstate clubs such as Adelaide (42,283), West Coast (26,663) and newcomer Port Power (35,000 for 1997, projected to eventually reach 45,000), Melbourne based clubs in most instances are lagging some distance behind. Even Tasmania believes that when granted entry to the AFL they will start with 13,500 members which will expand to 20,000 within five years. In 1996 the average club membership was 17,931 which was a significant rise from the 1992 average of 11,705. (Connolly 1996, p. 5)

The significance of the above membership figures does not lie in a comparison between Melbourne-based and interstate Australian Football League (AFL) clubs, but rather in the potential databases available to the various clubs. If analysed, manipulated and used to inform decision-making strategy, these will provide the football clubs with a readymade *marketing information system* (MIS). However, it should be noted that it is not only professional sporting organisations that have need for an MIS. All sporting organisations, even at the very local level, can gather information from their supporters, participants, suppliers and sponsors, which should frame their decision making.

DEVELOPING MARKETING INFORMATION SYSTEMS

To make informed decisions organisations need information, and lots of it. Yet the collection of this material is only a starting point for the construction of an MIS. Once compiled, this information must be integrated, analysed and used to guide the direction of the organisation. Stanton et al. (1995) believe that an MIS is an 'ongoing, organised set of procedures and methods designed to generate, analyse, disseminate, store and later retrieve information for use in decision making' (p. 48). Nevertheless, they also acknowledge that for the MIS to be successful the data should be not only of high quality but also used in a realistic manner and adopted as a source of decision making by the organisation. Figure 4.1 provides a basic design for the construction of an effective MIS. In this instance the population is divided into consumers and non-consumers, and relevant information is obtained using appropriate data collection methods. The information is then collated and integrated. From this resource base, marketing strategies can be formulated, along with mechanisms for monitoring effectiveness.

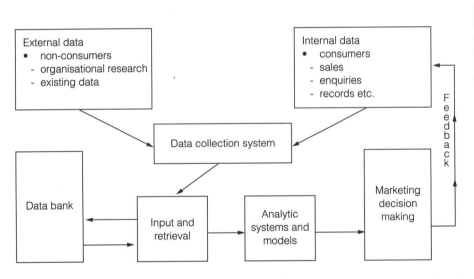

FIGURE 4.1

A basic design for a marketing information system

The current need for ongoing market research and the establishment of increasingly sophisticated MISs are the result of a dynamic, constantly changing sport environment. With less time for deliberation, increased accountability, growing consumer expectations and the ever-expanding scope of marketing activities, sporting organisations need rapid access to reliable information that will result in clear, appropriate decision making. Fortunately for sport, the quantity and quality of available information are constantly expanding. How such information is used is the real key to organisational success.

In order to develop an extensive MIS, sport marketers need to collect general market data, data on individual consumers, and data on competitors and their participants.

General market data includes all that information which relates to the broad environment in which the sport operates. Within its area of operation, most commonly referred to as its *critical trading radius*, the organisation needs to establish size, demographics, the consumer habits of residents and workers, the way such individuals choose to spend their leisure time, and any specific trends that will impact positively or negatively on the sport. This information is particularly important for sports hoping to expand nationally and be successful. The profile of the specific sport fan needs to be well represented in the new market for the sport to have any hope of success. The Sydney Swans believe that there is a potential AFL base of approximately 640 000 supporters in the city, and the Australian Rugby League (ARL) obviously felt that the predominantly Aussie Rules city Perth would support rugby league when it introduced the Western Reds to the national competition.

Once *individual consumer* data have been collected and entered into the appropriate database, the sport marketer has a myriad of information available with which to establish marketing strategies. Name, address, phone number, gender, age, occupation or student type, purchase patterns and payment methods are a small representation of the type of information that can easily be collected by sporting organisations. Both the Sydney Kings in 1995 and the Footscray Football Club in 1996 offered season tickets as inducements for fans to supply their names, addresses and phone numbers when responding to fan surveys.

A third source of information for sporting organisations relates to *competitors* and their participants. It is critical that sporting organisations not only be aware of who their competitors are, but also know the consumers of a rival's products or services. In many instances a number of sports can successfully operate in the same area as their fans may be dissimilar. Basketball, tennis, soccer and netball appear to be quite different in their support base. So, apart from observing general promotional strategies, these sports would be best served by focusing on information that is internal to the organisation and sport specific. Nevertheless, if a sport is jockeying for position in the marketplace, competitor pricing, promotion, and product breadth and depth need to be noted. This is particularly important when junior competitions and leagues are involved. Juniors will invariably gravitate to those sports which provide them with opportunities at the local level.

DATA SOURCES FOR A MARKETING INFORMATION SYSTEM

There are two major sources of data for any MIS: external and internal data. *External data* may be primary or secondary and have been collected by the sporting organisation or an external agency. *Internal data* are all that information, such as basic enquiries, that the organisation collects during the day-to-day operation of its business.

External secondary data

There are numerous sources of secondary data that sporting organisations can use to assist in the formation of a strategic marketing plan. The most obvious starting point is *government agencies* such as the Australian Bureau of Statistics (ABS). *Involvement in Sport Australia* and *Sports Attendance* are two potential information sources. *Involvement in Sport Australia* (Castles 1993) showed the numbers and demographic characteristics of persons involved in sport at some time in the previous twelve months, the type of involvement and whether or not that involvement was paid for, while *Sports Attendance* (McLennan 1995) was the result of a survey designed to assist sporting organisations to understand their spectators. Both documents provide basic information useful for a number of sporting bodies.

Libraries and *chambers of commerce* also are useful sources of information, especially at the local level. Data related to trends and uses of local events and facilities should be held there, as well as the various municipal rules and regulations that govern the conduct of sport events. Larger community libraries, along with those attached to institutes of higher education, often contain much of the government or commercial data that have been collected in relation to sport. Chambers of commerce will hold data relating to the income and expenditure patterns of local industry, which can assist sport marketers in establishing profiles that may match their organisation.

An increasing amount of data is being gathered in various research units in Australian *universities*. While much of this information is proprietary, some of the findings are being presented at conferences and appearing in academic journals. Likewise, a growing number of sport-marketing academics are being used as market research consultants and are bringing an ever increasing repository of skills and knowledge to their task.

Advertising media are constantly engaged in the collection of secondary data. While it may not be specific to the focus of the sport marketer, information related to demographics and psychographics may be useful for sponsorship or advertising. This is particularly the case when the characteristics of the media information match a particular sport's own data.

A final source of secondary data is *private organisations* such as Brian Sweeney and Associates. Their publication *Australians and Sport* annually looks at sports participation, attendance, television viewing and sponsorship awareness. Similarly, Roy Morgan Research, most commonly associated with the Morgan Gallup Poll, has established a variety of services and products that can provide significant data to sporting organisations. The Roy Morgan *Monitor* covers areas such as tourism, entertainment and leisure, and the organisation annually conducts more than 60 000 personal interviews. The collection of such data provides wide-ranging information on consumer behaviour and media usage, and as such can be an invaluable secondary source for the sport marketer. For more specific data it is even possible in some instances for organisations to contract for an industry-related question to be included in a survey.

Primary data

Primary data may be internal or external and are a product of collection methods and purpose.

The most common type of internal data is data collected from enquiries, letters and telephone calls. Moreover, these may be in the form of complaints or praise. However, accounts, credit card purchases and general sales also can provide a wealth of information indicating consumer trends in relation to a sporting organisation's product or service. Other sources of internal information can include an organisation's employees, contractors, suppliers and sponsors. All can offer the sport marketer useful advice, and any such comments should be heeded.

However, there is little doubt that the best source of data available to the sport marketer is that which is purpose driven by the organisation. In this way direct answers to specific questions can be obtained about the habits and consumption patterns of sport participants and consumers. Moreover, the collection of primary data through market research is not difficult. All that is required is access to the information source, time, energy and good questions!

MARKETING RESEARCH IN SPORTING ORGANISATIONS

Basically, *market research* in sporting organisations seeks to answer six questions about consumers in relation to their consumption of the product. Initially, sporting organisations need to know WHO their consumers are, but this is only the tip of the iceberg. WHY they choose the particular sport product, and WHEN and WHERE that consumption takes place, are equally important. WHAT that consumption entails in terms of pre- and post-event activities, and HOW the product is used, also are critical in terms of establishing a complete consumer profile.

In no particular order, the information requested generally falls into the categories of general and sport specific.

General information

Usually, the *general* information requested focuses on *demographics* such as gender, age, occupation, household size, place of residence and methods of transport.

Similarly, information is often elicited regarding *psychographic* issues, which were addressed at length in Chapter 3. Fundamentally, psychographic information conveys data related to the what and how of consumer behaviour, such as how many times in a given period a person visits a particular establishment (e.g. restaurant, hotel or facility), the number and type of vehicles in the household, and the various electronic items they use. This latter issue is becoming more and more important as sporting organisations endeavour to ascertain how many of their consumers not only use personal computers but also have access to the Internet. With many sporting organisations establishing interactive home pages, new opportunities for establishing enhanced databases are plentiful.

An equally important general question relates to *where consumers get their information*. Frequency and type of newspapers read, radio stations listened to, television stations and programs viewed, and magazines read, both general and specific, are crucial factors in determining promotional strategy. Research has indicated that television is the major source of event information, with radio rating poorly. However, there are two other issues that need to be considered. The variable word-of-mouth is a constant response, and a market research strategy needs to be developed to control this. Moreover, although general questions about magazines read invariably result in a sport-specific magazine being the most common response, magazines targeted towards women often feature strongly. With the increasing female acceptance of, and adherence to, many sports and recreational activities, perhaps it is time that sport marketers reallocated a portion of their advertising budget to this expanding market segment.

Sport-specific information

Sport- or activity-*specific* questions frequently relate to attendance patterns, influences to purchase or consume, and levels of satisfaction with various aspects of the event.

In relation to *attendance*, organisations need to be aware of both the *depth* of product or service use (i.e. how many years consumers have been buying the offering) and the *breadth* of use (i.e. the variety and level of consumption of the activities, products and services offered).

Likewise, organisations need to know what influences the consumer's decision to *purchase* this particular product when faced with a diverse and ever expanding range of options in the sport or entertainment marketplace.

Finally, organisations need to be apprised of the customer's levels of *satisfaction*, that is, their perceptions of the range and quality of the merchandise and concessions sold, of the scope and type of services offered, and of the way in which the organisation conducts its business.

By asking such questions of sport fans and consumers, organisations can establish comprehensive profiles of their customers, which in turn allows the organisation to strategically market its products or services in a diverse marketplace. As Huggins (1992) notes:

> . . . the principal focus of the marketing function in sport is not so much to be skilful in making sport fans or participants do what suits the interest of sport as to be skilful in conceiving or doing what suits the interest of the fans or participants without changing the sport itself. (p. 40)

MARKET RESEARCH AND STRATEGY

Mullin et al. (1993) suggest that:

> . . . the most critical factor in marketing success is the marketers' ability to collect accurate and timely information about consumers and potential consumers and to use this data to create marketing plans that are specifically targeted to meet the needs of the specific consumer groups. (p. 115)

To ensure that such activities become both useful and operational, the data gathered should be incorporated into an MIS.

THE MARKET RESEARCH PROCESS

In many respects the days are gone when sporting organisations could rely on general sport market research to inform their decision making. It is not difficult for sporting organisations to conduct their own market research, to engage a specialist to assist in part of the research, whether it be questionnaire construction, data analysis or interpretation, or to contract a consultant to deliver product-specific information. Organisational decisions should be based on the needs and expectations of the consumer, and the only way this can be ascertained is to ask. While the phrase 'use it or lose it' is a sport cliché that is often used and abused, when applied to market research there is not a more appropriate sentiment.

Selection methods

Surveys
The survey is the most popular mechanism for gathering sport-related data. However, whether done personally or by telephone, this method does have a number of strengths and weaknesses. Nevertheless, the personal survey is still potentially the most useful of all research methods as it allows the sport marketer to source first-hand information regarding the purchase and consumption patterns of sport fans. For this reason organisations such as the Footscray Football Club, the Canterbury-Bankstown Rugby Leagues Club and the South East Melbourne Magic Basketball Club regularly engage in this type of research.

The limitations of this type of research include:

- Errors in survey construction can result in skewed data.
- Surveys are often labour, time and even cost intensive.
- There may be an element of interviewer bias.
- Potential respondents may simply refuse to cooperate or be less than candid with responses.

Telephone interviews are further limited by day and time of call and are restricted to individuals who make their phone numbers available. This automatically excludes households without telephones and those who choose to have an unlisted number. Yet despite such limitations, this data collection technique, especially when triangulated with other methods such as focus groups and observation, is still the most revealing.

Mall or shopping centre intercepts

Mall or shopping centre intercepts involve collecting data from individuals as they go about daily activities. This is a less time-consuming method of collecting data than going door-to-door, but rejection rates can be high. Potential respondents are always more likely to assist the research process if they are provided with a small token of appreciation or are entered in a raffle for membership tickets, sport-related products or perhaps even a vacation.

Focus groups

The Sydney Swans is just one organisation that is using focus groups to assist in the creation and refinement of marketing strategy. A focus group is a small group of interested individuals gathered to talk about the issues that an organisation and its consumers believe are important. Usually the size of the focus group is less than ten, which provides everyone present with an opportunity to contribute. This method encourages individuals to engage freely in dialogue with each other, with the data collector in this instance prompting, guiding and recording. Trends and issues emanating from focus groups are often the catalyst for more structured, follow-up research.

Observation

Although not always undertaken in a formal manner, the observation technique should be used by the sport marketer on an ongoing basis. From Bill Veeck with baseball during the 1940s, to Kerry Packer and World Series Cricket in the 1970s, to Michael Wrubleski and the National Basketball League (NBL) in the 1990s, good sport promoters have recognised the value of getting out and both talking to the fans and watching their behaviour. In many instances this simple act can inform the sport marketer about which aspects of their market strategies are having the desired result and which need some work done on them. Ideally, the observation could lead to the focus group, which could lead to the structured survey, which should then lead to action based on rigorous data collection.

Experimentation

Experimentation can be useful to the sport marketer in specific circumstances. In this instance the researcher or promoter manipulates one variable while holding all others constant. Changing the venue, time, or day of event, or altering uniforms, are just a few of the variables that professional sport clubs manipulate during a pre-season competition in order to gauge reaction to such changes. If the changes prove popular, they may be adopted for the regular season. However, if not, the previous modus operandi is utilised.

Sampling

To obtain a truly *random sample* everybody in attendance must have an equal chance of being surveyed, and in most cases this is not feasible due to issues such as restricted access. Data collectors can attempt to survey every *n*th person who walks through the event entrance. However, usually this requires diligent counting by a large number of data collectors. Moreover, rejection can be high the closer the event is to starting. If it is an event with seating, it is preferable to identify seats prior to collection. Hence anybody purchasing a ticket has a chance of sitting in a particular seat in a specific area.

In reality, unless a truly random sample is obtained, generalisations only can be made to the population sampled. Anything more is guesswork, intuition or at best an indication. Stanton et al. (1995) state that this type of sampling, known as *convenience sampling*, is quite common in market research (p. 62).

Sample size

If a truly random sample is required, the sample size is predetermined. Information regarding this is available in most basic statistics texts. For sporting organisations that are using the convenience method, sample size should be large enough to enable the sport marketer to be comfortable in the knowledge that any decision making that flows from the market research will be well grounded. Purely anecdotal evidence suggests that in many instances 750 respondents is an acceptable sample size, as anything above this usually provides only minor statistical variations in response.

Research design

Although types of research design are as varied as the sports products and services being researched, there are a number of basic principles that should be adhered to. They include:

- Sport marketers should only ask questions they need to know the answer to. If responses to perceived personal questions, such as income levels, are not needed, they should not be asked, as incorrect responses can bias results.
- For ease of analysis, questions should be closed, mutually exclusive and free of ambiguity.
- While questions should be thematically linked, each response should provide a unique piece of information. This approach means that a questionnaire or survey can be reduced to sections, which can then be used and manipulated as a stand-alone instrument.
- The research design should be of sufficient scope to provide all necessary

information, but short enough to encourage broad-based participation in the process.

- Mullin et al. (1993) suggest that the sport marketer needs to have a feel for the kind of answers expected. While it could be argued that this may introduce bias into the project design, most research is initiated through some type of intuitive process.

Potential uses of marketing research

Sport-marketing research generally can have numerous outcomes, although the following are the most common uses:

- It can enhance the flow of communication between the organisation and the customer.
- It may facilitate the creation of promotional strategies or the development of sponsorship proposals.
- It should assist in general decision making and programming.

Sportview 4.1 illustrates how a small-scale market research project may be devised, constructed, administered, analysed and interpreted.

THE INAUGURAL CATHAY PACIFIC AUSTRALIAN PGA PAR 3 GOLF CHAMPIONSHIP

SPORTVIEW
4.1

In 1995 the organising committee of the inaugural Cathay Pacific Australian PGA Par 3 Golf Championship commissioned a small market research project from a group of sport marketing students at a Sydney university, specifically an on-course consumer behaviour survey (Moore et al. 1995). The major objective of the research was to provide the organising committee with consumer information that would enable the construction of a database. Other objectives related to the provision of a mechanism for the evaluation of the current championship and the establishment of criteria for future promotion strategies and market research.

The questionnaire was the result of the collaboration between the chairman of the organising committee and the research group, and resulted in the collection of 100 surveys over the three days of the championship (the estimated attendance for the three days was 900). Surveying was conducted over a two-hour period each day, with each member of the research team covering the entire course three times each day.

The researchers believe that the following exogenous variables may have been influential in encouraging visitors to attend the championship: the novelty factor associated with an inaugural event, the long weekend factor, and the general abundance of sport available to sport consumers at that time of year, which included the AFL Grand Final, the Bathurst 1000 motor race and the ARL Grand Final the previous week.

Consumer information gleaned from the survey included gender, postcode spread and density, occupation, golf club membership, media analysis, reasons for attending the tournament, and ratings for features such as food and beverage, staff helpfulness and availability, toilets and leader boards. Respondents were also asked about future consumption patterns related to the tournament. General comments were also asked for, and frequencies for these were established.

The research team established a number of significant points, such as that local and non-local respondents had different reasons for attending the event and that there was a low attendance rate by golf club members. The research team brought these and other issues to the attention of the organising committee and suggested topics and areas for future research. These included scheduling, merchandising, golf vs sport fans and an education process aimed at ensuring understanding of the specific nature of the competition.

SEGMENTING THE SPORT MARKET

In constructing strategy, marketers may treat the marketplace as aggregated or segmented. One differs from the other in the following manner.

Market aggregation strategy views the marketplace as a homogeneous or a single unit. Realistically, this has extremely limited applicability to sport, as the latter is such a complex phenomenon.

If *all* activity had the same meaning for *all* people, it would be easy for sport marketers to establish a single marketing strategy that was generalisable to all cases. However, as this is not the case, sport marketers must establish specific promotional strategies that target different groups within the community—*market segmentation* strategy. On any given weekend, Australian sport attracts millions of spectators and participants who participate for a myriad of reasons. Moreover, members of the same family or household may witness or participate in a particular activity for a variety of motives. In an attempt to encourage such groups to initiate or maintain their involvement in the sport or activity, different strategies must be developed that are specifically aimed or targeted towards such groups.

What is market segmentation?

Stanton et al. (1995) suggest that *market segmentation* is the process of dividing the total heterogeneous market for a product or service into several segments, each of which tends to be homogeneous in all similar aspects. Mullin et al. (1993) further suggest that segmentation is central to an understanding of consumers as it recognises differences in consumer behaviour, which directly informs marketing strategies. Consequently, the task facing sport promoters is first to determine how consumers use sport products or services to meet individual needs, and then to determine which factors are common. This allows the sport marketer to categorise or group customers according to the type of people they are, the way they use the product or service and finally their expectations of it.

Segmentation and strategy selection

The advantage of market segmentation is that it is a consumer-oriented philosophy and as a result endeavours to satisfy as many needs and wants in the marketplace as possible. Moreover, by segmenting the marketplace sport promoters can more judiciously allocate marketing resources, and this should result in greater returns on the investment or 'more bang for the bucks'.

Although the segmentation possibilities are endless, there are a number of broad-based variables that provide an effective starting point for segmentation strategy. Commonly, consumers are segmented on the basis of demographics, psychographics and behaviour towards the product. This latter category is further divided into the benefits wanted from the product and product usage, or how the product is used. Figure 4.2 schematically represents such variables.

The market segmentation process

Demographic segmentation
Demographic segmentation is the most common form of segmentation. Segmentation based on gender and age was discussed in some detail in Chapter 3. However, other important demographic determinants include religion, income, occupation, level of education, marital status, geography and stage in the family lifecycle. Social class also is an important consumer demographic. However, it is usually an amalgam of other demographic variables.

Although all demographic variables are potentially important, *stage in the family lifecycle* has the greatest impact on sport consumption. Traditional lifecycle stages include singles, married couples with and without children, 'empty nesters' and elderly singles. However, single parents, older childless couples and divorced individuals are increasingly representing alternative stages in the family lifecycle. Stages in the family lifecycle directly impact on consumer behaviour, and it is essential for sport marketers to provide mechanisms that encourage customers to remain loyal from childhood to senior years.

Geographic issues such as regions, city size, the urban–rural dichotomy and even climate can also influence strategic sport marketing. The types of activities practised by Tasmanians in June will be very different from those in North Queensland at the same time of the year. Moreover, the transient nature of sections of Australian communities, especially the ongoing migration

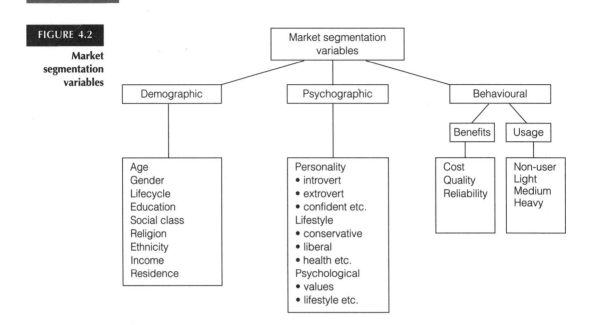

FIGURE 4.2

**Market
segmentation
variables**

of southerners to warmer climates, should result in ongoing opportunities for sport in such areas. It may also be safe to assume that spectator expectations in country and regional areas are quite different from expectations in the city. Yet even cities cannot be treated as homogeneous for the sport marketer. While ease of event access, parking and travel time are often important to the suburban commuter, public transport and additional entertainment possibilities may be far more important to the inner city dweller.

Psychographic segmentation

While demographic information can inform the sport marketer *who* the consumers are, this information alone does not tell *why* they consume. To partially answer this question consumers need to be further categorised according to psychographics.

Psychographic segmentation is based on variables that are associated with personality types or lifestyles. This approach attempts to explain consumer behaviour in terms of the reasons for purchase and the needs it meets. In the process, categories of values and lifestyles are established, such as outer-directed, inner-directed and need-driven (Mullin et al. 1993) or socially aware, visible achievement, traditional family life, young and optimistic (Stanton et al. 1995).

However, while the nomenclature may differ, basically the sport marketer must cater not only for the consumer who is confident and assertive, believes that there are advantages in being associated with the sport product and wishes to be seen to be involved with it, but also for the consumer who wishes to satisfy *intrinsic* as opposed to *extrinsic* needs. Such intrinsic needs may vary from personal development to pure escapism. Hence an individual may purchase a sailboard because they can, or because they like the scene associated with sailboarding and wish to fit in or belong. Likewise they may see the purchase as an opportunity for individual growth through the development of new skills, or they may just wish to 'sail away'.

Irrespective of the reasons for consumption, all individuals must be catered for if possible. Chapter 3 provided an expanded analysis of the impact of psychographic behaviour on sport.

Behavioural segmentation

Behavioural segmentation refers to the benefits and usages attributed to the consumption of the product.

Stotlar (1993) comments that *benefit segmentation* is based on the unique benefits of a product or service that motivate a consumer to purchase, that is, on the different benefits that the consumer expects from the product or service. An important feature of this concept is that the consumer is purchasing the benefit, not the product. For example, an athlete may purchase an electrolyte replacement drink not because they are thirsty or like the taste, but because they believe that it will replace essential elements the body has lost during intensive exercise. Hence the athlete is purchasing the benefit, a more rapid recovery, rather than the product, a sport drink. However, the most obvious case of benefit segmentation in sport relates to the purchase of athletic shoes. Shoes that correct pronation or supination, provide arch support and cushioning, or glow in the dark are just a small sample of the potential benefits of athletic footwear.

Benefit segmentation is not applicable to sport products only. A person may choose to attend a basketball game not because they have an innate love of the sport, but because a friend is going. In this instance the benefit inherent in going to the game is the opportunity for social interaction. If the friend were going to the zoo, the idea of attending the basketball game would be moot. In this instance the chance for social interaction is just one benefit that the sport promoter provides. Similar benefit segmentation strategies can focus on the entertainment aspect of the event or the opportunity to escape from the rigours of the daily grind and indulge in recreative activity, to be involved in the production and presentation of an event or activity, or simply to be seen at an event. Sportview 4.2 examines a number of the motivations and reasons for both competing in triathlons and joining clubs in New South Wales.

TRIATHLON ASSOCIATION OF AUSTRALIA

SPORTSVIEW
4.2

Chang and Johnson (1995) set up research aimed at investigating motivations for competing in triathlons, reasons for joining triathlon clubs and the impact of different features of triathlon membership on the renewal intentions of existing members. Previous research in the area of membership had examined member wants, and the authors found this somewhat limiting. The present research used conjoint analysis to examine the relative appeal of various attributes of club membership.

The research clearly identified four distinct market segments among the Triathlon NSW membership: mainstream members, frequent racers, true believers and value seekers. Mainstream members were the largest segment of Triathlon NSW membership and did not display any high or low valuations for the membership attributes being studied. Frequent racers displayed higher valuations for race discounts and lower valuations for the less tangible attributes of membership. True believers had high valuations for most attributes of membership; however, this group provided the highest level of support for the proposition that Triathlon NSW membership should be compulsory. Value seekers were those athletes who were very price sensitive and this was the only attribute that they considered important.

Chang and Johnson suggest that the existence of four distinct benefit segments may merit the offering of a range of membership packages or even the ability to pick and choose different elements of the membership package. Finally, they argue that the management of clubs and associations should undertake studies of this order to gain a better feel for the benefits expected by members from their organisations.

Usage segmentation focuses on the amount of the product or service consumed by the customer. The usage pattern for a product or service is especially applicable to spectator sport. In attempting to define the consumer in respect to usage patterns, broad categories including non-user, light user, medium user and heavy user are established. Chapter 7, which examines the sport promotion mix, discusses usage patterns in light of the escalator principle, and so only passing reference will be made to it at this stage.

While it is often desirable to encourage consumers to elevate their level of consumption, this is not always possible or even desirable. For example, Spolestra (1991) believes that in terms of the consumption of professional sport, the season ticket or membership is not for everyone. Consumers, due to lack of finance, time or even interest, find that attending every game is not possible. Hence he argues that the concept of seat sharing, whether corporate or with friends, results in maximum use of a particular seat. By adopting an approach called *full menu marketing* the organisation provides numerous packages that allow fans to consume at a level with which they are comfortable. In this instance the market has been segmented based on usage.

Multiple segmentation

The establishment of a segmentation strategy depends on a number of features such as size, reachability and receptiveness of the target market. As such, multiple segment strategies are often developed, which enable the sport marketer to construct different yet coordinated strategies for delivering a product or service. The establishment, maintenance and ongoing addition to an organisation's MIS will assist sporting organisations to become increasingly discerning and creative in their target market segmentation strategies.

PLANNING SEGMENTATION STRATEGY

In 1995, Graham Halbish, former chief executive officer of the Australian Cricket Board (ACB) identified four target audiences that had developed since the World Series Cricket era:

- the *purist*, who understood the nuances of the game and often had a history of active participation in the sport;
- the *sport enthusiast*, who followed a wider range of activities;
- the *follower*, who, while unlikely to attend matches, avidly followed the game via the media; and
- the *entertainment seeker*, who sought action and excitement.

Each segment was important for distinct reasons. While purists were perceived as essential for Test Match Cricket longevity, enthusiasts were important for their current level of interest. Similarly, while followers were important because of their desire for cricket information, entertainment seekers provided for an important segue into the female and youth market. The task facing the ACB therefore was, and is, to ensure that the four target markets are offered a product that suits their needs. As Halbish pithily commented, the other imperative is to make sure that individuals from different market segments are not seated beside each other.

At a macro level, Pitts et al. (1994) established the *sport industry segment model* articulating the segments represented in Figure 4.3:

- The *sport performance segment* relates to the spectatorial or participative products offered to the consumer.
- The *sport production segment* is concerned with those products designed to produce and/or enhance a quality product.
- The *sport promotion segment* involves those products used as promotional tools.

The use of models such as this is but one example of how sport marketers need to be creative in establishing strategies to segment their markets. Pitts et al. (1994) also point out that the challenge facing sport marketers is the identification of new ways of segmenting the industry, and of combining segments, which could lead to the discovery of more meaningful market segments.

Shoebridge (1993) argues that emerging market segments constantly force

FIGURE 4.3   The sport industry segment model

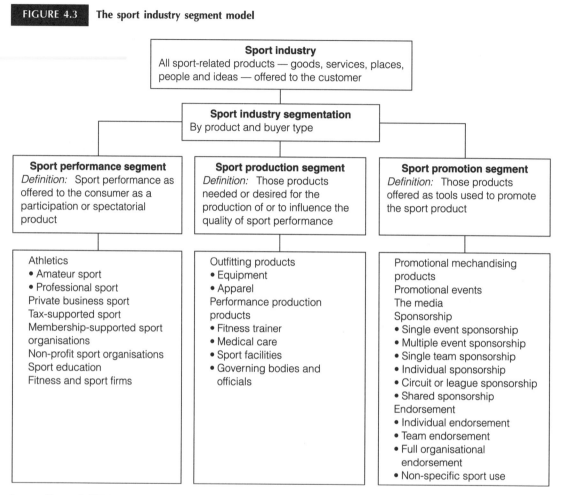

Sport industry
All sport-related products — goods, services, places,
people and ideas — offered to the customer

Sport industry segmentation
By product and buyer type

Sport performance segment
Definition: Sport performance as
offered to the consumer as a
participation or spectatorial
product

Sport production segment
Definition: Those products
needed or desired for the
production of or to influence the
quality of sport performance

Sport promotion segment
Definition: Those products
offered as tools used to promote
the sport product

Athletics
• Amateur sport
• Professional sport
Private business sport
Tax-supported sport
Membership-supported sport
organisations
Non-profit sport organisations
Sport education
Fitness and sport firms

Outfitting products
• Equipment
• Apparel
Performance production
products
• Fitness trainer
• Medical care
• Sport facilities
• Governing bodies and
  officials

Promotional mechandising
products
Promotional events
The media
Sponsorship
• Single event sponsorship
• Multiple event sponsorship
• Single team sponsorship
• Individual sponsorship
• Circuit or league sponsorship
• Shared sponsorship
Endorsement
• Individual endorsement
• Team endorsement
• Full organisational
  endorsement
• Non-specific sport use

Source: Pitts et al. (1994, p. 18)

marketers to re-examine their marketing strategies. He suggests that in the
1990s strategies must be established to cater for the adversarial shopper, the
8–12-year-olds, very-early product adopters, the over-45s, the over-50s, teen-
agers and debt-laden families. When these groups are linked with an
expanding Asian market, changes in family structure, lifestyle and workforce,
and an elevated level of competition, new segmentation possibilities are
endless. As sporting organisations approach the new millennium, how they
respond to the potential inherent in such growth and diversity will have a
direct impact on their ongoing viability.

Given that the sport marketplace is so dynamic and constantly in a state
of change, sport marketers must not only recognise change, but also be
strategically ready to respond to it quickly. Moreover, the speed at which

change occurs will only increase in the future, and sporting organisations, already sensitive to market share if mergers and franchise relocations are any indication, will need to be increasingly creative in their segmentation strategy.

SUMMARY

In the 1990s, ongoing data collection is essential for the adaptation of an organisation to a volatile and changing marketplace. Moreover, such data need to be collected in a systematic ongoing manner and stored in a marketing information system (MIS). The MIS should not only allow for ready accessibility, but also enable ongoing decision making and strategy selection.

The major sources of information for an MIS include both external and internal data. External data may be classified as primary or secondary and involves data that have been collected by the sporting organisation or an external agency. It should be understood, however, that while some general market and sport market research may have universal applicability, the sporting organisation cannot do better than collect its own data.

Market research in sporting organisations seeks to answer the questions of who, when, where, what, how and why. While the survey is the most popular mechanism for gathering sport-related data, mall or shopping centre intercepts, focus groups, observation and even experimentation are becoming increasingly popular. Collected data should explore general market conditions, individual consumers and competitors. Internal data are information that the organisation collects during the conduct of its business.

A major advantage of solid market research is that it allows the sport marketer to divide the total market into several segments. Commonly, consumers are segmented on the basis of demographics, psychographics and behaviour. This latter category is further divided into the benefits wanted from the product and product usage. Finally, it should be remembered that the sport marketplace is in a constant state of change. Hence sport marketers must place themselves in a position to not just respond to change but even anticipate it.

TAI CHI—THE GENTLE ART OF RELAXATION

CASE STUDY

This case study was originally prepared by Ken Slinger, University of Western Sydney, Nepean.

Tai Chi, the oriental form of relaxation and exercise, has gained enormous popularity in Australia since its introduction in 1970. Currently the largest group offering Tai Chi classes to the community is the Australian Academy of Tai Chi. This institution is controlled and run by the Khor family. The founder, Gary Khor, was a Malaysian student attending university in the mid 1970s, who began conducting classes for his fellow students. As word-of-mouth publicity caused his classes to expand beyond the university campus, a second brother, Eng Khor, was brought from the United Kingdom to assist with this fledgling operation. From its early beginnings the academy has grown to 6000 members with 100 instructors spread across Australia's major cities. Increased awareness by the Australian community of health and relaxation has led to a rapid expansion of this form of exercise and relaxation.

In establishing the early market for Tai Chi, the founders were faced with the task of identifying their market. In addition, suitable locations or sites had to be acquired so that students could assemble in areas that provided firm footing, good lighting and easy access. Early sites were developed in Paddington and the upper north shore of Sydney. Community awareness was considered to be of prime importance; so demonstrations in shopping centres were conducted to make the community aware of what Tai Chi represents.

A profile of Tai Chi consumers identified an age range of 20–80 years, from all walks of life and most suburbs in Sydney. In addition to shopping centre demonstrations, external lessons and demonstrations in public parks and on beaches were also conducted. Brochures outlining the history of Tai Chi and its development in Australia were produced and distributed to interested members of the community. Testimonials were secured from doctors, physiotherapists and others testifying to the physical benefits of Tai Chi, while other testimonials were secured that acknowledged the benefits in the area of relaxation and stress reduction.

Tai Chi was conducted according to levels of competence. Most students would progress to Level 6, with a lesser number of competent students moving on to more advanced classes. To further supplement the promotional strategies, advertisements were taken out in regional newspapers, but ultimately word-of-mouth or a referral system was the best method of acquiring new students. To date, 65% of the students are female and 35% are male, with age or physical handicaps being only a minor barrier.

Source: Adjusted from Stanton (1995).

Questions

1   Develop a target market for Tai Chi in the following areas:
    (a) your city;
    (b) Australia.
    Consider the above in the light of demographic, psychographic and behavioural segmentation.
2   Develop a strategy for improving consumer perceptions of Tai Chi or changing any incorrect preconceptions.
3   Discuss expansion strategies for this form of exercise and relaxation.

REFERENCES

Brian Sweeney (1995). *Australians and Sport*, Annual Survey of Sporting Participation, Attendance, TV Viewing and Sponsorship Awareness, Brian Sweeney & Associates, Melbourne.

Castles, I. (1993). *Involvement in Sport Australia*, Australian Bureau of Statistics, Canberra.

Chang, M. and Johnson, L. (1995). 'Segmenting the Triathlon Association membership market: an Australian example', *Sport Marketing Quarterly*, 4 (4), 25–28.

Connolly, R. (1996). 'After the first merger comes the flood', *Sunday Age, Sportsweek*, 19 May, p. 5.

Halbish, G. (1995). 'Developing professional sporting leagues', Keynote address to the Sport Management and Marketing Conference, Sydney, August.

Huggins, M. H. (1992). 'Marketing research: a must for every sport organisation', *Sport Marketing Quarterly*, 1 (1), pp. 37–40.

Malhotra, N. (1996). *Marketing Research: An Applied Orientation,* Prentice-Hall, Englewood Cliffs, NJ.

McLennan, W. (1995). *Sports Attendance*, Australian Bureau of Statistics, Canberra.

Moore, D., Allport, S. and Kelly, A. (1995). *The Inaugural Cathay Pacific Australian PGA Par 3 Golf Championship Report*, Commissioned research report, Sydney.

Mullin, B., Hardy, S. and Sutton, W. A. (1993). *Sport Marketing*, Human Kinetics, Champaign, Ill.

Pitts, B., Fielding, L. and Miller, L. (1994). 'Industry segmentation and the sport industry: developing a sport industry segment model', *Sport Marketing Quarterly*, 3 (1), pp. 15–24.

Shoebridge, N. (1993). *The Secrets of Successful Marketing*, Text Publishing, Melbourne.

Spolestra, J. (1991). *How to Sell the Last Seat in the House*, 1, SRO Partners, Portland, Oregon.

Stanton, W. J., Miller, K. E. and Layton, R. (1995). *Fundamentals of Marketing*, 3rd edn, McGraw-Hill, Sydney.

Stotlar, D. (1993). *Successful Sport Marketing*, Brown & Benchmark, Dubuque, Iowa.

PART II

Strategy determination

5

The sport product

CHAPTER OUTLINE

Stage 1—Identification of marketing opportunities

Stage 2—Strategy determination

Step 5—Determine core marketing strategy

Marketing mix—sport product

Stage 3—Strategy implementation, evaluation and adjustment

Chapter 5 introduces the first variable in the marketing mix: the sport product. This chapter also moves to Stage 2 of the strategic sport-marketing planning process (SSMPP): strategy determination. During this stage, marketing mix variables are reviewed and combined in such a way as to determine the core marketing strategy. It is first important to identify and understand the product and its attributes. Key tools to assist in determining the core marketing strategy are introduced, including perceptual mapping and product lifecycle.

After studying this chapter you should be able to:

1   Identify the difference between core and product extensions in sport.
2   Describe the characteristics of a service.
3   Understand why sport is classified as a service product.
4   Identify the dimensions of quality service.
5   Understand the strategic importance of product positioning.
6   Understand the strategic significance of the product lifecycle.

THE FORD AUSTRALIAN OPEN—CONTRIBUTING TO THE SERVICE ECONOMY

The 1995 Ford Australian Tennis Open was held at Flinders Park (now Melbourne Park), Melbourne over the period 16–29 January. It is a major event in world tennis, being one of four Grand Slam tournaments. Most of the world's top players come to Melbourne for the tournament which also attracts a considerable number of spectators and substantial media coverage. A total of 312,000 spectators passed through the turnstiles for sessions of the 1995 event. Approximately 120,623 visitors attended the Open with 82.5% (99,608) from Victoria, 10.4% (12,530) from interstate and 7% (8,486) were from overseas. Expenditure in Victoria by interstate visitors was estimated to be $10 million and $10.7 million by overseas visitors. Total economic impact increased national Gross National Product by $39 million. The impact on Victorian Gross State Product was $50 million with $30 million of private consumption expenditure. Prizemoney for the event was $8.25 million. (National Institute of Economic and Industry Research 1995)

Melbourne Park is the home of Australia's premier tennis event: the Ford Australian Open. The contribution of this tournament to the Victorian and Australian economy is highlighted above. Given the significance of this tournament, Tennis Australia and the Victorian government were naturally keen to retain the status of the Australian Open as one of four Grand Slam tournaments. In the mid to late 1980s, there was a possibility that the event could lose this prestigious standing, and also be relocated to Sydney. Tennis Australia, with the assistance of the Victorian government, responded by moving the tournament from Kooyong, a traditional tennis venue replete with wooden stands, limited seating capacity and grass courts. The world of tennis had clearly outgrown one of Australia's traditionally important sport facilities. The event was moved to the new tennis facility with the retractable roof, now known as Melbourne Park.

By the 1990s, a professional tennis tournament of the standing of the Australian Open had to provide the very best in terms of facilities and prizemoney to attract the world's leading players. Quality facilities were also required to cater for the 312 000 spectators who attended the 1995 event. The Australian Open of the 1990s provides a very good example of how the sport product has changed during the last twenty years. Players will not accept substandard facilities and prizemoney. Spectators also expect first-class facilities, a first-class product and first-class service at the event. The purpose of this chapter is to examine the place of the sport product in the marketing mix and illustrate the importance of service in the provision of the sport product.

THE SPORT PRODUCT

Boyd and Walker (1990) describe a *product* as being 'anything that satisfies a want or need in terms of use, consumption or acquisition' (p. 385). Moreover, the authors note that a product is a problem solver in that it is purchased because of the benefits provided. Essentially, consumers buy benefits, not the product.

Quality is another feature of perceived product benefits. McCarthy and Perreault (1990) define *quality*, from a marketing perspective, as 'the ability of a product to satisfy a consumer's needs or requirements' (p. 219). As the authors point out, this definition focuses on the consumer's view of what quality may mean, or of a product's suitability for some specific purpose. In sport, the product is easily discernible; however, the quality of the core product is something over which the sport marketer has no control. This is a distinctly unique aspect of sport and sport marketing. For this reason, it is important to recognise a broader definition of the product than simply the game.

Mullin (1985) identifies the playing of the game as the *core product* and all the related activities, such as food and beverage, merchandise, half-time entertainment, video screens and the facility itself, as *product extensions*.

Returning to the Australian Open, the new Melbourne Park facility and all the services provided within and during the tournament are crucial in measuring the overall success of the event. Ultimately, once players have agreed to play in the Australian Open there is little organisers can do to ensure quality matches. Even matches receiving 'top billing' such as Sampras vs Agassi or Seles vs Graf do not always guarantee quality contests. The quality of the supporting product extensions, however, can be guaranteed. It is at this point that similarities are observed between the importance of quality service provision and quality product extensions. Often, most product extensions possess an element of service provision, and hence quality is important.

As a consequence, product extensions have the capacity of ensuring that spectators at the tennis have an enjoyable day despite oncourt results.

Branch (1992) supports the need to broaden sport product position and program concept. He observes that:

> Forward-thinking professional sport marketers realise that the game, sport's *'core'* or primary product, is *not* the organisation's *only* or most important product . . . diversifying sport's program concept in this manner, the core product accrues substantial 'value added' qualities. In other words, the event becomes a more consistent buy for sport consumers. The challenge is to focus less on the game's outcome and more on a positive customer experience. (p. 25)

Sportview 5.1 demonstrates the relevance of this argument by emphasising the success of the National Basketball Association's (NBA) Charlotte Hornets basketball franchise. The Hornets entered the NBA as a new franchise in 1988, primarily comprised of cast-offs from other teams. Oncourt success was not realistic; so attention to detail and customer satisfaction with the experience of the event became benchmarks for the Hornets' marketing efforts (Macnow 1990).

<table>
<tr><td>SPORTVIEW
5.1</td><td></td></tr>
</table>

A WINNING GAME PLAN

'Down on the court, the Charlotte Hornets (NBA-USA) were slogging through a contest that looked more like a playground pick-up game than a battle between professional teams in the NBA. Kelly Tripucka, one of the Hornets' top scorers, connected only once in 11 attempts. J. R. Reid, the team's highly touted rookie, was clearly overmatched by David Robinson . . . But up in the stands of the Charlotte Coliseum, no one seems to mind. The 23,388 fans—the 43rd consecutive sold out crowd for a Hornets game. Although the Hornets have won less than a quarter of their games since entering the NBL, they have attracted fans and made money beyond all expectations.

'The Hornets may be the most thoroughly packaged franchise in sport, with everything from half time shows to players' uniforms designed down to the most minute detail. How well does it work? Consider these figures:

- In their inaugural season, the Hornets led the NBA in attendance, drawing more than 950,000 fans despite losing 62 of 82 games.
- The franchise turned a larger profit than any other NBA team.

'The club's fans spend money not just on tickets but also on ancillary products. In 1989, fans spent an average of 39 cents per person at every game on shirts, mugs, key rings, and other licensed souvenirs.

'Attention to detail and total customer satisfaction with the experience of the event are benchmarks for the Hornets' marketing efforts. "We've borrowed the philosophy from Disney that the small things count" says general manager

Scheer. "To us, taking the fans for granted is the ultimate sin". What plays in Charlotte now is the Hornets. And though they've lost more than they've won so far, they are playing to great reviews.'

Source: Excerpts from Macnow (1990, pp. 82–4).

The Charlotte Hornets also illustrate an example of another important concept in product planning: *branding.* 'Branding means the use of a name, term, symbol, or design—or a combination of these—to identify a product' (McCarthy & Perreault 1990, p. 235). The Hornets represent a brand within the NBA competition. Brands are important to their owners as they help consumers to recognise a company's products; and if brand recognition and acceptance are high, there exists the potential for high brand loyalty. In sport, teams and clubs such as the Hornets are examples of a brand, and it is through team and club loyalty that prominent brand recognition is achieved. The issue of branding will be considered in more detail in Chapter 12 when the role and purpose of promotional licensing are reviewed. Developing highly recognisable brands as trademarks and logos is an important source of revenue and promotion for sporting organisations and athletes. These trademarks form the basis of merchandise and licensing programs, an important form of product extensions.

This section has stressed the importance of quality service provision in the product extensions; so it is appropriate now to consider in more detail how and why sport is a service product.

SPORT AS A SERVICE

Services marketing has increased in importance across a wide range of industries during the last decade. In Australia, the Bureau of Industry Economics (1995) has noted that:

> . . . despite easing in recent quarters, services output is growing faster than any other sector of the Australian economy. Production rose by 1.1% in the June quarter 1995, contributing to the 6.5% growth in the last year. This is the twelfth consecutive quarter of growth in aggregate services output and leaves services production 16.6% above the level recorded in the trough in production in 1991. (p. 48)

As a consequence of this strong production growth, employment in this sector increased by more than 90 000 jobs in the June 1995 quarter. Significantly, tourism-related activities and cultural and recreational services were major contributors to this strong production and investment. Exports in tourism services grew in real terms by over 10% between the June quarter 1994 and the June quarter 1995. Major sporting events such as the Ford Australian Open and Formula 1 Grand Prix have the capacity to add to the strong performances indicated in the tourism-related, cultural and recreational service activities. The impact on the Australian economy of a major event such as the Ford Australian Open was indicated at the start of this chapter.

Service defined

Why is sport considered a service? This section will answer this question by discussing the characteristics that distinguish a good from a service. A common theme of authors writing on sport marketing (Mullin 1980, 1985; Mullin et al. 1993; Shilbury 1989, 1991; Sutton & Parrett 1992) has been their agreement on how the unique characteristics of sport as a product require marketing personnel to adopt different strategies from those traditionally espoused. Although many of these writings are devoid of specific references to services marketing, the discussions pertaining to these unique characteristics align sport to the attributes of a service.

Zeithaml et al. (1985) summarise the characteristics distinguishing a good from a service. This summary helps in describing sport as a service.

- *Intangibility*: Services cannot be seen, tasted, felt or smelled before they are bought. Services are performances rather than objects. For example, is it possible to describe what product benefits people take home with them after playing sport? Or the benefits derived from watching a game of basketball? There is no tangible take-home product in this example.
- *Inseparability of production and consumption*: Services are simultaneously produced and consumed. The product cannot be put on the shelf and bought by the consumer. The consumer must be present during production. For example, consider getting a haircut, attending a sporting contest or visiting a physiotherapist. You need to attend.
- *Heterogeneity*: Services are potentially variable in their performance. Services can vary greatly depending on who performs them. Many different employees can come into contact with the consumer; therefore, consistency becomes an issue. Few sporting contests are the same from one week to the next, and the consistency of service delivery by people working at such an event can also vary.
- *Perishability*: Services cannot be stored. Hotel rooms not occupied, airline seats not sold or tickets to a sporting contest not sold cannot be reclaimed. Simply, it is lost revenue and indicates the importance of understanding that services are time dependent.

Perhaps the most significant difference between a good and a service is the simultaneous production and consumption of a product. The implications of this for marketing will be examined further in Chapter 13, when the convergence of the marketing and operations functions are considered in relation to the 'place' of the facility in the marketing mix.

A *service*, then, is predominantly any activity or benefit that is intangible and does not result in ownership.

Both spectators and participants take from the game a series of experiences, none of which are physically tangible. Students of sport marketing should be careful not to confuse some of the tangible products that can be purchased as a consequence of the game or sport (product extensions) with the game or sport itself (core product). Without the sport, the merchandise would not exist.

Classification of services

When classifying services we need to determine the extent to which the customer must be present. To assist in making this determination, Lovelock (1991) uses a four-way classification scheme involving:

- tangible actions to people's bodies,
- tangible actions to goods and other physical possessions,
- intangible actions directed at people's minds, and
- intangible actions directed at intangible assets.

Table 5.1 illustrates Lovelock's schematic with examples.

Considering the classification used in Table 5.1, where would sport be placed? This is an interesting question, as the answer might depend on whether we were being specific about physical participation or attendance. Physical participation could be classified as a people-based service directed at people's bodies. Attendance at sporting events could more accurately be classified as a people-based service directed at people's minds. The context of participation

What is the nature of the service act?	Who or what is the direct recipient of the service?	
	People	**Possessions**
Tangible actions	*Services directed at people's bodies* Health care Passenger transportation Beauty salons Exercise clinics Restaurants Haircutting	*Services directed at goods and other physical possessions* Freight transportation Industrial equipment repair Janitorial services Laundry and dry cleaning Landscaping/lawncare Veterinary care
Intangible actions	*Services directed at people's minds* Education Broadcasting Information services Theatres Museums	*Services directed at intangible assets* Banking Legal services Accounting Securities Insurance

TABLE 5.1

Understanding the nature of the service act

Source: Lovelock (1991, p. 26).

in sport is important in framing marketing strategies. The most obvious example is the formation of marketing strategies aimed at attracting players to participate in a competition or sport and the marketing strategies required to attract people to attend a sporting event. In either case, it is necessary to ask why such a classification scheme is important.

Lovelock (1991, p. 27) notes the following questions, which help to answer this question:

1   Does the customer need to be physically present:
    (a) throughout the service?
    (b) only to initiate or terminate the service transaction?
    (c) not at all?
2   Does the customer need to be mentally present during service delivery? Can mental presence be maintained across physical distances through mail or electronic communications?
3   In what way is the target of the service act 'modified' by receipt of the service? And how does the customer benefit from these 'modifications'?

If, as is the case in sport, customers need to be present to play or watch a live event, they must enter the service factory, returning us to the importance of simultaneous production and consumption. When spectators or participants enter the sport factory, this has an obvious implication for the sport marketer. The sport factory is best known as the facility, and the implications for managing the customer in the sport factory or facility will be specifically investigated in Chapter 13. The major implication of the consumer entering the sport factory is that sport spectatorship, in particular, is a service experience.

In sport, it is hard to overcome the winning (I had a good day/night) or losing (I had a bad day/night) syndrome. Although this special range of emotions will never be removed from the sport product, their importance can be diminished by ensuring that the quality of service is very good. Again, the importance of the product extensions through quality service provision is highlighted. Slowly, sporting organisations are beginning to recognise the need to plan for service quality.

SERVICE QUALITY

Service quality research has become prominent in the marketing literature during the last decade. Much work has been conducted to identify the key attributes of quality service. These attributes have been developed from the perspective of the consumer. Extensive research using focus group interviews, conducted by Parasuraman, Zeithaml and Berry during the 1980s, identified the ten dimensions of service quality shown in Table 5.2. Parasuraman et al. (1985) note that 'regardless of the type of service, consumers used basically similar criteria in evaluating service quality' (p. 46).

Dimension	Description	TABLE 5.2
Tangibles	Appearance of physical facilities, equipment, personnel and communication materials	**Dimensions of service quality**
Reliability	Ability to perform the promised service dependably and accurately	
Responsiveness	Willingness to help customers and provide prompt service	
Competence	Possession of the required skills and knowledge to perform the service	
Courtesy	Politeness, respect, consideration and friendliness of contact personnel	
Credibility	Trustworthiness, believability, honesty of service provider	
Security	Freedom from danger, risk or doubt	
Access	Approachability and ease of contact	
Communication	Keeping customers informed in language they can understand and listening to them	
Understanding the customer	Making the effort to know customers and their needs	

Source: Zeithaml et al. (1990, p. 22).

Figure 5.1 illustrates the application of the ten dimensions in relation to the way the consumer views quality: 'Perceived service quality is the result of the consumer's comparison of expected service with perceived service' (Parasuraman et al. 1985, p. 47). Figure 5.1 illustrates how word-of-mouth, personal needs, past experience and external communications build up a level of expected service quality. Word-of-mouth is a particularly strong source of pre-consumption information that determines the likelihood of purchase.

The lack of tangible clues creates difficulties for consumers in making decisions about service product purchase. In relation to purchasing a good, it is often possible to try out the product before purchase, or at least to see it in action. This would be the case with the purchase of a car or computer. As services are time dependent, it is often not possible to try out the product before purchase. Consumer recommendation about a service is a powerful influence in pre-purchase decisions. Similarly, past experience with a service provides the same opportunity to develop perceptions about the quality of the service being considered. Finally, external communications, via advertising, create levels of expectations about service quality.

The gap that ultimately exists between 'expected' service and 'perceived' service is the result of the four factors consumers bring to product consumption. Companies should ensure that they do not promise more than they can actually deliver, as unrealistic expectations created by a company can negatively affect the level of perceived quality, when in reality the level of service quality was good. By implication, a firm needs to understand customer expectations as well as to have an intimate knowledge of the product attributes, which are the genesis of the expected service levels and product positioning.

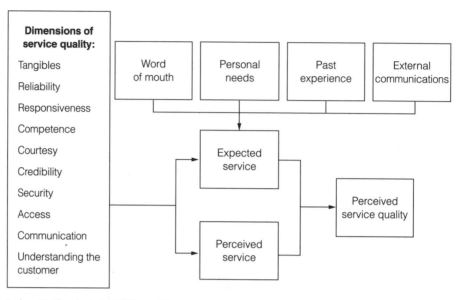

FIGURE 5.1

Customer
assessment of
service quality

Source: Zeithaml et al. (1990, p. 23).

POSITIONING THE SPORT PRODUCT

Positioning the sport product in the marketplace is strategically important as it plays a pivotal role in marketing strategy. Product positioning links the market research and market segmentation phases described in Chapters 4 and 5. In essence, *positioning* is the perceived fit between a particular product and the target market. To a large extent, the success of a product within a chosen market depends on how effectively it has been positioned. The sport product, like any other product, is subject to the same range of preferences and perceptions by consumers.

Defining position

Use of a *perceptual map* to define positioning is helpful. The perceptual map is formed by asking consumers to rank certain product attributes. In much the same way as attitude is measured, key attributes of the sport product are identified. In a hypothetical example, two simple bipolar scales measure level of excitement of the sport and expense, or cost to attend. The two attributes are put together to form a two-dimensional diagram as is illustrated in Figure 5.2.

Location of the product in a *product space* is called a *position* and is a crucial step in defining the market that a product is targeting. In the example shown in Figure 5.2, only sport products are considered. This is important as the sports chosen here include the major professional sports played in

Australia. An astute marketer would realise that the sport product should be positioned within a larger competitive frame than just sport, as professional sport is part of the much larger entertainment industry. However, to ensure that this example does not become too complex, it has been restricted to just sport entertainment. Costs for entry to the sports shown in Figure 5.2 are based on 1996 ticket prices. It is also important to note that under normal circumstances the market researcher would ask the sport consumer about the attributes used in this perceptual map. Spectators would be asked, for example, to rate the excitement level of rugby league, or cricket or basketball.

Figure 5.2 highlights the intense competition that exists for the consumer's disposable income during the winter season. The Australian Football League (AFL), for example, is seeking a segment of spectators looking for high levels of excitement at moderate to low cost. Rugby league, through the Australian Rugby League (ARL) competition, is a direct competitor and as a consequence a substitute for the AFL given that both games are played during the winter. The genuine likelihood of substitution, of course, assumes that both codes are played in the same market. In Sydney, Perth and Brisbane this is the case. It is only a matter of time before it is also the case in Melbourne. In Melbourne, the National Basketball League (NBL) also appears to be a major competitor to the AFL. Figure 5.2 shows that the product attributes of the AFL and NBL are similar, as is demonstrated by the product space both occupy.

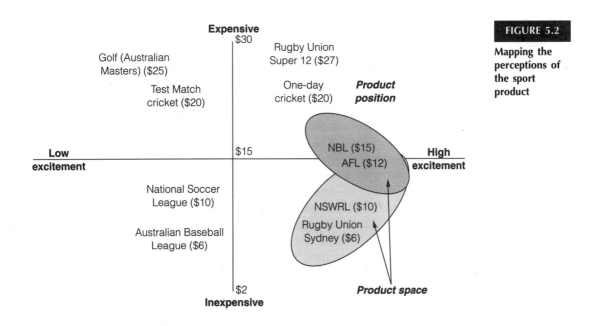

FIGURE 5.2

Mapping the perceptions of the sport product

Establishing position

Establishment of a desired position in the marketplace is a priority for the sport marketer. This can be achieved in two ways: by physical design and through advertising.

Physical design refers to the rule changes and modifications that can be made to render a sport more attractive to certain segments of the market. Cricket is the best example of this. The two forms of the game shown in Figure 5.2 exemplify the way in which a sport has been modified to capture different segments of the market.

Establishing a product position through *advertising* is being used more and more by sport marketers. The most notable campaign aimed at repositioning a sport was the NSW Rugby League's (NSWRL) advertisements featuring Tina Turner. In 1989 the NSWRL embarked on an advertising campaign aimed at presenting rugby league as a glamorous, racy and exciting game. This was necessary as the league was emerging from a period where the game was beset by image problems such as excessive on-field violence and a struggling image at both club and league level. The 'What you get is what you see' and following 'Simply the best' campaigns were extremely effective in creating a new and different image for the game. In effect, the game was being repositioned to broaden its appeal, which had been predominantly to the blue collar male market. Between 1983 and 1990, when the league embarked on its turnaround strategy, attendances doubled and television ratings rose by 70% indicating some success in broadening the appeal of the game. This is also indicative of the phases through which products pass in varying stages of their lifecycle.

PRODUCT DEVELOPMENT

Kotler et al. (1989) note that 'a company has to be good at developing new products. It also has to be good at managing them in the face of changing tastes, technologies and competition' (p. 354). Every product, including sport products, seems to pass through a *lifecycle*. Typically, this follows a consistent pattern in that the product is conceived or born and develops through several phases of maturity before dying as new and improved products emerge. In sport, it is also true that various sports oscillate within this described lifecycle.

There are some differences, however. In general, it is unusual for a sport to die. It is possible to trace the history of many sports worldwide and to note how the majority have stood the test of time. Not all sports have always been successful, but they have continued to exist and experience varying levels of success. Rather than the actual sport dying, sporting competitions, events, tournaments and clubs or teams tend to disappear or require marketing strategies designed to extend their lifecycle. Relocation of teams, rule changes, mergers and the provision of new facilities all constitute ways in which various forms of the sport product endeavour to avoid decline. The other major difference is that sporting organisations do not often release new products in the same way as the car and computer industries do. The sport product is again seen to be reasonably stable.

The ARL, like the AFL, is an example of a sport that has had to rejuvenate its products. Expanding to form national competitions was one way that this was achieved. In rugby league, the previously described Tina Turner advertising campaign was an integral part of relaunching a sport that was losing market share or, in product lifecycle terms, was in decline. Other strategies included expanding the competition to Queensland, the ACT and Western Australia. Within Sydney itself, some clubs were closed or relocated to overcome declining inner city populations. For example, the Balmain Tigers survived 87 years on the dedication of its fans and working class traditions. As the demographic profile of the Balmain region changed, the club was forced to look elsewhere to ensure that it maintained the necessary financial infrastructure to continue to participate in the league. The club's name was changed to the Sydney Tigers, broadening its appeal, and it relocated to a new facility in Parramatta.

The product lifecycle curve

Figure 5.3 illustrates the *product lifecycle (PLC)*. The typical PLC curve is S-shaped and characterised by four different phases:

1 *Introduction* is a period of slow sales growth. Profits are non-existent at this stage because of the heavy expenses of introducing the product to the market.

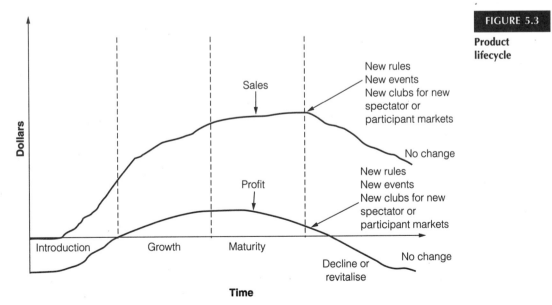

FIGURE 5.3

Product lifecycle

2 *Growth* is a period of rapid market acceptance and increasing profits.
3 *Maturity* is a slow period of sales growth because the product has been accepted by most potential buyers. Profits stabilise or decline because of increased marketing designed to defend the product against competition.
4 *Decline* is the period when sales show a strong downward drift and profits erode.

In the late 1970s and early 1980s a number of traditional Australian sports entered the decline phase of the PLC. Cricket, the Victorian Football League (VFL) and NSWRL all struggled as Australians' appetite for sport and leisure options began to diversify. A subsequent surge in interest for individual sport and recreational activities such as jogging, triathlon, aerobics and cycling saw the profits and previous market dominance of these sports begin to erode. Also in 1979, the NBL was formed, capitalising on the trend towards the professionalisation of sporting competitions. Entry of the NBL was indicative of the heightened intensity of competition that has emerged in the professional sport sector.

The NBL presents an interesting example of the way in which the PLC can be used to assess the phases of development of this product. Sportview 5.2 explains in more detail the progress made by the NBL since its inception in 1979. What can be understood from this information is that by 1995 the NBL had reached the maturity stage. Attendances and the level of support for the NBL seemed to have plateaued. This was not a special feature of season 1995, but a trend that had become apparent during the 1993 and 1994 seasons. Attendances had peaked at about 80% of stadium capacity, sponsor interest had levelled, and the NBL was still experiencing problems in attracting good television ratings. The challenge for the NBL was what to do to arrest the decline.

One solution examined during 1996 was to change the season in which the NBL plays, moving the NBL season to the summer. Not only would this provide the impetus to relaunch the NBL as a summer game; it would also, as would be shown in the perceptual map, have the capacity to alter its direct competitors, including an increased capacity to obtain more television time. Moving to summer would see the intense competition provided by the AFL and ARL reduced, at the risk of moving into cricket's competitive space. Also, the Australian Baseball League (ABL) and National Soccer League (NSL) would become relevant competitors. Neither the ABL nor NSL has the same product intensity as either the AFL or ARL. Cricket, in particular one-day cricket, does have the competitive intensity to create difficulties for the NBL. Unlike the football codes, programming of cricket is not as intense and as weekend orientated as that of the AFL and NSWRL. In winter, the AFL often schedules matches on Friday night, Saturday afternoon, Saturday night, Sunday afternoon and Sunday night, with a move to schedule some Monday night matches also. In terms of both television and live attendance at matches, this creates difficulties for basketball. Cricket on the other hand, has fewer matches, and they tend to be concentrated in one major city on any given weekend. The opportunity to rejuvenate the NBL is therefore presented through the season change that will take effect in the summer of 1998.

THE NBL—PRODUCT DEVELOPMENT

A substantial drop in attendance figures forced the NBL to review its marketing strategies, in a bid to generate more excitement and momentum in the early part of the 1993 season. After ten rounds, the NBL—which trumpeted a sensational growth in attendances throughout the 1980s and early 1990s—was down by almost 270,000 fans. (Brown 1993, p. 6)

The ten-team NBL competition commenced in 1979 as an outlet to provide a regular opportunity for its elite players to play top-line basketball. It also quickly became the promotional vehicle for basketball in Australia. The gate for the first season was 196 000 for all home and away games. By 1995, as is shown in the table below, attendances had risen to 1 097 678 from 201 games played across the country. An average of 5461 fans attended games in 1995. From 1979 to 1984 attendances grew 82% to 355 828 spectators; but in the five years to 1988 they jumped 130% clearly demonstrating the sport's appeal, and in the five years to 1993 they rose to just over 1 million. Seasons 1993 to 1995 show that growth then slowed and that the NBL in terms of attendances had plateaued.

The success of the NBL in capturing the public's imagination in the 1980s can be traced to several reasons. It was a highly entertaining game, played in a comfortable warm stadium, enjoyed by men and women, and revered by children. Hype generated by the NBL was also fostered by enormous goodwill from the print media and radio media. There was no question that this most American of sports had taken off in Australia, but to continue to grow it needed television to play a more significant role (Brown 1992). The Seven network, which held the rights to televise basketball in Sydney and Melbourne prior to 1992, was reluctant to give basketball a greater profile. Channel Ten took up the rights to televise the NBL in 1992 on the promise that the NBL would be shown in prime time. As season 1992 unfolded the Ten network realised that NBL programming was suffering from low ratings. The only exception to this was Perth. Following the break for the 1992 Olympic Games, the Ten network removed the NBL from prime time television.

Television remains a source of frustration for the NBL. In 1995, the NBL made the following observations in relation to television and its impact on product development:

With television we found ourselves in a difficult situation. In order to make television work, the NBL will have to become much more flexible in its scheduling (playing in non-competitive days and times), consider changing the time of year we play, clean up the court clutter (to increase NBL branding and strengthen television advertising). All of these strategies may have a cost to the clubs. This cost will not be initially met by television rights revenue. But without making some

NBL attendances 1984–95

Year	Total	Games	Average	Annual % Increase
1984	242 022	209	1158	—
1985	317 372	187	1697	31
1986	394 685	189	2088	24
1987	483 467	192	2518	22.5
1988	536 493	166	3232	11
1989	662 439	170	3897	23.5
1990	887 443	195	4550	34
1991	825 645	194	4256	(7)
1992	945 117	173	5463	14.5
1993	1 083 490	199	5447	14.6
1994	1 127 033	198	5692	4
1995	1 097 678	201	5461	(2.6)

Source: NBL (1994 and 1995).

or all of these changes, television rights revenue may never reach the level to be able to finance the changes. Almost every aspect of the NBL/Club business now comes back to creating success on television. Marketing, merchandising, attendance, rights money and sponsorship levels all point to television needing improving. The television ratings are a mystery. Our worst rating performance in recent history comes at a time when a new ARM Quantum survey shows that basketball has increased its stranglehold on the youth in this country. Basketball ranks as the top sport played by boys (10–17) at 59% thirteen points above the next team sport, cricket (47%). For girls, basketball ranks third at 31% behind swimming (52%) and netball (36%). There are more mysteries in the result of the survey that indicates what the youth market are watching on television. Basketball is way out in front at 50% ahead of cricket at 38%—significantly improving its position since the last youth monitor three years ago. Finally, in the 10–17-year group, basketball is the best attended sport at 22% ahead of rugby league at 17%. (NBL 1995)

Stages of the product lifecycle

It is worth returning to the stages of the PLC shown in Figure 5.3 for further examination.

Introduction

The introductory stage is characterised by the need to communicate the existence of the product to potential consumers. This can be very expensive, and accounts for the high start-up costs for a new product. The principal objective in this stage is to build awareness. Returning to the NBL example, building awareness of the new competition in 1979 was the primary objective for competition organisers. Successfully achieving this goal was inhibited as basketball was not a traditional sport in Australia. Typically during the introductory stage, profitability is low or negative and sales near zero. Attracting 190 000 spectators in the first year of the NBL competition compared to just over 1 million in 1995, illustrates the initial difficulties of developing a market segment for basketball. The other important consideration in this introductory stage is identifying the channels through which the NBL is distributed. Each club in the league was based in a major capital city or regional centre, with the intent of developing product awareness in that city or region. The most difficult phase of developing product awareness was trying to build team loyalty and team rivalry.

Growth

As product awareness began to build for basketball it moved into the next stage of the PLC: the growth stage. The NBL attendances increased to 242 022 by 1984 and to just over 800 000 by 1990. In this period considerable growth was achieved as many clubs moved to larger playing facilities. During the growth stage, the range of product offerings tends to increase, and refinements are made to the way in which the product is offered. The NBL found it necessary to provide large comfortable facilities as well as quality product extensions. It was through product extensions that the NBL made its greatest change to product offerings. Merchandise and licensing programs emerged, associated television programming appeared, and basketball began to identify and open up new market segments. To overcome the high cost of enticing new consumers to NBL games, the clubs began to recognise the importance of retaining their members and loyal supporters. This marked the transition from the growth to the maturity stage. The clubs themselves became the most important marketing vehicles for basketball. Brand loyalty via individual clubs became important, and club memberships began to stabilise post 1990.

Maturity and revitalisation

The mature stage is characterised by a plateau in sales—in the NBL's case, sales in the form of attendance, memberships, sponsorships and merchandise. As has already been discussed in this section, action needs to be taken to extend the PLC. This returns us to the reasons why the NBL is considering a change of season, to recycle or extend the capacity of the NBL to capture further market share. Given that the NBL is only a relatively new sport product in Australia, it will be worth watching what other action the NBL will take to extend the PLC of basketball.

Variations from the product lifecycle curve

The PLC is a useful tool for the sport marketer to assist in strategy development for sports and sporting league and associations. The S-curve indicated in Figure 5.3, however, can be misleading. Not all products progress incrementally through the stages of the lifecycle described, making it harder to discern at what stage of the PLC a product can be classified. Another complication is the time taken to progress through the stages of the PLC. It is very hard to predict how long it will take a product to move from an introductory stage

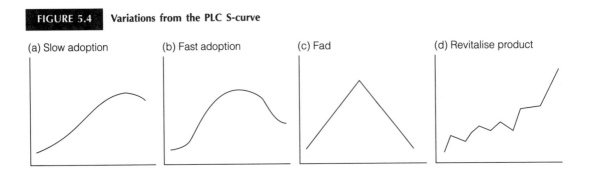

FIGURE 5.4 Variations from the PLC S-curve

(a) Slow adoption   (b) Fast adoption   (c) Fad   (d) Revitalise product

to maturity. Indeed, the NBL has been caught in this situation of taking at least two years to identify maturity, and a subsequent levelling off of interest.

Figure 5.4 illustrates some of the more common variations from the normal S-curve shown in Figure 5.3. The first curve (a) shows a product that has a long introduction stage because it is adopted slowly by consumers. The second curve (b) illustrates products such as one-day cricket, which are rapidly accepted and have a shorter introductory stage. The third curve (c) represents 'fad' products that typically have a rapid rise and rapid fall. Finally, the fourth curve (d) shows a product that has been frequently revitalised, going through stages of decline followed by growth. The Olympic Games is a good example of the fourth curve as it has ebbed and flowed in terms of growth and popularity during the last 100 years. At present, the Olympic movement could be described as being in a growth phase, although as recently as 1980, leading up to the 1984 Los Angeles games, the Olympic Games were in a stage of decline. Los Angeles proved to be the catalyst that provided the necessary revitalisation for the Olympic movement.

Like all the models presented in this book, the PLC provides the sport marketer with a framework on which to base decision making. There will always be variations on the models and theories discussed. However, it is incumbent on the sport manager to temper theory with the peculiar nature and development of each product.

SPORT AND TELEVISION

Earlier in this chapter we discussed the benefits provided by a product as being vital to the consumer's decision to purchase. In sport, television has emerged as an important substitute for attendance at the live event. Another question is whether sport on television is the same product as the live event.

Sportview 5.2 has highlighted the importance of television to the NBL in developing its product to its full potential. The exposure and promotional benefits to be gained by a sport from televising its games or events have been central to most sport-marketing strategies in the professional sport sector.

At issue also has been the revenue aspect of televising sporting contests versus the live game. That is, consumers have the choice to either attend the event or stay at home and watch it on television. For sports where consumers may decide to stay home and watch the event on television, this choice represents direct lost revenue. It is, however, also revenue that may find its way back to the sport indirectly in the form of television rights as a consequence of high program ratings. Alternatively, the short-term lost revenue may result in a long-term revenue gain as the consumer is enticed to attend future games because the televised game was entertaining and enjoyable. The relationship between television and sport has always been prickly as the balance between live coverage, delayed coverage and 'blacking out' home markets has created tension between respective sports and the television networks. Other tensions are observed in the form of scheduling, as television looks to the most favourable programming options to maximise its investment via television rights.

In this book we consider the televised form of sport to be different from attendance at the live event. In other words, the benefits offered by watching the game on television are different from those gained by attending. Television offers different features, including commentary, slow motion replays, live interviews and, depending on the sport, close-up action, which can sometimes detract from observing the build-up to the central action.

The television–sport relationship will be considered in greater detail in Chapter 9. Specifically, Chapter 9 will examine why television has become such an important component of the economics and marketing of professional sport. Television will also be discussed in Chapter 13 in relation to its role in distributing the sport product.

SUMMARY

This chapter has defined and described sport as a product. A product is anything that satisfies a need or want and is acquired to do so. In relation to sport, two important concepts have implications for sport marketing. The first is the core product, defined as the actual game, over which the sport marketer has no control. The sport marketer must be very careful not to overpromise in terms of how good the game will be, or how well specific athletes may perform. The second concept is the importance of product extensions to the overall marketing effort. It is here that the marketer can ensure that acceptable levels of quality are achieved. Discussion in this chapter has also focused on the importance of delivering quality service. The dimensions of quality service have been discussed and the areas requiring attention in the delivery of product extensions indicated. These include anything that impacts on spectators' attendance and enjoyment of an event.

Issues of strategy were also considered when discussing product position-ing and the product lifecycle. In both cases these techniques allow the marketer to assess the relative standing of a product in relation to competitors and the phases of product growth. The perceptual map was used to illustrate the concept of product space and the way in which this defines direct and indirect competitors. Perceptual mapping also highlights the importance of key product attributes and their ability to entice consumers to purchase or attend games. Level of excitement was used as an example of one key product attribute. In this example, it was possible to determine the direct competitors of the NBL and other sports. The NBL was also used to illustrate the application of product lifecycle analysis, which revealed some interesting challenges confronting the NBL in its quest to arrest the plateau in the fortunes of its competition.

Finally, the importance of television to sport was noted. A distinction was made between the television product and the live product. It was posited that televised sport is a different product from the one viewed live. Different benefits are offered; so a different range of options is considered in the pre-purchase process.

CASE STUDY

THE TRADITION CONTINUES—THE AUSTRALIAN MASTERS

This case study was originally prepared by David Cross and Mark Gladman as part of their studies towards the Graduate Diploma of Sport Management at Deakin University.

The Australian Masters is an important event on the Australasian Professional Golfers' Association (APGA) Tour. Australians, and in particular Victorians, have been extremely supportive of the tournament since its inception in 1979. It has grown to a stage of maturity where it is able to attract international players, national and international television, and worldwide recognition. It has also been able to attract substantial prizemoney, although in recent years the level of prizemoney has slipped in comparison to one or two other tournaments on the Tour circuit. The tournament since inception has been positioned to be among the top one or two tournaments on the APGA Tour. Like its namesake, the US Masters, it is an invitation-only event with a traditional gold jacket presentation to the winner. The theme 'The tradition continues' is a feature of the advertising and promotion, recognising the desired positioning of the event.

A well-known expression in business is 'A quality product will always sell'. To some extent this may be true; however, in marketing circles this attitude would obviously cause some discomfort. The golf product is unique. A marketing study published in documents promoting the Australian Open Golf Tournament indicated that 33% of all adult Australians watch golf. Brian Sweeney & Associates' market research in 1991 showed that, of a sample of 1500 males surveyed throughout Australia, 93% of males aged sixteen or over expressed an interest in golf, as either a player (39%), an onsite spectator (7%) or a television viewer (47%). Major viewers were those aged 45 or over and those in white collar occupations.

At the same time trend data indicated that golf had increased its popularity. There had been a 6% increase in the percentage of the total population playing golf between 1987 (20%) and 1990 (26%). Similarly, television audiences had jumped 6% to 42% of the total population, which placed golf equal third in the viewing stakes. It is clear that the passion Australians hold for golf suggests that the golfing product has considerable scope for promotional opportunities, especially in the context of a special event such as the Australian Masters.

The International Management Group (IMG) owns the Australian Masters, and the event has been conducted at the Huntingdale Golf Course in Melbourne since its inception. The IMG is the dominant sport management enterprise worldwide. Founded in the 1960s by international entrepreneur and author Mark McCormack, IMG has grown from a one-office, one-client concern to a multinational enterprise operating over 45 offices in more than twenty countries. The IMG's marketing strategy for the Masters commences immediately the current event concludes. Priority is given to the design of new sales strategies and sponsorship packages in order to begin the process of obtaining sponsor finance.

Carlton and United Breweries (CUB), as a secondary sponsor of the 1991 Masters, conducted its own market research to determine the worth of sponsorship and advertising during the event. Although the results of this research were made available to IMG, no other market research or sponsor evaluation was undertaken. The 1991 sponsor, Pyramid Technology Corporation, enjoyed excellent corporate publicity, as Channel Seven topped the ratings. Research conducted by CUB also supported the positive impact of Pyramid's involvement.

The IMG's management of the Australian Masters varies considerably from textbook marketing. In analysing its market, IMG places very little importance on market segmentation, target marketing and positioning. By inheriting a successful or proven product, IMG is able to develop sponsorship strategies based on the assumption that the success of the past events was due to correct segmentation strategies by the previous tournament owners. The IMG's strategies acknowledge that promotion of the tournament to the general community is important; however, the target market is in fact the corporate sponsor, not the golfing community. The marketing strategies consist solely of those required to generate sponsorship sales. This is further evidenced by the high number of free passes allocated to corporate sponsors. Almost 90% of attenders do not pay. The IMG's international reputation and network clearly give them easier access to potential corporate sponsors and to a greater range of high profile players.

A ten-year agreement was struck between IMG and Channel Seven and is the cornerstone of the promotional strategy for the tournament. The Masters usually achieves good television ratings averaging 24, reflecting the advertising pursed by Channel Seven in the weeks leading up to the event. Also, IMG's international standing allows worldwide television coverage to approximately

52 countries. Television coverage is a critical component of the promotional strategy devised to maximise product awareness as well as to provide the launching pad to attract the necessary corporate sponsorship.

The IMG owns a proven product, which in more recent years has shown evidence of having plateaued. Prizemoney has stabilised, as have television ratings, and the flow of higher profile players has slowed. Greg Norman in particular has been absent during the 1995 and 1996 events. The challenge confronting IMG is how to boost an event that is showing signs of flagging. It is also confronted with the challenge of boosting prizemoney to over $1 million in order to keep pace with the high profile tournaments. Prizemoney remained stagnant at $750 000 in 1995 and 1996.

Questions

1 Discuss the importance of a comprehensive analysis of the market in relation to the staging of the Australian Masters.
2 What advantages would a more formal marketing management approach bring to this event?
3 How would you describe the stage that the Masters has reached in product lifecycle terms?
4 Describe how the theme used for the event, 'The tradition continues', impacts on product lifecycle decisions.
5 Describe why control of the media is so important to a special event such as the Australian Masters.

REFERENCES

Boyd, H. W. and Walker, O. C. (1990). *Marketing Management: a Strategic Approach*, Irwin, Homewood, Ill.

Branch, D. (1992). 'Rethinking sport's product position and program concept', *Sport Marketing Quarterly*, 1 (2), pp. 21–7.

Brian Sweeney & Associates (1991). *The Fifth Annual Survey of Sporting Participation, Attendance, TV Viewing and Sponsorship Awareness*, Brian Sweeney & Associates, Melbourne.

Brown, M. (1992). 'The big gamble', *The Age Green Guide*, 14 February, pp. 1–2.

——(1993). 'NBL rethinks its strategy as crowds fall', *Sunday Age Sports Extra*, 27 June, p. 6.

Bureau of Industry Economics (1995). *Australian Industry Trends*, 23, Australian Government Publishing Service, Canberra.

Kotler, P., Chandler, P., Gibbs, R. and McColl R. (1989). *Marketing in Australia*, 2nd edn, Prentice-Hall, Englewood Cliffs, NJ.

Lovelock, C. H. (1991). *Services Marketing*, 2nd edn, Prentice-Hall, Englewood Cliffs, NJ.

Macnow, G. (1990). 'A winning game plan', *Nation's Business*, March, pp. 82–4.

McCarthy, J. E. and Perreault, W. D. (1990). *Basic Marketing*, 10th edn, Irwin, Homewood, Ill.

Mullin, B. J. (1980). 'Sport management: the nature and utility of the concept', *Arena Review*, 3 (4), pp. 1–11.

——(1985). 'Characteristics of sport marketing', in *Successful Sport Management*, eds G. Lewis and H. Appenzellar, Michie Co., Charlottesville, Va, pp. 101–23.

Mullin, B. J., Hardy, S. and Sutton, W. A. (1993). *Sport Marketing*, Human Kinetics, Champaign, Ill.

National Basketball League (1994). *Chief Executive Annual Report*, NBL, Melbourne.

——(1995). *Chief Executive Annual Report*, NBL, Melbourne.

National Institute of Economic and Industry Research (1995). *The Economic Impact of the 1995 Ford Australian Open at Flinders Park, Melbourne*, report prepared for the Flinders Park Tennis Centre Trust, Melbourne.

Parasuraman, A., Zeithaml, V. A. and Berry, L. L. (1985). 'A conceptual model of service quality and its implications for future research', *Journal of Marketing*, 49, Fall, pp. 41–50.

Shilbury, D. (1989). 'Characteristics of sport marketing: developing trends', *ACHPER National Journal*, Autumn, pp. 21–4.

——(1991). 'Marketing scores with game plan for sports', *Marketing*, July, 18–22.

Sutton, W. A. and Parrett, I. (1992). 'Marketing the core product in professional team sports in the United States', *Sport Marketing Quarterly*, 1 (2), pp. 7–19.

Zeithaml, V. A., Parasuraman, A. and Berry, L. (1985). 'Problems and strategies in services marketing', *Journal of Marketing*, 49, Spring, pp. 33–46.

——(1990). *Delivering Service Quality: Balancing Customer Perceptions and Expectations*, Free Press, New York.

6

Pricing strategies

CHAPTER OUTLINE

Stage 1—Identification of marketing opportunities

Stage 2—Strategy determination

Step 5—Determine core marketing strategy

    Marketing mix—sport product, pricing

Stage 3—Strategy implementation, evaluation and adjustment

CHAPTER OBJECTIVES

Chapter 6 introduces price as one of the marketing mix variables. Pricing strategies are discussed in this chapter in relation to overall organisational and marketing goals. Pricing as a process is defined as setting or adjusting a price charged to a customer in exchange for a good or a service. The techniques used to determine price and the role of price in the marketing mix form the basis of this chapter.

After studying this chapter you should be able to:

1 Distinguish between factors that influence the pricing process.
2 See pricing in the context of organisational strategy.
3 Determine demand and supply relations and the price sensitivity of markets.
4 Apply a strategic pricing approach in setting or adjusting the price of sport products.

HEADLINE STORY

MAXIMISING GATE RECEIPTS OR MAXIMISING TOTAL INCOME?

Mass attendance is important to our game. This means that there is a large gap between the costs of the competition (approximately $26 per attendee) and the gate admission prices (currently $11 per adult attendee and $1.50 per child attendee) which are very low on world standards. This gap will be met by TV rights and commercial sponsors who are offered exposure by the AFL and its clubs. (Australian Football League, 1994, p. 25)

The Australian Football League (AFL) made a deliberate choice to keep its admission prices to league games below the admission prices of comparable sporting codes around Australia. We could wonder why a governing body like the AFL does not charge higher prices, as it is the leading spectator sport in Victoria, South Australia and Western Australia and is increasing in popularity in Queensland and New South Wales. Hard core fans are probably prepared to pay a lot more to see their heroes play every weekend.

Pricing, as a process, can simply be defined as setting or adjusting a price charged to a customer in exchange for a good or service. Pricing a product or a range of products properly is of utmost importance to an organisation. The level of pricing determines how many customers are inclined to buy the organisation's products. At the end of the day, the price multiplied by the number of products sold must at least cover the costs of production. This is, however, a simplified version of reality, which will be elaborated on during this chapter.

In Chapter 5 it was shown that the sport product is made up of different components: the core product and product extensions. Although the core product may be the main attraction for customers, product extensions, in terms of potential income, make up a considerable part of overall revenue for sporting organisations. This is one reason why the AFL does not price its core product at a higher level. The core spectator product is priced relative to the product extensions, or in other words, the total product mix.

In this chapter, the pricing process will be examined from a strategic perspective. After presenting a strategic pricing model, the different steps of this model will be discussed.

THE STRATEGIC PRICING PROCESS IN SPORT

In the section above, the importance of recovering the costs of production through setting the right price was highlighted. Cost of production, however, is only one of the variables to take into consideration when setting or adjusting price. The strategic pricing process incorporates both internal characteristics of the organisation and its products (e.g. goals and objectives) and external characteristics (e.g. competitors' pricing behaviour). This will enable the marketer to create a pricing strategy, beyond the short-term future of the organisation. Figure 6.1 describes the strategic pricing process for sporting organisations.

FIGURE 6.1

The strategic pricing process in sport

STEP 1: DETERMINE PRICING GOAL(S)

Although there exists a subtle difference between introducing a product and setting a price and adjusting the price of an existing product, determining the pricing goal must occur for both. It is vital to recognise the influence price has on customers' perceptions of the product. A relatively high-priced product will often be perceived as a high quality product. Pricing, in other words, has a strong impact on the positioning of the product.

Determining the pricing goals should be a direct derivative of the organisation's reason for being (i.e. its mission) and the resulting marketing goals. Marketing goals of different organisations and derived pricing goals are shown in Table 6.1 and will now be discussed.

TABLE 6.1 **Marketing goals and derived pricing goals**	**Marketing goals**	**Derived pricing goals**
	Maximise shareholder value	Maximising profit Maximising sales growth Maximising revenue
	Be the most innovative in the business	Market skimming
	Deliver the highest quality products	Premium price
	Be accessible to all members of the community	Full cost recovery Partial cost recovery

Maximum shareholder value

Private enterprises and privately owned sport franchises often pursue goals designed to maximise shareholder value. In order to achieve maximum shareholder value, pricing goals would include maximising profit, maximising sales growth or maximising revenue.

Maximising profit is often seen as a short-term goal concentrating on current financial performance assuming little influence of competitors (i.e. to undercut the set price).

Maximising sales growth is a long-term pricing goal. Although profits could be higher, the organisation aims to sell its products at a lower price to as many customers as possible. The goal is to obtain a large share of the market and reap the subsequent long-term benefits.

Maximising revenue can be the pricing goal of, for example, the organisers of Wimbledon. Having an infrastructure (buildings, equipment and personnel) in place, every extra customer adds to the revenue of the organisation. The organisation itself is incurring little extra cost by providing services to that one extra visitor, and this makes it extremely attractive to sell the extra tickets, such as ground passes.

Most innovation

If an organisation aims to be an innovative company, the pricing goal may be to *skim the market*. Nike, as an athletic footwear manufacturer, establishes a price high enough for a small segment of the market to buy its products. As soon as competitors introduce similar products, Nike lowers the price to sell to the segment below the 'early adopters'. Nike skims the market by receiving the maximum price from the different segments in the market. Nike can adopt this strategy because it ensures that it is the first to introduce a new, trendy, high quality product.

Highest quality products

If an organisation aims to deliver the highest quality products, a *premium pricing* strategy may be an alternative pricing goal. In order to communicate the high quality of the product (e.g. a world title boxing contest), a corresponding high price is set. Customers, valuing the high quality features of the product, will pay the premium price, and the organisation will achieve an above-average return.

Community accessibility

Not-for-profit organisations, government organisations and many sporting organisations often set pricing goals such as partial cost recovery or *full cost recovery*. Public hospitals, for example, may set prices in order to recover their costs because they do not need to make a profit as their main goal is to serve the community. National sport-governing bodies can price their products in order to break even, incorporating funding from the federal government *(partial cost recovery)*. Setting or adjusting the price depends not only on the goals of the organisation but also on the other elements of the pricing process. This will become clear in the following sections.

STEP 2: DETERMINE MARKET SENSITIVITY TO PRICE

How sensitive customers are to a change in price is important in determining a range in which the final price may be set. It is also vital to know the estimated size of the market and how the market is segmented. In this section it is assumed this information is available. The concepts of demand and supply, price elasticity and non-price factors are important in determining market sensitivity to price. Given the marketing focus of this book, we will start discussing the concept of demand first.

Demand and supply

Demand

The quantity demanded of the product by potential customers depends on the price assigned to the product. In general terms, *the higher the price of a product, the lower the quantity demanded.* Figure 6.2(a) shows that for a certain product a *demand curve* can be drawn that shows the linear relationship with the price. The quantity demanded also depends on the prices of other factors such as product (substitutes and complements), income of customers, expectations of future prices and the size of the population.

Substitutes are products that can be used in place of another product (e.g. spectator tickets to a football match and to a basketball match). If the price of a product (football tickets) increases, the quantity demanded of the substitute (basketball tickets) is likely to increase as well because consumers will elect to purchase the cheaper substitute.

FIGURE 6.2

Demand, supply and market equilibrium

(a) Demand and supply in equilibrium at unit price $100

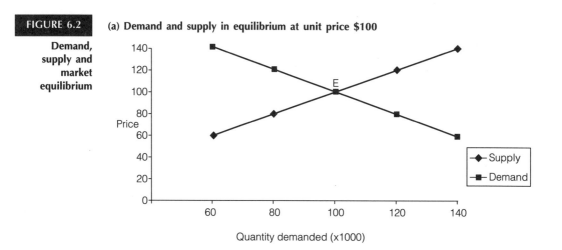

(b) Excess supply at unit price $120

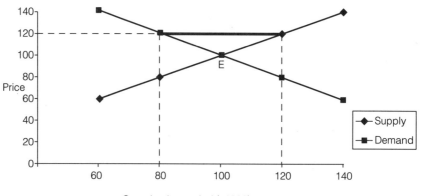
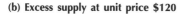

(c) Excess demand at unit price $80

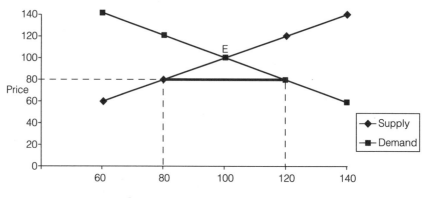

Complements are products used in conjunction with another product (e.g. golf clubs and a golf course membership). If the price of a product (golf course membership) decreases, the quantity demanded of this product and its complement (golf clubs) will increase.

Generally, when the income of customers rises, demand for most goods will also rise. Expectations of higher prices in the future may prompt customers to buy now, and hence demand will increase. In general, the larger the population, the greater the demand for products.

Supply

When a product is providing attractive returns to producers, more organisations will be inclined to supply the product to the market than when the price is relatively low. In general terms, *the higher the price of a product, the greater the quantity supplied.* Figure 6.2(a) shows that for a certain product a *supply curve* can be drawn that shows the linear relationship with the price. The quantity supplied also depends on resource prices, technology, the number of sellers and the expectations about future prices.

In general, when resource prices increase, the quantity supplied will decrease. Similarly, technological improvements and increasing efficiency will result in an increase in the quantity supplied because a greater quantity can be produced at the same cost. The more sellers there are, the greater the quantity supplied. Expectations about future prices are a more complicated issue. When a sporting goods firm expects prices of tennis racquets to rise after the final at Wimbledon, it may choose to hold back the racquets in stock in order to sell them at a higher price. Racquet manufacturers, however, may decide to increase production and supply more racquets to the market.

Market equilibrium

Figure 6.2(a) shows that at the point where demand equals supply the market is in *equilibrium* (E). This point represents the price that the market is prepared to pay, given the quantity supplied. Figure 6.2(b) shows that at a price of $120 there will be a supply of 120 000 racquets but a demand for only 80 000. There will be excess supply of 40 000 racquets. Figure 6.2(c) shows that the reverse situation will occur at a price lower than the equilibrium price (e.g. $80). In that situation, there will be excess demand of 40 000 racquets.

If the demand for tennis racquets after the Wimbledon final increases, the demand curve will move to the right. This will result in an increase in the quantity supplied (i.e. a movement along the supply curve) because the price will go up to establish a new equilibrium. Let us assume that people will keep demanding the new quantity. With this increase in demand, new producers will be lured to the market because of the higher price, supply will go up, and the supply curve will move to the right. This again will result in a decrease in price. Equilibrium will return to the point where it is not attractive enough for new suppliers to enter the market. The only change will be that the total quantity supplied has increased.

It goes beyond the scope of this book to further elaborate on demand and supply issues.

Price elasticity of demand

We have now explored the influence that price can have on the quantity of products supplied and demanded. What we do not know is how sensitive a customer is to a change in price. Will an increase or decrease in the price of a product result in a great or small change in the quantity traded? *Price elasticity of demand* is a measure projecting this relationship. It is calculated as the absolute value of the change (%) in the quantity demanded, divided by the change (%) in price. The absolute value can range between 0 and infinity. A value between 0 and 1 represents inelastic demand; a value greater than 1 represents elastic demand; a value of exactly 1 is called unit elastic demand.

Figure 6.3(a) shows that *inelastic demand* occurs where the decrease (%) in the quantity demanded *is less than* the increase (%) in price. In other words, the organisation will benefit from raising price because the number of customers lost will be less than the gain in revenue. For example, the number of customers will not vary greatly when the price of tickets for the World Championship Soccer Final is increased.

Figure 6.3(b) shows that if the decrease (%) in the quantity demanded *equals* the increase (%) in price, the elasticity of demand is 1 *(unit elastic demand)*. This means that total revenue will not change.

| FIGURE 6.3 | Price elasticity of demand |

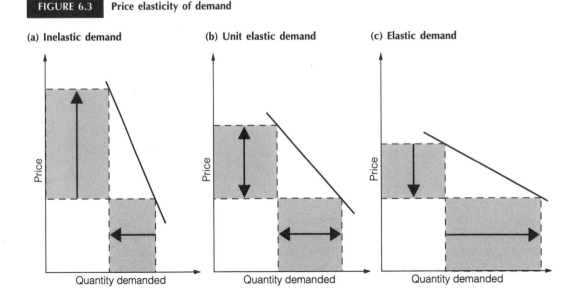

(a) Inelastic demand   **(b) Unit elastic demand**   **(c) Elastic demand**

In Figure 6.3(c) it is shown that if the decrease (%) in the quantity demanded *exceeds* the increase (%) in price, demand is considered to be *elastic*. In this case, the organisation will benefit from reducing price because the gain in number of customers will be greater than the loss in revenue. For example, the number of customers will vary greatly (i.e. increase) when the price of a golf course membership is lowered.

Factors determining elasticity

The size of the elasticity of demand is mainly determined by three variables:

- the substitutability of the product,
- the amount of time since the price change, and
- the proportion of customer income spent on the product.

The more *substitutes* there are available for a product, the easier it is for a customer to replace one product with another when price increases, and hence the higher the price elasticity. A range of professional sports are playing in the metropolitan area of Melbourne less than one kilometre apart. An increase in the admission price for one sport will force customers to search for cheaper alternatives. A substantial price increase will result in an even more substantial loss of customers. However, existing customers of a basketball club, for example, will not immediately be able to go to a football club because they may have purchased long-term memberships.

The greater the amount of time since the price change, the more opportunities customers will have had to find alternatives, and hence the greater the elasticity of demand.

The higher the proportion of customer income spent on club membership, the higher the elasticity of demand. If expenditure represents a large part of an individual's income, every extra dollar on top of that expenditure will be scrutinised and can make them decide not to purchase. If, however, a very rich person has to make the same decision, money spent on membership represents only a small portion of total income, and a price increase will not greatly affect the decision to buy. This last example shows that price elasticity of demand can differ not only between products but also between consumer groups, and provides the marketer with the opportunity to differentiate between customer segments.

Different issues related to price elasticity of demand are explored in Sportview 6.1.

AFL KICKS A GOAL ON MARKETING STRATEGY

SPORTVIEW
6.1

'The AFL's marketing strategy since the early 1980s has boosted football and helped to reverse the game's long-run decline in attendance, say two Melbourne economists. Research conducted by Mr Peter Fuller and Mr Mark Stewart at RMIT has rejected the belief widely held among football fans "that the AFL is conspiring against the best interests of the game. To the extent that increased attendance at football matches is deemed the yardstick by which football administrators are judged, we can only endorse their recent actions," Mr Fuller and Mr Stewart have concluded.

'The AFL's decision to hold down ticket price rises in the late 1980s, the construction of the new Great Southern Stand at the Melbourne Cricket Ground, the closer competition, the player draft from 1986, and the continued program of ground rationalisation were major factors in boosting game attendances. But Fuller and Stewart have found that the AFL could now push prices up further without suffering any loss in gate takings. In both Victoria and South Australia, attendance was in decline from 1948, "indicating football was becoming proportionately a less popular form of entertainment," the economists have found, using an analysis based on attendances as a proportion of each State's population.

'Crowds hit rock bottom in Victoria in 1987 and in South Australia in 1989. However, some of the game's popularity has been restored since those low points. According to Fuller and Stewart, this is partly because the real cost of admission has been held down in the minor round games, and partly because of improvements in administration. "Increased competitiveness allowing people the opportunity to attend games at different times, ground rationalisation and the move to the National competition (especially in South Australia) seem to have played a part in this," they said. The research has suggested that the player draft and the salary cap have helped by making games more even.

'Analysis of the impact of price changes on crowd size shows that a 10% increase in ticket prices (adjusted for inflation) eventually reduces attendances by around 6%. This means "the AFL could increase gate receipts by charging higher prices. The implication is that in terms of revenue derived from attendance, both the AFL and the SANFL are under-charging," according to Fuller and Stewart.'

Source: Excerpts from Henderson (1996, p. 5).

Non-price factors

Non-price factors influence buying situations and reduce the importance of price in the buying process. Non-price factors include an intangible perception of a product, resulting in a perceived value. In other words, some customers may be willing to pay a higher-than-average market price *(premium price)* to receive product benefits. Other customers, however, may be willing to forgo these benefits in return for a lower-than-average market price. For marketers, it is therefore important to understand key product attributes in order to increase the perceived value and hence charge a premium price.

In the sport industry, non-price factors are very important. The rules of demand and supply and price elasticity can be applied to sport's core product and extensions. In addition, different combinations of core and extensions can increase the perceived value of the total product, justifying extra expenditure for customers. The core product cannot be remixed, but in combination with different product extensions the perceived value of the total package can be increased. The Back Stage Club at the Brisbane Entertainment Centre, a large multifunctional entertainment facility, home of the Brisbane Bullets basketball franchise, serves as an example:

> Through the Club, members have the opportunity to mingle socially with touring entourages and other special guests. The first 250 Back Stage Club members to respond to notice of an event [for example a Bullets game] can purchase up to six tickets each—and pay a AUD$15 per ticket premium giving them access to VIP car parking and an exclusive entry foyer. (*Panstadia International*, 1994, p. 33)

Also, the more important the product is to the consumer, the less important price will become. For example, a $100 repair on a bicycle of $2000 will enable the owner to ride the bicycle again. The perceived value of the $100 expenditure is likely to be higher than that of another $100 expenditure on something less important (e.g. a television repair) to the bikerider.

If the marketer is able to increase the perceived value of the product, customers will become less sensitive to price (i.e. elasticity will decrease), and the organisation will benefit from raising price. This also applies to the reverse situation. If the marketer is able to filter out the product attributes less valued by customers (e.g. cushioned seats or undercover seats in a sport stadium), customers will become more sensitive to price (i.e. elasticity will increase), and the organisation will benefit from lowering price.

It is clear from these examples that different segments of customers are targeted as part of the pricing strategy. The next section will show the impact of the cost–volume–profit relationship.

STEP 3: ESTIMATE THE COST–VOLUME–PROFIT RELATIONSHIP

Cost–volume–profit analysis, also called *break-even analysis*, examines the interaction of factors influencing the level of profits. These factors, as identified by Anderson and Sollenberger (1992), are:

- selling prices,
- volume of sales,
- unit variable cost,
- total fixed cost, and
- sales mix.

The first four factors will be discussed in this section, with sales mix left to the section on constraints by other marketing mix variables (product mix).

In general terms, the *total costs* of production represent the minimum financial figure (i.e. *break-even point*) that needs to be recovered from sales in order to at least break even (total costs = total revenue). Total costs are made up of a fixed cost and a variable cost component. *Fixed costs* are the costs that an organisation has to incur in order to operate (e.g. costs of plant and equipment, taxes, insurance) regardless of the level of production. *Variable costs* fluctuate in direct proportion to changes in the activity of the organisation. The costs of direct materials like leather for shoes is a good example. Pertaining to the goals of the organisation, the break-even point may vary. For an organisation with a partial cost recovery goal, this point is relatively lower than for a full cost recovery organisation. Both organisations, however, need to be able to ascertain their cost of production, enabling the organisation to arrive at a minimum price for its products by dividing the cost of production by the (estimated) number of products sold.

For a large athletic footwear manufacturer, total costs are made up of a fixed and variable component. In order to produce, for example, 10 000 pairs a day, a certain infrastructure needs to be evident. Plant, equipment and labour are needed in order to start operations and represent the fixed costs of operations, which are independent of the output level. Raw material to manufacture the shoes is the major component of the variable costs, which vary with the output of the plant. Although certain levels of production will be more efficient, in this example it is assumed that the variable cost per unit of production is the same. In Figure 6.4 a *break-even chart* is shown.

It can be derived from Figure 6.4 that the higher the total costs, the smaller the average fixed cost in each unit of production (e.g. pairs of shoes). In other words, the fixed cost component will decrease with volume of production. If a factory with building costs of $10 million produces 100 million pairs of shoes over its productive lifetime (e.g. ten years), the fixed cost component in every pair of shoes is $0.10. The relationship between total

FIGURE 6.4

The break-even chart

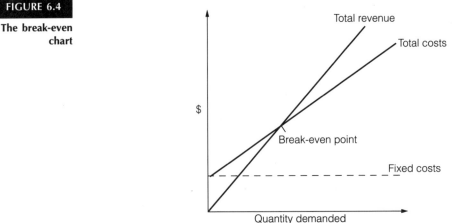

Unit price	Break-even point (pairs of shoes)	Unit variable cost	Total fixed costs (per year)
10	2 000 000	5	10 million
100	105 264	5	10 million
200	51 282	5	10 million

TABLE 6.2

The relationship between unit price and the break-even point

fixed costs, price and *unit variable cost* can be shown in the *break-even formula*:

$$\text{Break–even point (pairs of shoes)} = \frac{\text{Total fixed costs}}{\text{Unit price} - \text{Unit variable cost}}$$

The formula shows that, with a variation in the unit price, the amount of shoes sold to break even varies. This relationship is shown in Table 6.2.

When we turn our attention to service products, and many sport products are service products, the unit variable costs in the break-even formula are much harder to determine. Many costs are both fixed and shared across different services. In a large stadium, the building, its equipment (e.g. indoor courts, tennis nets, computers) and labour (a majority often is multiskilled in order to deliver different services) are all needed to provide the total mix of services provided by the facility. The variable costs per unit are hard to determine. What are, for example, the variable costs of providing basketball spectator services when one extra ticket is sold? Most costs have to be incurred, irrespective of the number of customers on the day or over a longer period. We can state that most costs are fixed. This is why it is very attractive to entice that one extra customer: with little to no extra (variable) cost, the revenue from one extra customer is almost pure profit. This explains why, in the health and fitness industry, competition is based primarily on price. An organisation has to incur little extra cost in order to gain a substantial increase in revenues.

This also indicates the importance of managing the non-price factors in the sport industry. Because we know that most costs are fixed, it becomes a matter of sophisticated marketing in order to increase the perceived value of the sport product. This should lead to sufficient and sustainable market share to at least cover the costs of operation.

STEP 4: DETERMINE PRICING STRATEGIES OF MAJOR COMPETITORS

As in any strategic-planning effort of an organisation, it is important to monitor competitor behaviour and adjust actions accordingly. The first question that needs to be answered is: *Who* are the major (potential) competitors? Do they operate in the same *market* (e.g. an amateur soccer team and a professional basketball team) or even in the same segment of the market (e.g. a central-business-district golf course and a working-class-suburb golf course)?

Organisations can then determine when to respond to price changes by competitors.

The next step is to determine how competitors are positioned in terms of their relative prices, providing an organisation with an indication of the competitive *price range* for which the product is on offer. It would also be very useful to know which *strategies* of competing firms are successful.

Finally, if an organisation is able to find out what the probable *responses* of competitors would be to a price change, different pricing scenarios can be developed in order to make the appropriate choice.

STEP 5: DETERMINE CONSTRAINTS ON PRICING BEHAVIOUR

Laws and regulations are the most obvious constraints on pricing behaviour. Most of these are a direct result of government intervention in regulating the market behaviour of organisations. Some cases of *price fixing* (i.e. agreement between organisations about price) can be regarded as disadvantageous for the public and are therefore forbidden by law. In order to keep government-owned facilities accessible to all members of the community, local government can set a maximum price level *(ceiling)*. Even when a management company is hired to manage the local pool, local government can constrain it in its pricing strategies. Regulatory organisations, like national sport organisations, can set membership fees for members, clubs and associations in order to optimise participation levels.

Social responsibility constraints can also affect the pricing behaviour of organisations. If, for example, the local professional soccer club feels that disabled members of the local community should be able to enjoy a game of soccer, it will have to adjust its facility in terms of access and seating arrangements. This will have a direct impact on the fixed cost component of the total costs of the club, and hence it may decide to set different unit (i.e. admission) prices to recover those costs. The pricing strategy of this club will be different from that of a club focusing solely on profit maximisation. Legal and social responsibility constraints therefore limit the pricing range for the product.

STEP 6: DETERMINE CONSTRAINTS BY OTHER MARKETING MIX VARIABLES

The variables of the marketing mix all impact on each other. Constraints of product mix, place dependence and promotion mix are discussed in this section.

Product mix

Prices in supermarkets are based on the overall mix of products rather than the individual products. Some products are priced at an attractive price level (e.g. soft drinks during summer) in order to entice customers to do the rest of their shopping in the same supermarket. The AFL example at the beginning of this chapter also exemplifies the importance of looking at the overall product mix before pricing individual products. The AFL's admission prices are low compared to other sporting codes. These prices attract larger crowds, enhancing the atmosphere for attractive television coverage and as a consequence the attractiveness of the total product for television sponsors. The AFL can offset the loss of income from gate receipts against the increase of income from television, sponsor contracts and other in-stadium purchases.

Place dependence

A majority of sport products are produced and consumed in a facility specifically designed to produce those sport products. The capacity of the facility limits the number of customers that can be serviced at a certain point in time and as a consequence the maximum total income. The location of the facility determines the catchment area of potential customers and hence partly determines the profile of the customer. In general terms, dependence on the place of distribution further limits the possible pricing range of the products of the organisation. Place dependence will be discussed in more detail in Chapter 13.

Promotion mix

The *promotion mix* (i.e. the means through which communication with the target markets will take place) can be constructed after product, price and place information is available. A low price strategy often needs an intensive promotional effort in order to sell as many units as possible. If the promotional tools for intensive promotion are not available due to limited funds, the organisation will be limited in pursuing a low price strategy. The promotion mix is constraining the pricing strategy. A pricing strategy never stands on its own as it needs to be backed by sufficient promotional efforts.

One of the characteristics of services is that they cannot be stored. Services are time dependent, and this is the focus of the next section.

STEP 7: DETERMINE TIME DEPENDENCE

The visitor at the Olympic Games witnesses production and at the same time consumes the product. The customer is therefore part of the production process. When the Games are over, nobody will ever be able to consume this (past) product again. Dependence on the time of consumption makes it attractive for the Games organising committee to sell as many tickets as possible, because the tickets for today's event cannot be sold the next day.

Time dependency makes sport suitable for *price discrimination*. Price discrimination implies that different groups of customers pay different prices for basically the same product. In the case of a health and fitness club, part of the *peak demand* (i.e. full utilisation of capacity) between 5 pm and 7 pm can be moved to a low demand time slot by offering the same product at a lower price during an off-peak time. Senior citizens and parents with home duties, for example, may be able to take advantage of this offer. Pre-selling tickets to the Olympic Games is another example of price discrimination. By offering the same tickets at a lower price, the organising committee fills up seating capacity with customers who are able to plan and purchase in advance.

STEP 8: DETERMINE FINAL PRICE

Throughout this chapter it has been shown that many factors impact on the pricing process of a certain product. Figure 6.5 summarises these factors and

The possible pricing range

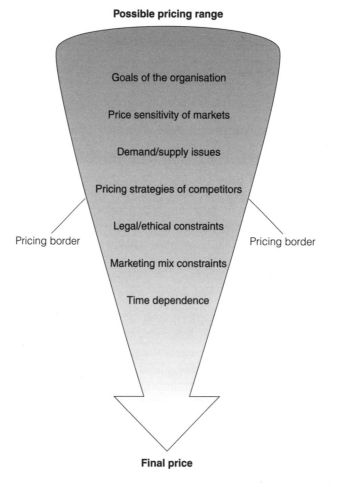

Possible pricing range

Goals of the organisation

Price sensitivity of markets

Demand/supply issues

Pricing strategies of competitors

Pricing border   Legal/ethical constraints   Pricing border

Marketing mix constraints

Time dependence

Final price

shows how the possible pricing range of the product narrows down after taking the influence of these various factors into consideration.

Final price determination is based on either cost, competition, demand or a combination of the three. Most of the time, one method provides the basis for decision making, although the others often contribute. As was shown in this chapter, *cost-based* price determination proves to be more difficult for service-based sport products. The break-even analysis was presented as a cost-based approach. Many providers in the health and fitness industry will base their pricing on *competition*. It was shown that in this industry it is important to fill the capacity of the facility and hence to attract those few extra customers from the direct competitors. It is likely that the larger spectator sport organisations base their pricing on *demand*. In this method, the value of the product to the buyer is estimated. Westerbeek and Turner (1996) found that:

> . . . together with an increase in televisual appeal and hence income, the AFL was able to devise strategies in which demand characteristics of their markets (like elasticity of demand) could be used to optimise net income. Mass attendance at games was deemed more important than maximum profit from gate receipts. By undercharging at the gate [it was found that demand was inelastic at the current pricing level], income from TV and sponsorship could be raised, leading to greater total income rather than maximising gate receipts. (p. 394)

In this chapter's opening example, the AFL will have estimated the value of its television product to the broadcast network and its sponsor product to the sponsors. In closing this chapter it can be concluded that, ultimately, the AFL based its pricing strategy on the perceived value of its total product mix.

SUMMARY

In this chapter, price as one of the variables of the marketing mix was discussed in the context of setting or adjusting the price of a sport product. In order to arrive at a final price, a strategic pricing model was introduced. To enable the sport marketer to set appropriate prices, it is important to set pricing goals in concert with the overall organisational and marketing goals. Then the sensitivity of markets to changes in price can be determined, and as a consequence the elasticity of demand. This information, combined with marketing data such as the size of the market and the number of competitors, is used to estimate cost–volume–profit relationships, leading to the creation of a break-even chart with an emphasis on a cost-based pricing strategy. When the organisation is able to base its pricing on the demand in the market, in other words, powerful enough to lead the way in setting price, the emphasis will be on demand-based pricing. It may, however, be more important to find out about the pricing strategies of competitors and to determine constraints (legal, social, other marketing mix variables) on pricing behaviour in the industry. This can lead to a competitor-based pricing strategy. When taking into consideration the time dependence of many sport products, a combination of cost-based, demand-based and competitor-based pricing will often be exercised in setting the final price or adjusting the current price.

THE HIGH PRICE OF BEING THERE

'Is it a bit rich, even for the traditionally wealthy rugby fraternity, to pay more than $100 to watch the Wallabies this season? Or is it merely value for money in an era when the marketers and administrators are constantly reminding us that sport is now fully integrated into the entertainment industry, and should be priced as such? Perhaps the only certainty in a time when the various major sports are forced to accommodate the inflationary spiral of player payments is that the cost of watching the stars will continue to rise.

'In those cases where demand far exceeds supply—notably Bledisloe Cup rugby, the AFL Grand Final, State-of-Origin rugby league and major World Cup soccer games—the premiums are likely to become especially prohibitive. Rugby, particularly, seems determined to place itself alongside a visit to the Opera or a night out watching the Sydney Symphony Orchestra in terms of its cost structure. In other sports, this may be seen as misguided elitism, but if crowds at Super 12 games are any guide then the pockets of the rah-rah wallahs remain as deep as ever. Indeed, it will be impossible to buy a ticket for just one Wallabies match this year as the Australian Rugby Union has made it compulsory to buy a package for two Tests if you want to see the Wallabies at all. And depending on whether you live in Brisbane or Sydney, this can work out to be as much as $70 per match.

'The working man's game, rugby league, is taking a similar route, charging up to $53 to see its showpiece State-of-Origin series. Prices at club grounds have also risen sharply in some cases, partly because clubs like the Sydney Bulldogs and Penrith have spent heavily on improving facilities.

'If there is a moral to the story it can be found in the country's most popular spectator sport, Australian Football, which continues to draw people by the hundreds of thousands each weekend. The AFL remains perhaps the most egalitarian of all the football codes, offering better facilities each season without bumping up ticket prices. There is a convincing argument that in Sydney and Brisbane the AFL may be enticing supporters away from league, not least because they can afford it.'

Source: Excerpts from Cockerill (1996, p. 32).

Questions

1   If sporting organisations consider themselves as competing in the entertainment industry, what restricts them in terms of pricing their product compared to other entertainment competitors?

2   Given the price of rugby league State-of-Origin tickets, is demand elastic or inelastic? Justify your answer.
3   Are rugby league and Australian Rules football likely to compete on price?
4   Identify the potential negative side effects of maximising profits from gate receipts in sport.

REFERENCES

Anderson, L. K. and Sollenberger, H. M. (1992). *Managerial Accounting*, 8th edn, South-Western Publishing, Cincinnati, Ohio.

Australian Football League (1994). *AFL Strategic Plan 1994*, Melbourne.

Cockerill, M. (1996). 'The high price of being there', *Sydney Morning Herald*, 5 April, p. 32.

Henderson, I. (1996). 'AFL kicks a goal on marketing strategy', *The Australian*, 23 July, p. 5.

Panstadia International (1994). 'The centre of attention', 2 (2), pp. 32–4.

Westerbeek, H. M. and Turner, P. (1996). 'Market power of sport organisations: an Australian case study', *Conference Proceedings: 4th International Conference on Sport Management (EASM)*, Montpellier, France.

7

The sport promotion mix

CHAPTER OUTLINE

Chapter 7 introduces the sport promotion mix. In this chapter the traditional elements of the promotion mix are discussed, including advertising, public relations and publicity, and sales promotion. In addition, elements special and important to sport are added, including sponsorship and promotional licensing. Many of the components of the sport promotion mix are the subject of separate chapters. This chapter introduces these elements and specifically examines the types of promotion and product demand, as well as concentrating on the importance of sales promotion for sport.

After studying this chapter you should be able to:

1 Articulate the concepts related to promotion strategy.
2 Recognise the components of the promotion mix.
3 Establish procedures for selecting the correct promotion mix.
4 Develop strategies to determine the applicability of personal selling.
5 Comprehend the importance of the escalator principle.
6 Develop programs and techniques to increase sales.

THE MONEY-BACK GUARANTEE

Bill Veeck, the great pioneer in North American sport marketing during the 1940s and 1950s always argued that promotion must be more than simply amusing or entertaining . . . it had to create conversation. His contention was that when a fan left the ball game he had to talk about what he has seen. To this end he offered 'the money back guarantee' (Veeck & Linn 1962, p. 119).

In what was a complex world, Veeck articulated three simple principles that set him apart from other sport promoters. He insisted that a city owed nothing to a baseball (sport) team; that baseball (sport) was not a civic monument and had to be hustled; and, most importantly, that 'everyday was Mardi Gras and every fan was King'.

In the process of expressing these three principles Veeck recognised three major dimensions of sport: the fans, the game and the periphery. Furthermore, while acknowledging the importance of a winning team, he argued that the game itself had to be attractively packaged and aggressively promoted, and that the comfort and satisfaction of the fan had to be ensured.

Nevertheless, Kahn (1972) argues that more than anything Veeck liked to win. He contends that Veeck's objectives were to have a winning team and great promotion, failing that, a winning team and poor promotion, and if all else failed a losing team with great promotion. The fundamental belief in this instance was that great promotion would assist in maintaining consumption or minimise supporter drop-off during on-field decline.

In the Australian context, World Series Cricket during the late 1970s, Australian Rugby League (ARL) in the mid 1980s, the National Basketball

League (NBL) in the late 1980s and the Australian Football League (AFL) in their 1996 centenary year not only heavily promoted their respective core products; they also increasingly highlighted the product extensions. While superstar athletes, media-created celebrities, entertainment, excitement and glamour may have resulted in a different type of fan consuming sport products, the success of night and midweek contests suggests that sport promoters have tapped into an emerging sport spectator trend: a trend where the athletic contest is only a part of the total entertainment package.

In an era when contemporary sport consumers are derided by long-suffering traditional fans as 'theatre goers', it is clear that sport events are no longer confined to the playing field with the spectators 'looking in from the outside'. Fans are now part of the event and construct the spectacle while simultaneously consuming it. The Mexican Wave, various team chants, the interaction of team mascots with the crowd and the use of contemporary music are all examples of the nexus between on-field and off-field activity. Promotion is now an integral and vital part of the sport experience. How the sport marketer and promoter manipulates the promotion mix will be vital to the success of the game and even the long-term viability of the sport.

PROMOTION STRATEGY DEFINED

Broadly, a *promotion strategy* is a controlled integrated program of communication designed to present an organisation and its products or services clearly to prospective customers. Furthermore, it communicates needs-satisfying attributes in order to facilitate sales. This in turn contributes to long-term profits. Figure 7.1 schematically represents the variables inherent in promotion strategy. The most important component of promotion strategy is that which relates to communication. *Communication* occurs when an individual attends to a message *and* attributes importance to it. Once information processing occurs, communication is said to have taken place (Cravens 1994).

In the late 1970s, the establishment of World Series Cricket was an excellent example of a controlled promotion strategy. During the period 1977–79, the World Series was positioned as an alternative to the traditional game. In the process, it not only used the best athletes the sport had to offer; it also radically altered the tone of cricket by creating stylistic changes in the game's production and presentation. In numerous ways the sport was repackaged as a television spectacle to captivate the home viewer. Multiple camera angles, coloured uniforms, onscreen graphics and various auditory devices were introduced, which elevated the entertainment level of the game. Not only cricket devotees were captivated, but also sport and entertainment fans in general.

Simultaneously, other promotion strategies were implemented, which resulted in multiple layers of cricket consumption. This occurred not only at

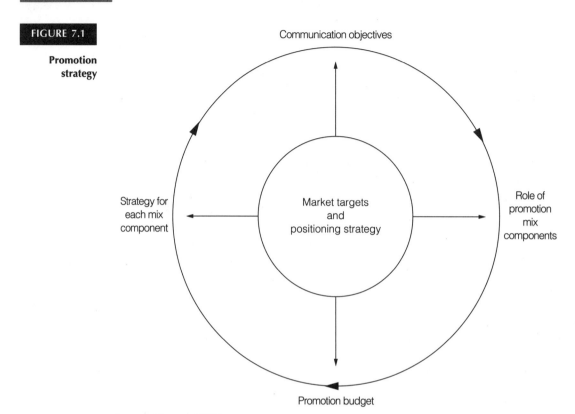

Source: Cravens (1994).

the ground, but also on television, on radio, in newspapers and magazines, and in department stores and supermarkets across the country. World Series Cricket sold books, fruit, paint and even lunch boxes, as well as cricket apparel. The message being communicated was one tinged with excitement, glamour, aggression, superstars and non-stop entertainment. Judging by the numbers that turned up to see World Series Cricket limited overs games, in hindsight it is obvious that not only was the promotion strategy adopted by the organisation successful for cricket worldwide; it also marked a watershed in sport marketing in Australia.

PROMOTION AND PRODUCT DEMAND

The ultimate goal of promotion strategy is to stimulate demand for a particular product. However, before strategies are developed there is a need to understand the type of demand that exists, which may be:

- generic, or
- brand, and
- direct or indirect.

Generic demand is the demand for a particular product category. At a national level, a government policy may promote sport and recreation as a means to increasing health and fitness levels among the population at large. In this case tennis clubs, fitness centres, sports stores, and recreational and tourist accommodation can all benefit from the generic campaign. Occasionally a market leader unilaterally engages in generic advertising when industry sales are down.

At a league, competition or association level, sport marketers engage in promoting the sport or competition while leaving clubs to their own marketing devices. For example, during the Australian Open, Tennis Australia will create a generic demand for tennis by promoting the sport in general. It is then up to local clubs and associations to establish localised promotion strategies allowing them to tap into the generic demand.

Most consumer promotion is directed towards increasing *brand demand*. The Sydney Flames, the Tassie Islanders and the Melbourne Tigers of the Women's National Basketball League (WNBL) all adopt specific promotion strategies in an attempt to encourage consumption and support of their particular teams—the brands. In the process, the demand for the generic product (i.e. WNBL) is increased. Occasionally brand switching may occur when a Flames fan becomes a Perth Quit Breakers fan, but in the main the promotion strategy results in increased industry (i.e. WNBL) sales, or in this case an increase in the number of fans attending women's basketball games.

The majority of consumer promotion is an attempt to stimulate *direct demand* for a specific product. Sporadically, a manufacturer may promote an element of a product, which may stimulate demand for that component, which in turn may directly stimulate *indirect demand* for a particular brand. For example, lycra manufacturers promote the attributes of lycra, which indirectly stimulates demand for products made using the substance, such as fitness and cycling apparel.

Irrespective of the type of demand, the audience targeted by the promotion strategy invariably remains the same. Current and future customers, stockholders, the public at large and special interest groups are all existing or potential consumers. However, responses to promotion strategies will vary based on the myriad of consumer behaviour factors discussed in Chapter 3. As a response to such differences, sport promoters need to tailor marketing strategies in order to attract specific consumer groups. This is done by acknowledging the stages in promotion strategy development and then manipulating the promotion mix.

STAGES IN PROMOTION STRATEGY DEVELOPMENT

In establishing promotion strategy development an organisation needs to undertake the following steps.

As Figure 7.2 shows, first an initial analysis of the specific *situation* is required, when the following questions should be addressed: What is the

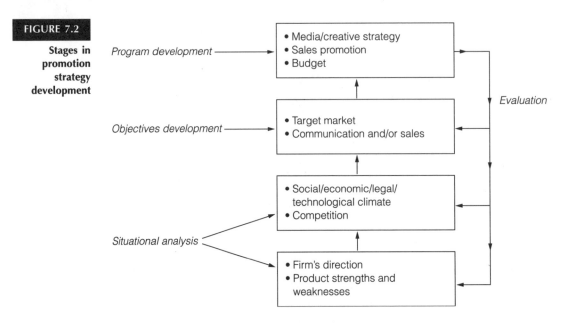

FIGURE 7.2

**Stages in
promotion
strategy
development**

Program development

- Media/creative strategy
- Sales promotion
- Budget

Evaluation

Objectives development

- Target market
- Communication and/or sales

- Social/economic/legal/
  technological climate
- Competition

Situational analysis

- Firm's direction
- Product strengths and
  weaknesses

general direction of the firm in the prevailing social and economic climate? What are the product or service's strengths and weaknesses compared with those of competition? Are there legal, technological or distribution issues that need to be factored into the decision making?

Once an analysis of the situation has been undertaken, *objectives* need to be developed. Considerations here should take into account the composition of the target market, what the sales objectives are and, equally importantly, the message to be communicated.

Once the objectives are known, *programs* need to be established that will enable the objectives to be accomplished. These may include the creative and media strategies to be employed, the sales promotion to be utilised, reseller support programs, and the budget that underpins the breadth and scope of the programs.

Concurrently with program execution, a system of *evaluation*, or for monitoring the effectiveness of such strategies, needs to be rigorously implemented. These evaluative mechanisms need to be specifically linked to the stated objectives. By clearly defining the stages in promotion strategy development, an organisation not only establishes a framework for future activities but also, by constantly using it as a reference source, creates an excellent evaluative mechanism.

DEFINING THE PROMOTION MIX

The *promotion mix* consists of advertising, public relations and publicity, sales promotion, promotional licensing and personal selling, which includes sponsorship and telemarketing. How these elements are combined, and in what measure, depends on the target market, the organisational objectives and the promotion strategy that is to be utilised.

Advertising

Advertising is a non-personal communication by an identified sponsor. This is the most obvious form of sport and event promotion. On a regular basis, sport producers such as the AFL, Uncle Toby's Ironman Series and the ARL advertise their products on television and/or radio, as well as in the daily newspapers, with the intent of informing potential consumers and shaping their choices. In regard to events this information would contain the names of the sponsoring organisation and the organisation paying for the advertisement, the time and place of the event, the featured acts, sports or athletes, perhaps cost and, invariably, a telephone number for further information. Advertisements for a fitness centre could include information as to the range of services offered. Advertisements for sport equipment such as tennis racquets could also include the particular facts of the equipment and also, for specific versions, technical specifications.

The major advantage of advertising is that the advertiser can control the time, placement and content of the advertisement. The major disadvantage is cost per exposure per consumer, especially with mass advertising. An expanded analysis of the role of advertising in sport marketing is covered at length in Chapter 8.

Public relations and publicity

Two other forms of communication are public relations (both proactive and reactive) and publicity. *Public relations* is discussed at length in Chapter 11.

Publicity is a non-personal communication that is neither paid for nor sponsored by a promoting organisation. The best example of this is the amount of copy, space and time given to sport and related activities in the media. The various football codes dominate the back pages of newspapers during the winter, while cricket predominates during the summer. Less regular publicity is given to sports like basketball, netball, motor racing, hockey and bowls. Activities such as golf, tennis and horseracing may attract significant publicity at specific times of the year. The Ford Australian Open and Wimbledon, the major golf tournaments around the world, and the Melbourne Cup all heavily feature at the appropriate time. Moreover, similar scenarios occur whether on television or radio or in the newspapers.

The major advantage of publicity is that it is free. However, the disadvantages can be numerous. The relevant sporting body cannot control the time and placement of the story, nor can it control the slant a particular journalist or writer may place on a story. Undoubtedly, publicity can be either positive or negative, and as a consequence it is up to sports to promote the former and minimise the latter. Similarly, it is incumbent on sport promoters to have a public relations strategy in place to negate the effects of adverse publicity. The need for publicity is also discussed in Chapter 11.

Sales promotion

Sales promotion is the set of promotion activities that stimulate and support advertising, personal selling and publicity. Usually such activities are temporary in nature and may involve price or non-price strategies. Sales promotion based on price invariably involves 'two-for-one' deals, group discounts or, in some circumstances, 'half-price tickets', which is a popular concept in the theatre industry. The decision the sport promoter needs to make in this instance is whether the promotion takes place when a strong drawing team comes to play or the reverse. Mullin et al. (1993) suggest that you 'try the promotion with each, and determine which increase the attendance more' (p. 186).

The use of give-aways, such as caps, drink bottles, posters or sport memorabilia, is an example of non-price promotion. Although such promotion can occasionally offer an adult premium, more often than not it is directed towards children, which in turn influences family attendance and consumption. Spolestra (1991) contends that:

> . . . for a premium to excite fans enough for them to buy tickets, the premium needs to have a perceived value equal to the price of the tickets. To get the most fans to buy tickets because of that premium, it is better to offer a weekend game against a decent opponent during the middle of the season. (p. 12)

Irrespective of whether the sport marketer chooses to run with a price or non-price promotion, Spolestra also argues that energies should be directed not to increasing average attendances, but to increasing the number of sold-out games. By increasing the number of sold-out games, average attendances will increase.

Personal selling

Personal selling is paid personal communication by an identified sponsor. It uses oral presentation to prospective consumers or purchasers. Evans and Berman (1987) suggest that the key features of personal selling are:

1 identifying prospects,
2 determining the customer's needs,
3 selecting a sales strategy,
4 communicating with the buyer, and
5 evaluating the sales strategy.

The two most obvious varieties of personal selling are the 'face-to-face' presentation and the increasingly common telemarketing.

Face-to-face presentation

Face-to-face presentation is most closely related to *sponsorship*, and the growth of this component of the promotion mix in the sport marketplace has risen exponentially over the latter half of the twentieth century. This is evidenced by corporations such as Nike, McDonald's, Coca-Cola and Shell, who are prepared to invest a significant part of their marketing budget in direct sport sponsorship. The fundamental underpinning of this position is the belief that sport, especially on television, delivers a captive audience to the company. As a result, organisations are prepared to pay large sums in an effort to connect with clearly segmented consumer markets. This issue of sponsorship will be discussed in depth in Chapter 10.

Telemarketing

Telemarketing is not as advanced in sport in Australia as it is in North America; however, the concept is well known. Insurance companies, credit card organisations, banks, telecommunications agencies and general market research firms are constantly in phone contact with Australian homes both day and night. By accessing existing databanks the telemarketer usually has some knowledge about the potential client's consumption patterns. In North America the selling of season tickets and requests for alumni contributions to universities are clear examples of telemarketing. In both instances, representatives of the respective organisations phone previous or current consumers (i.e. fans or students) in an attempt to either initiate or elevate patterns of consumption. Relevant information is held in existing databanks.

In the case of university students, alumni are asked to recall their positive experiences with the university and then requested to pledge a donation, either one-off or continuing, to one or a number of universities. Invariably at the forefront of many such requests are college athletic programs. Such donations may assist capital works programs, student athlete scholarships, or ongoing awards and honours. Whatever the case, the donation, gift or commitment is usually solicited by telephone and relies on known information about the client.

Similarly, with season tickets, at the end of one season an organisation's telemarketers quickly need to swing into action for the next. Existing season ticket holders are quizzed as to their future intentions, and lapsed members and season ticket holders can be once again reminded of membership benefits. Both current and previous consumers should be well known to the organisation through inhouse databases. By pre-selling a large percentage of seats, merchandise and services, an organisation establishes its product as a premium article, which assists not only in sponsorship development but also in future pricing strategies.

While the former are examples of telemarketing at a macro level, this promotional tool also has strong relevance to community sport. Local recreation centres can canvas former clients as to their reasons for their failure to continue to use the facility's services and, in the process, discern how their needs are currently being met. The benefits of doing this are numerous. The centre can be made aware of service shortfalls, and it may also be apprised of changing demographics or psychographics within the catchment area. Conversely, it may stimulate reconsideration of facility use. In such instances useful information may be provided that can frame future marketing strategies.

Likewise, information regarding the facility's services can be provided to local industry with the intention of assisting the latter to conduct its business. This can take the form of offering group or corporate rates for specific programs or services, conducting contra arrangements where relevant expertise or products are exchanged, or even providing onsite consultancy and health, fitness and well-being services. In many cases it is the function of the telemarketer to initiate interest and, if appropriate, instigate some action.

Finally, the local junior sporting club engages in a form of telemarketing when it contacts parents and interested individuals to assist in the operation and organisation of the club's affairs. In such cases money is not always the focal point of the request; more often than not it is labour, time and expertise. Nevertheless, conceptually it is still the same as telemarketing for season tickets, for alumni support or for tracking information on fitness centre defection. In each case there is an exchange process taking place with the intent of creating a win-win situation. The exchange may not always involve physical goods, as feelings, perceptions or beliefs can form part of this process. Nevertheless, benefits and costs are clearly established and comprehended by both parties to the agreement. If this happens, the telemarketer has done their job well.

Promotional licensing

According to Mullin et al. (1993), *promotional licensing* can be defined as 'the acquisition of rights to affiliate or associate with a product or event for the purposes of deriving benefits related to the affiliation or association' (p. 204). Officials of the Atlanta organising committee for the 1996 Olympic Games suggested that corporations pay as much as $50.7 million to have an official association with the games.

Licensing can involve the use of a logo, an association, the right to designations such as 'official', the right of service or the privilege to conduct promotion activities. Merchandise examples of sport promotional licensing are numerous. Caps, shirts, windcheaters, jackets, scarves and keyrings are merely the tip of the iceberg in licensed goods. Products on supermarket shelves, in service stations and in hardware stores often carry the name of a sport, team or athlete, which on sale will return a percentage to the licensing agent. Sportview 7.1 illustrates this relationship between one such product and sport.

NABISCO BLANKETS CANADA WITH CARD PROMOTION

In 1992 Nabisco was facing declining sales in the cereal division in Canada and trailed Kellogg Canada Inc. by a wide margin. To reverse this trend, Nabisco designed a program which would advertise its association with two Canadian Major League Baseball teams—the Toronto Blue Jays and the Montreal Expos. In the process the company ran the largest Canadian sport promotion ever.

Beginning with a specially designed set of 36 baseball trading cards, Nabisco mounted a multifaceted promotion designed to focus attention on its cereal brand. During the regular season, packages of Nabisco cereal in 15 000 retail stores throughout southern Canada contained three baseball cards. The cards were supported by in-store displays and price incentives for retailers in the 2000 outlets that represented 80% of Nabisco's cereal business. To spur interest in the program, Nabisco also mailed a single card to 4.3 million Canadian households.

Encouraging continued interest, Nabisco ran a bingo game that was tied into the card packs and offered more than 9000 prizes. A bingo card was printed on the inside of each cereal box and two bingo tokens were included with each card pack. To support the program in-stadium, a total of 20 000 card albums (each containing eight cards) were given away at two exhibition games between the Montreal Expos and the Toronto Blue Jays. Media support for the program included 30-second spots on English-speaking television and French-speaking radio.

The two baseball clubs negotiated with their former players for permission to use their likeness and Nabisco paid the players a small fee which, in most cases, was donated to charity. In addition to the cost of the retail component, Nabisco paid the Canadian baseball clubs between $85 000 and $100 000. By mid-summer Nabisco's sales were up by 15% and levelled out at 10% by the season's end.

Source: Adjusted from *Team Marketing Report* (1992).

There is no doubt that the growth in promotional licensing over the last decade has been prolific. However, in some instances it has created dissent as to use of trademarks, images and logos. These issues, and others, will be discussed at length in Chapter 12.

SELECTING THE PROMOTION MIX

Selecting the correct promotion mix is potentially one of the more difficult decisions facing the sport promoter. As is the case when selecting the appropriate marketing mix, the blend of promotion activities engaged in, to entice the consumer, must reflect the type and nature of the product or service and the specific characteristics of the consumer. Not only would a billboard on a major freeway for a marginal sport or niche product be inappropriately placed, the expense involved would be disproportionate to the 'cost per exposure'. In such instances, a combination of selected advertising in a sport-specific magazine, publicity in local or community newspapers, and telemarketing using inhouse databases is a more appropriate way of connecting with potential consumers. Conversely, national sporting organisations employ promotion strategies such as national advertising on radio, television and newspapers; they promote sport-specific magazines; they are the beneficiaries of a colossal amount of publicity across all media; and they engage in telemarketing and personal selling to increase attendances at events. In this instance the use of billboards on major arterial routes would be most appropriate, especially if a significant event in the sport were about to occur, such as a final, a playoff, a State-of-Origin or a blockbuster match-up.

Yet it is equally important for local, community and regional clubs and organisations to establish an appropriate promotion mix. Moreover, while the scope and size of their mixes may be vastly different from those experienced at national or professional level, conceptually they are very similar. Sportview 7.2 demonstrates how aspects of the promotion mix combine to create a successful promotion.

| SPORTVIEW 7.2 | **A RATHER BALD VIEW OF THE SPORT WORLD** |

In February 1993 Brad Ewing, marketing manager for the Houston Rockets of the National Basketball Association (NBA), decided to run a promotion to ensure a sellout at an upcoming home game against the Charles Barkley-led Phoenix Suns. The promotion capitalised not on Barkley's skill or on-court demeanour but rather on his shaved head. In establishing the promotional strategy Ewing wanted to make sure that the game sold out, got publicity on local television, encouraged people to come and witness the promotion even if they did not have game tickets, and create an event that people would positively talk about even if the home team did not win.

This promotion encouraged Rockets fans to have their heads shaved, by qualified hairdressers, on a large stage out the front of The Summit, the Rockets' home court. As an inducement, male fans were offered a five-game pass and female fans were offered a season ticket. The marketing department believed that perhaps 20–30 people would take advantage of this offer. How wrong they were.

When the organisation stopped the promotion five minutes before game time, nearly 200 fans (including twenty females) had decided to imitate Sir Charles's bald pate and the promotion had been an outstanding success. The game was a sellout, hundreds of people gathered to watch the 'shearing' take place, they bought merchandise, they moved into the arena and watched the game on television from one of the many bars on the mezzanine, and they bought tickets for upcoming games. Furthermore, the event was not only covered on all the local television stations; it also featured on the nationally watched ESPN Sportscenter that evening. The fact that the Rockets won the game was merely icing on the cake for a very successful evening.

SALES PROMOTION, TICKETING AND PARTICIPATION

In 1995, the Sydney Swans chief executive officer undertook a series of research projects that enabled the organisation to formulate a promotion strategy aimed at 'selling' the team to what the chief believed to be a potential AFL spectator base in Sydney of 650 000. In June 1996, Smith reported that:

> . . . from this research the club launched a series of acquisition, retention and cross selling programs that led to a 50% increase in membership, the development of a solid database, a strategic alliance with East's Rugby League Club, Swan-link—a transport joint venture with the NSW Department of Transport, and a four-fold increase in the sale of Swans merchandise. (1996a, p. B6; 1996b, p. 42)

By undertaking this research and implementing a number of key recommendations, the Swans management demonstrated a fundamental knowledge of the attendance frequency escalator principle discussed below, and instigated programs and techniques to increase sales. Only time will tell whether they are as successful in preventing defection.

The attendance frequency escalator

One of the key issues that faces the sport industry is how to encourage existing consumers to elevate their levels of involvement while at the same time introducing new consumers to sport products and services. This is as true for recreational activities and merchandise as it is for professional sport.

The consumption of sport was initially thought to be analogous to a *staircase*. In this instance, the consumer would make an initial foray into the product by purchasing a single game ticket or buying a single piece of apparel or merchandise. The consequences of an incorrect choice would not be great. Once the consumer was happy that the right decision had been made, they would increase their level of consumption to a point with which they were comfortable. In other words, they would take a number of steps up the sport consumption staircase. Marketing in this instance was focused on the new consumer, ignoring the contribution that an existing member, fan or participant could make to the sport or organisation. Potentially, the satisfied customer is an organisation's best salesperson.

While the staircase analogy may have had initial applicability to the sport industry, the sheer complexity of potential sport consumption choices created a need for a framework that exhibited greater flexibility and fluidity. Furthermore, the initial staircase structure did not allow for non-direct or non-consumers. The *frequency escalator* provides a mechanism for addressing such shortcomings.

Mullin (1985) contends that the distribution of existing consumers 'is a continuous series of steps on an escalator that runs from one through to the number of games in a season' (p. 161). Conceptually, this can be applied not just to the sport spectator, but also to the snow skier, fitness centre member, tennis player or golfer, who may indulge in their activity of choice from infrequently to daily. When these are combined with pre-consumers, who are divided into non-consumers and indirect consumers, the possible levels of consumption are quite vast. Hence the escalator principle recognises both the fluid nature of consumption and the increasing levels at which consumption is possible. To explain the process Mullin (1985) created the categories shown Figure 7.3.

Non-consumers

While non-consumers may be divided into *aware* and *non-aware* categories, establishing promotion strategies aimed at such groups is problematic. The sport promoter either does not know the constituency of the group or realises that a conscious decision not to consume the sport offerings has been made. While advertising campaigns that both inform and educate may have some success in introducing new consumers to a product, such strategies are little more than one part of an extensive promotion campaign. Nevertheless, non-consumers are now a significant part of the sport consumption process and need to be acknowledged accordingly.

Indirect consumers

Indirect consumers listen to sport on the radio, watch it on television, read about it in the newspapers, and discuss it with friends and colleagues. In all respects this group is extremely important. If fans refused to listen to or watch the game, buy the merchandise, or associate the sport with a particular manufacturer, the potential for corporate involvement in sport would be severely limited. Only 16 000 tennis fans can watch the Ladies' and Mens' Final of the Australian Tennis Open live, but many millions can be transfixed by the event on television.

In this instance it is the task of the sport marketer to attempt to convert the indirect consumer to one who purchases the live or actual experience or commodity. Given that in most instances such consumers are predisposed towards the sport product, the inducements that can be utilised to offer the 'one-off' experience are numerous. Moreover, if such inducements are tied to an appropriate advertising campaign, the potential to add to the direct consumer base is enhanced. Nevertheless, it should be recognised that indirect consumers are an integral part of any attendance or participation act, and as such their level of commitment must be appreciated and acknowledged.

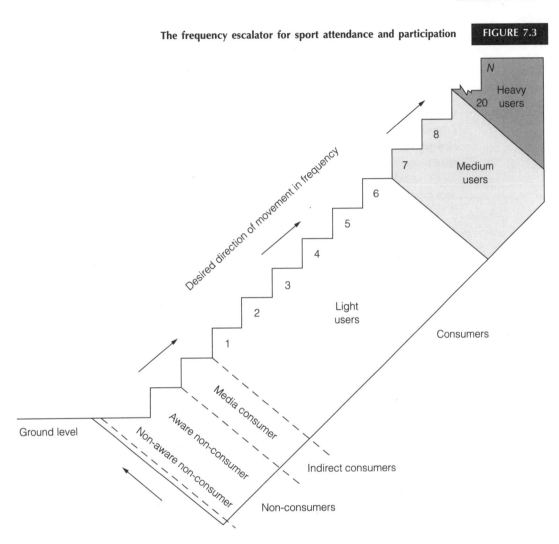

The frequency escalator for sport attendance and participation   FIGURE 7.3

Source: Mullin (1985, p. 163).

Moreover, strategies should be implemented that ensure their ongoing support at the level with which they are comfortable. Junior supporters' clubs on television, sport-specific magazines and home pages on the World Wide Web (WWW) all provide for a specific level of sport consumption.

Direct consumers

Direct consumers are categorised into *light, medium* and *heavy users*, and promotions should be designed to encourage consumers to move towards the heavy end. Shilbury (1994) suggests that sport marketers should initially aim for a 60% heavy, 10% medium, 30% light combination of consumers, and this idea has merit. The selling of 60% of tickets pre-season enables early financial strategy and fiscal planning, while the 10% allocated to medium users, or mini-season ticket holders, provides a mechanism for light users to elevate their level of consumption without making the leap to a full season ticket. This is especially important in sports such as basketball, where the season is invariably long and many games are played. By reserving 30% for the walk-up crowd the sport marketer ensures access to infrequent game attenders, first-timers and fans who wish to see an individual game due to a strong match-up, star players or game promotion.

The advantage of this ticketing strategy is that it allows for fluidity in fan movement. The suggestion inherent in the sport attendance frequency escalator is that the consumer is moved by the sport or organisation towards increased levels of consumption. It also argues that, given the variety in light, medium or heavy use, the movement from one category to the next is rather seamless with a relatively ill-defined transition phase. This is in contrast to the sport participation staircase, where the consumer makes a conscious decision to move to the next consumption level. In this case, stages are discrete and may be mutually exclusive.

The key issue related to the sport attendance frequency escalator is: How do sports encourage increased consumption levels? In this instance strategies and programs need to be developed that will not only enhance awareness of the benefits resulting from additional investment on the part of the consumer, but also result in increased sales.

By encouraging different levels of participation and hence segmenting the market, the sport marketer strives to ensure maximum consumption of the event—the *sellout*. It should not be forgotten that the first objective of sports attendance is to sell out the stadium. The second objective is to repeat the first as often as possible. Spolestra (1991) argues that it is much more fun to go to a sold-out event than one that is only half-sold. Sellouts create premium tickets, which in turn elevate the profile of the event. This in turn increases the desirability of the product, which itself leads to increased sales. Once an event has been sold out the sport marketer can then focus attention on providing excellent service to the fans on hand.

However, the sport marketer should not create a perception of a sellout merely in an attempt to create premium tickets. In the early 1990s the Sydney Kings organisation had to work assiduously to combat the notion that their basketball games were always sold out. Although this was not the case, basketball fans, believing this to be true, often stayed away from games when excellent seats were still available.

PROGRAMS AND TECHNIQUES TO INCREASE SALES

The four major areas that need to be concentrated on with respect to sales are:

- indirect consumers,
- light users,

- medium users, and
- heavy users.

While the first three groups are encouraged to elevate their usage level, anti-defection programs need to be implemented for the heavy usage category in an attempt to prevent them from 'falling off' the escalator.

Indirect to light

Converting indirect consumers to light users is not that difficult and is best accomplished using advertising and sales promotion. The consumer has already shown a predisposition towards the product by being a media fan or purchasing related merchandise. What needs to be done is to provide them with an incentive to walk into an arena and see first-hand that which has been previously mediated for them. The number of possibilities here are endless. The most obvious is providing a tangible connection between the products consumed at home and the event itself. Media competitions, game-redeemable coupons and event-associated product purchases all provide an attractive entry into the initial consumption experience.

Light to medium

Moving the light user to the medium user category can be achieved through sales promotion and personal selling. Consumers at this stage are still predominantly price sensitive; so offering reduced prices for bulk purchases and discounts on selected associated goods will often encourage light users of the product. Given that there are various levels of medium usage, predesignated seating, newsletters and invitations to pre- or post-game functions and special events may be appropriate incentives.

Medium to heavy

Encouraging the medium user to become a heavy user is rather more difficult than the previous scenarios, as more often than not medium users have reached a saturation level in terms of their personal consumption. This may not be a problem if the season is not excessively long or expensive. To encourage heavy usage, organisations need to make this individual feel very special. In this instance the emphasis should be on personal selling and premium sales promotion. While group-specific deals and give-aways can be negotiated for this group, these may be only a start of the service offered. Sport promoters need to think about the range of value-added extensions that can increase the heavy user's enjoyment of the product, such as valet parking, special dining, boxes and access to play-off or finals tickets. They also need to be aware of those club resources which may facilitate the heavy user's or member's conduct of their own business. These may include the use of athletes to promote facets of the member's business, the use of organisational space and expertise to conduct business seminars and workshops, or even the provision of networking opportunities across this category of membership. In such instances all participants should be working towards a win-win situation.

Anti-deflection programs

Although all products and services have natural attrition rates, this does not mean that defection should be meekly accepted. Programs aimed at minimising defection should be firmly entrenched and constantly evaluated in any promotion strategy. By being aware of the client's purchase and usage habit through constant monitoring of databanks, changes in patterns of behaviour may be quickly noticed. Immediately a decline in usage is evident, sales staff or other appropriate individuals need to contact the client quickly to discern reasons for consumption fall-off. By responding to consumer issues and concerns in a prompt manner, organisations are more likely to maintain their heavy usage consumers.

SUMMARY

Establishing promotion strategies is a complex yet exciting task. Advertising, public relations and publicity, sales promotion, personal selling, including sponsorship and telemarketing, and promotional licensing are crucial to the success of any sport product, event or service and as such are vital to the promotion mix. Furthermore, the sport marketer not only needs to be fully conversant with the components of the promotion mix, but also needs appropriate application skills in any given situation.

Once the promotion strategy has been established, it is incumbent on sport marketers to analyse consumers within the framework of the frequency escalator to monitor ongoing consumer behaviour. Programs and techniques to increase sales and prevent defection need to be established and implemented, to ensure continued consumption of the product and to facilitate maximal gain from the specific promotion activity. Contemporary sport marketers also need to be able to offer the 'money-back guarantee'.

CASE STUDY

NCAA RECORD CROWD FOR WOMEN'S BASKETBALL

On Sunday 3 February 1985 the University of Iowa women's basketball team smashed the NCAA single-game attendance record. This historic landmark for women's sport and women's basketball in particular appeared to be the result of a very unique set of circumstances which combined to make the day a sport and cultural phenomenon. The factors that contributed to the record crowd are as follows.

Outstanding fans

The University of Iowa has exceptional collegiate sport fans. They have a loyalty that goes beyond winning and losing—men's and women's basketball games sell out on a season-ticket basis. Moreover, Iowans love basketball in general, a fact attested to by record crowds for highschool state playoffs.

A straightforward appeal
The University of Iowa women's basketball coach appealed to the fans 'straight from the heart'. The fans were challenged to do two things: first, help break the NCAA record set by Kentucky; and second, help cheer the underdog Iowan team against the powerhouse Ohio State.

Team effort
All parts of the university gathered behind the team. The entire athletic department supported the effort, with the men's coach going on television and radio to encourage people to attend the game.

Media support
The media also got behind the effort. Talk shows, sportcasts and game broadcasts all helped promote the game.

Marketing, publicity and promotion
Several specific elements were employed, including a direct letter from the coach to the fans that appeared in the local newspaper and that was mailed to 200 highschool coaches and teams. Press releases resulted in a number of pre-game stories—a 60-second radio spot featuring the coach was aired on local stations and a 30-second television spot was aired during state-wide telecasts of the men's basketball games (which regularly drew up to one million viewers). Moreover the network did on-air promotions during men's games complete with graphics. Eight thousand flyers offering two half-price tickets were distributed at the men's basketball game one week prior to the women's game—3000 of these were redeemed. The major sponsor of the women's team (Wendy's) distributed the coach's letter with the half-price ticket offer on the reverse side to all their customers during the week prior to the game. The area's largest employer, Amana Refrigeration Inc., also distributed the letter with the half-price offer.

Follow up
In an attempt to identify the key market for women's athletics, and to thank those who attended, a memento was sent to those who attended, filled out a name and address card and deposited the card in a box when leaving the venue. There were 17 000 respondents, representing approximately 9000 households. Commemorative T-shirts were offered for sale after the event and the coach appeared on many radio and television programs to thank fans for their attendance. Finally, to stem the negative feedback from the 5000 people who could not get into the match, a press statement was issued offering the memento to all those who were turned away.

The University of Iowa's women's athletic program received tremendous national, regional and local publicity. CBS Sports, CNN, Sport Time Cable Network and Sports Illustrated all contacted the university for follow-up stories.

For the record
Ohio State defeated Iowa (56–47) but a new attendance record had been set (22 157 people, of which 14 821 had paid). The previous record of 10 622 had been shattered.

Source: Adjusted from White and Grant (1985).

Questions

1 What are the major lessons from this successful promotion?
2 There is no professional sport competition within 380 kilometres. How should the University of Iowa athletic department respond if a major sport franchise were relocated close by?
3 What aspects of the promotion may not be applicable in the Australian context?

REFERENCES

Cravens, D. W. (1994). *Strategic Marketing*, 4th edn, Irwin, Ill.

Evans, J. R. and Berman, B. (1987). *Marketing*, Macmillan, New York.

Kahn, R. (1972). *The Boys of Summer*, Harper & Row, New York.

Mullin, B. (1985). 'Internal marketing—a more effective way to sell sport', in *Successful Sport Management*, eds G. Lewis and H. Appenzellar, Michie Co., Charlottesville, Va.

Mullin, B., Hardy, S. and Sutton, W. A. (1993). *Sport Marketing*, Human Kinetics, Champaign, Ill.

Shilbury, D. (1994). 'Ticketing strategy in the Australian National Basketball League', *Sport Marketing Quarterly*, 3 (4), pp. 17–22.

Smith, G. (1996a). 'A strategy to sell the Swans', *The Age*, 6 June, p. B6.

——(1996b). 'Swans kick goals with marketing research', *Marketing*, June, Niche, Melbourne.

Spolestra, J. (1991). *How to Sell the Last Seat in the House*, 1, SRO Partners, Portland, Oregon.

Team Marketing Report (1992). 'Nabisco blankets Canada with card promotion', 5 (1), October, pp. 3–4.

Veeck, B. and Linn, E. (1962). *Veeck—as in Wreck*, New American Library, New York.

White, J. and Grant, C. H. B. (1985). 'Report on NCAA record crowd', University of Iowa, Women's Athletic Program, Athletic Department Publication.

8

Advertising

CHAPTER OUTLINE

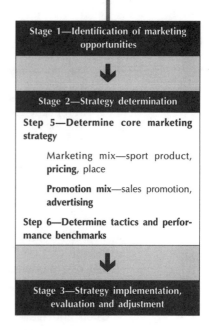

Stage 1—Identification of marketing opportunities

Stage 2—Strategy determination

Step 5—Determine core marketing strategy

Marketing mix—sport product, **pricing**, place

Promotion mix—sales promotion, **advertising**

Step 6—Determine tactics and performance benchmarks

Stage 3—Strategy implementation, evaluation and adjustment

Chapter 8 introduces advertising as a component of the sport promotion mix. Advertising is a non-personal paid message aimed to create awareness about a product or idea. This chapter examines some of the ways in which advertising is used in sport to promote sporting contests and events. The types of advertising are also described, and the creative techniques used to develop ideas and communicate them to the public.

After studying this chapter you should be able to:

1 Articulate the concepts related to advertising.
2 Recognise the message capabilities of various media.
3 Establish procedures for selecting appropriate media.
4 Establish strategies for selecting the appropriate media mix.
5 Develop mechanisms for measuring advertising effectiveness.

'SIMPLY THE BEST'

The phenomenon of Tina Turner's involvement with the NSWRL reached its highpoint in 1993 with her arrival in Sydney for the Grand Final. Turner's song 'Simply the Best' had become an anthem for the code and was associated nationally with Rugby League. Over a four-year-period, Rugby League, through its association with the rock superstar, constantly elevated its position in the Australian sportscape. In the process Rugby League turned the administration of their game into a business and began to professionally market their product. (Hertz Walpole 1990)

According to John Quayle of the New South Wales Rugby League (NSWRL) the campaign was good-looking, tough and sexy. Jim Walpole of Hertz Walpole agreed, commenting that Tina Turner and Rugby League projected compatible images in that both were international and dynamic. He further believed that the use of Tina Turner in the advertising campaign not only promoted a game that was modern, energetic, vital and one for the young, it also marketed the game in a totally new way. It now had style, music, a rockstar and a new appeal. Libby Darlason acknowledged that the campaign was slick, sophisticated and clever, and generally conveyed the required image, that is, tough game, tough athletes, tough rockstar.

The Tina Turner campaign succeeded beyond all expectations. In the two years up to 1990, crowds increased by 65.5% and television ratings soared. Female audiences climbed by 37% in 1989 alone and the advertising campaign was nominated for Hollywood's Radio and Television awards. What was rated as a $2 million gamble in 1989 had turned into a deal for rugby league that can only be interpreted as Simply the Best.

The 'Simply the Best' advertising campaign, and the 'C'mon Aussie C'mon' cricket campaign of the late 1970s, are possibly the most successful sport advertising campaigns Australia has witnessed. In fact, the momentum gained by both campaigns pushed them beyond the boundaries of sport and into a wider cultural milieu. In both instances it could be claimed that the advertising campaign ensured the medium-term success of the sport and established new market segments for the respective games.

Although the 'Simply the Best' and 'C'mon Aussie C'mon' campaigns are obvious success stories, they are by no means unique. Australian corporations, and multinational organisations with an Australian arm, have been prepared to make a significant investment in the Australian Football League (AFL), the Ford Australian Open, the Australian 500 Motorcycle Grand Prix and, more recently, Melbourne's Inaugural Formula 1 Grand Prix and the Women's National Basketball League (WNBL).

Judging by the amount of money spent on advertising, both sport and sponsors obviously believe that it is money well spent. However, this may not be an unequivocal position. Shoebridge (1993) comments that 'although media advertising accounts for roughly half of the $10 billion spent on advertising each year, its popularity is waning' (p. 18). He further contends that companies are starting to inject more money into public relations, sales promotion and direct marketing, as opposed to television, radio and print campaigns, due to the amount of 'clutter' associated with mass media advertising.

Mullin et al. (1993) also suggest that a major problem in advertising is perceptual distortion and argue that the core of advertising is effective communication. Moreover, Sutherland (1993) suggests that how advertising works is somewhat of a mystery given that consumers have a tendency to believe that it has no effect on them personally. Nevertheless, the fact that advertisers keep advertising means that something is working on someone. It is the *who* and *how* that need clarification.

The dilemma for sport marketers is that, while they are firm in their belief that advertising their goods and services increases sales, or at least results in a predisposition towards their product, questions related to media to be used, target markets to be engaged, cost per exposure, messages to be communicated and the creative component all need to be addressed. While the act of advertising is relatively simple, the construction of effective advertising is quite complex.

Source: Adjusted from Hertz Walpole (1990).

RELATIONSHIP BETWEEN ADVERTISING AND PRODUCT LIFECYCLE

Before making decisions as to the appropriate media to be used, sport marketers need to understand the relationship between advertising and the phases of the product lifecycle, discussed in Chapter 5. During the goods or services *introductory* phase, advertising should be *informative*. In this instance the advertisement should provide all the salient information about the product. This may include special features, relevant technical specifications, pictorial or illustrative representations, place of purchase and/or consumption and even price. Basically, the sport promoter is stating what the goods or services are and where they can be obtained.

During the *growth* and *maturity* phases, advertising should be *persuasive* in nature. Consumers should be reminded as to the benefits and/or the desirable attributes that can be gained by consuming the product.

During the *decline* phase, *reminder* advertising should be used. The intent behind this is to provide impetus for consumers to reconsider purchase options or, if the event is cyclical, to remind past consumers that the event will return at some stage in the future and to keep that time free.

Annual events such as the various motor vehicle grand prixs are a good example of this process. Initial advertising emphasises information as to event location, date, ticket options and purchase sites, and promoter. As the day of the event approaches, advertising promotes the participants or stars, becomes more subjective and develops emotional overtones. The 1994 Australian 500 Motorcycle Grand Prix used the advertising slogan 'Come feel the noise', while the 1996 slogan featured Barry Sheene asking, 'But are you going to be there?' The Australian Formula 1 Grand Prix held in Melbourne during March 1996 simply suggested 'It's a great place for a race'. Intermittent advertising takes place through the year, usually associated with similar events, providing fans with broad details of the next race.

PURPOSE OF ADVERTISING

Stanton et al. (1995) state that *advertising* is the activities associated with presenting a paid, sponsor-identified, non-personal message about an organisation and/or its products, services or ideas. While advertising can take many forms, it is basically constructed around a message that is designed to build audiences and promote sales. Joel Hochberg, president of DDB Needham Worldwide, believes that:

> . . . an ad that doesn't sell product has no purpose. To work in the marketplace it must have relevance, originality and impact. If it is not relevant it has no purpose, if it is not original it will not attract attention and if it does not have impact it will leave no lasting impression. (*Marketing News* 1988, p. 3)

Hence it can be argued that, irrespective of context, the foundation of successful advertising is the ability to *communicate*. The willingness of organisations to part with large sums of money to use sport to communicate messages to consumers is evidenced by Sportview 8.1.

O'Hara and Weese (1994) establish a framework to 'better communicate product and service offerings to target groups' (p. 9). Entitled the *advertising management process*, this five-step program incorporates research, campaign planning, creative development, media planning, and implementation and evaluation. This process is schematically illustrated in Figure 8.1.

SPORTVIEW
8.1

THE ADMAN'S OLYMPICS

Advertising and the Olympic Games have always been synonymous. It is believed that more than 2 million people passed through Atlanta during the 1996 Olympic Games, and this made the event an advertising executive's dream. Officials from the organising committee stated that corporations paid as much as $50.7 million to be an official sponsor of the games. Moreover, as tourists strolled through exhibits by General Motors, AT&T and Budweiser, gigantic advertising from 'a Swatch watch the size of a nuclear sub dangling from the side of a historic building', to a six-storey-high Coca-Cola bottle adorned the city.

There is no reason why the Sydney Olympic Games in the year 2000 should not result in similar corporate involvement. The *Business Review Weekly* of April 1996 reported that local companies, Telstra and Ansett, had joined IBM and Coca-Cola as sponsors of the 2000 Games. Furthermore, waiting in the wings to leap on the Olympic bandwagon is McDonald's Australia. Only the US parent company's decision to become one of ten worldwide sponsors of the Olympic program (TOP) will stop them from coming on board. McDonald's Australia is prepared to pay $50 million for a four-year involvement with the Sydney Games. There is little doubt that the Games have become the adman's Olympics.

Source: Adjusted from Bragg (1996).

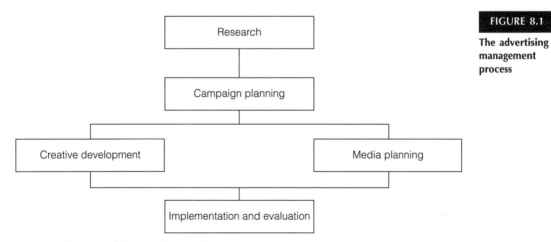

FIGURE 8.1

The advertising management process

Source: O'Hara and Weese (1994, p. 11).

The process is a simple yet effective way of establishing sports advertising strategy, as it links the five components of advertising management in a sequential manner. Following the data collection or research, a campaign is planned around a major theme. At this time how that theme will be creatively developed, and how it will be produced and presented for different media, are simultaneously established. During implementation an evaluative mechanism is established to ascertain the effectiveness or lack thereof of the campaign.

O'Hara and Weese contend that advertising must create exposure, generate processing and lead to long-term communication effects such as attitude and awareness. The comment by Andrew Hipsley, director of marketing for McDonald's Australia, that McDonald's is 'looking for a platform that would make an Olympics marketing program relevant and meaningful to consumers over a four year period' (Shoebridge 1996, p. 75), is a tangible example of the O'Hara and Weese framework.

Quite simply, the purpose of advertising is to influence consumers to respond positively to products or services. While this can be best achieved by establishing advertising campaigns that are linked to prior experience and are strategically focused, there are no fail-safe mechanisms to ensure success. While some advertising campaigns have been abject failures, others have had outstanding successes.

Sportview 8.2 illustrates how Holden used Greg Norman in its advertising campaign to establish linkages with the South Australian Golf Open and to cement the notion that golf is Holden's sport. There is no doubt that the thrust of this advertising campaign was to encourage consumers to purchase Holden motor vehicles rather than attend the South Australian Golf Open, or even play golf, but it is equally incontrovertible that the presence of Greg Norman in any event dramatically increases oncourse and media spectatorship. While this sportview is essentially about Holden using sport to advertise its product and not about golf advertising its sport, the connection between Norman, Holden and golf resulted in a winning situation for all concerned.

SPORTVIEW 8.2

CAPITALISING ON A UNIQUE OPPORTUNITY: GREG NORMAN AND HOLDEN

When Greg Norman, the number one golf player in the world and Holden's spokesperson, announced that he was playing in the Ford SA Open in Adelaide, a strategy was devised to capitalise on this situation for Holden. McCann-Erickson was briefed to develop a campaign that would achieve four key objectives:

1   Reinforce Holden's ownership of Australian golf.
2   Confirm Holden's partnership with Greg Norman.
3   Build Holden staff and dealer morale.
4   Leverage local media coverage of the event.

First, Norman and his caddy wore Holden logos on their golf shirts, and Norman drove a Holden Statesman to the course each day. Metropolitan newspapers and golf magazines were given colour pictures for Holden public relations stories. Second, a special 30-second television commercial, a full-page colour press advertisement for the Adelaide *Advertiser*, three supersites (billboards) on the way to the course and a series of locally produced and Holden-sponsored golf reports on five radio stations ran for the entire duration of the tournament. The results were outstanding. Norman won the event and metropolitan newspapers in Adelaide, Sydney, Melbourne, Canberra, Brisbane, Perth and Hobart quoted the campaign line when reporting on the tournament. The message was simple but extremely compelling: 'When I come home I always come home to a Holden.'

Source: Adjusted from *McCanndo* (1996, p. 2).

ADVERTISING STRATEGY

In establishing an advertising strategy the following issues need to be considered:

■ Has the target audience been identified, and can it be described?
■ What part does advertising play in relation to the totality of the promotional strategy?
■ Are the objectives sales or communication related, and how does this impact on both the media and creative strategy to be used?
■ Have instruments for monitoring and evaluating effectiveness been established, and are they in place?
■ What is the advertising budget?

It is important that the answers to all these questions be known before embarking on an advertising campaign.

Similarly, both the size of the community and the size of special interest groups or target audiences in the market can affect advertising strategy. However, despite any benefits one advertising medium may have over another, a mix of several is often the best strategy. Even the use of just two media, such as print and radio, can result in an interaction that makes each more effective.

The major issue facing the sport marketer's use of advertising is whether to stress reach or frequency. *Reach* refers to the identification of potential consumers, and *frequency* relates to the number of exposures required to access the consumer. Both are critical to a successful advertising strategy. When determining reach the advertiser must clearly decide which consumers are being targeted. When determining frequency the advertiser must decide how many exposures are necessary to reach the prospective consumer. In this instance factors such as price, stage in the product lifecycle, purchase frequency and competitive advertising need to be addressed. It should be remembered that it takes a number of exposures to communicate a specific message as there are always communication barriers to overcome.

Reach should be stressed over frequency when a product is being introduced or has a large target market. Frequency should be stressed over reach when products are frequently purchased and brand switching may take place, when the target market is relatively small, or when the message is difficult to explain and repetition is important in communicating the advertising idea.

ADVERTISING OBJECTIVES

Advertising objectives can be either sales or communication related.

Communication objectives endeavour to provide messages that are understood by consumers about the product or service as a result of the campaign. This type of advertising is predominantly used when a change of image is desired or there is an attempt to build or strengthen a particular demographic. It may also be appropriate if an organisation wishes to generate community goodwill or there is a need to counter a competitive campaign thrust. The advantages of adopting an advertising strategy based on communication objectives are twofold:

- It encourages the identification of process goals and requires that the campaign be evaluated in terms of those goals.
- Communication goals are less likely than sales objectives to be affected by other variables such as price or availability.

One disadvantage of communication objectives is:

- Attitude may be unrelated to purchase intention.

It could be argued that, given that the fundamental basis of advertising is to communicate, objectives should be communication linked.

Sales objectives indicate a target level of sales to be achieved as a result of the campaign. Advertising of this type is used when the desire is to increase membership, audience or product consumption. The obvious advantage of this type of advertising is:

- Sales are a result of purchase behaviour, which is the ultimate goal of the advertiser.

The major disadvantages of basing campaigns purely on sales objectives are threefold:

- The number of sales alone rarely provides much in the way of decision-making guidance.
- Advertising often has a lagging effect on sales; hence past, not present, advertising may influence current sales.
- Changes in competitive decisions may cause changes in current sales.

In releasing their respective campaigns for the 1996 Olympics, Nike, Reebok and Adidas adopted very different strategies. Nike dropped its name from global advertising and went with the 'swoosh' symbol, Reebok sponsored 3000 athletes, while Adidas played on its legendary association with the Games using the campaign line 'We knew then and we know now'. The advertising objectives of the three companies in this instance were communication based, as all companies wished to position themselves against their competitors. However, Phil Knight predicted that Nike revenues would reach $US6 billion by 31 May 1996 and $US12 billion by 2001, based on a 15% annual growth rate, which is indicative of the way sales objectives are linked to advertising (Jones 1996, B1).

When determining advertising objectives the issue of timeframe is critical. On some occasions sport marketers are limited in scope because the event, product or service may be a 'one-off' experience. Conversely, it may be part of a long-range plan with various steps along the way. In this instance advertising strategies can build on previous campaigns. Timeframes can also impact on the advertising media to be used, as some can be used with little advance notice while others require lead time. In general, for immediacy nothing is better than television, and for mass distribution newspapers are excellent.

ADVERTISING BUDGET

Costs distribution

In determining how the advertising budget should be allocated, the decision needs to be made whether the budget strategy should be massed or distributed.

When adopting a *massed* strategy the advertising budget is used heavily at the beginning of a campaign and falls away quickly as the weeks pass. In this instance, the percentage of advertising recall is initially high but then drops off quite quickly. This is an appropriate strategy to adopt for annual events, the commencement of seasonal or holiday activities such as snow skiing, or the introduction of a new product or model into the marketplace.

With a *distributed* campaign the advertising budget is used evenly throughout the year for a predefined period. In this instance the percentage of recall is initially low, but recall elevates with repeated weekly exposure. Activities such as professional sports that are constant, result in a playoff period and have a limited off-season, mainly use a distributed advertising budget. It should be remembered that all advertising campaigns have time limits in terms of their effectiveness. However, eventual advertising wear-out can be delayed by introducing variations on the theme. The time will come, however, when the advertising campaign will have either no effect or, more significantly, a negative impact on sport consumption.

Cost intensity

Irrespective of whether a massed, distributed or combination advertising strategy is adopted, the advertising budget should be determined by the importance of the campaign, which in turn should be based on expected returns from the investment.

While some types of advertising are cost intensive, others are labour intensive, and available resources need to be taken into account when establishing strategy. Radio, television, newspaper, magazine and supplement, outdoor advertising, direct mail, posters and premiums or give-aways are *cost intensive* in that they require more in terms of money than staff time. Conversely, press releases, contact with special interest groups, personal contact with business and community leaders, speakers, personal appearances, special event stations, involvement in community events and promotion stunts are *labour intensive* in that they require more in terms of staff time than money.

ADVERTISING SPORT SERVICES

According to George and Berry (1981), advertising *services* is quite different from advertising *goods*, and they articulate six guidelines for advertising services. They contend that performance is inextricably linked to consumer perception of a service; hence the service has to be sold to employees before it can be sold to consumers. Sporting organisation employees must not only be educated, motivated and encouraged to communicate the benefits of the service being offered; they must also inherently believe in its quality.

Likewise, positive word-of-mouth communication, the provision of tangible clues such as the facility in which the service is provided, making the sport service comprehensible by linking it with tradition and history, and establishing continuity of advertising through the use of constant themes and images, are all designed to establish a background against which the service can be assessed.

The final guideline of advertising sport services, only promising what is possible, is potentially the most crucial for the sport marketer. Although Bill Veeck offered the 'Money-back guarantee', in many instances this is not possible. In the lead-up to the 1996 Olympic Games, Australian swimming coach Don Talbot expressed in quantitative terms the anticipated level of success for the Australian swimming team. When this was not forthcoming, the Australian public believed that the Australian swimming team had not delivered on the promises made by Talbot. The result was a vigorous and sometimes acrimonious public debate that raged between the athletes, coaches, press and sport media consumers. Sport marketers should take the lesson of Atlanta on board and only ever promise that which they know they can deliver.

TYPES OF ADVERTISING

When establishing advertising strategies, sport marketers have a twofold task. Initially, a *creative strategy* must be implemented, which should be a response to the following questions:

- What is the purpose of the advertising?
- Who is it aimed at?
- What is promised?
- How will it be delivered?
- What will be the 'personality' or the essence of the product?

Next an organisation needs to establish a *media strategy*, which determines the best media for the message.

Hochberg (cited in *Marketing News* 1988) contends that all these questions have to be answered in conjunction with each other. However, for the purposes of this chapter mechanisms for establishing a creative strategy will be noted before potential media strategy is examined.

CREATIVE STRATEGY

The task of the creative strategy is to develop message ideas and execute them effectively. Effective message ideas should be based on consumer research findings, fit the overall marketing strategy, be appropriate for the target market, be simple or basic (one major point), and be developed so they are most resistant to counterattack. It should be remembered that, if an organisation's *unique selling proposition* (USP) is price, it is very easy for competitors to attack in the marketplace. While creativity is usually situation or even person specific, and hence highly individual, there are a number of more general creative approaches that organisations can utilise.

Umbrella advertising relies on an established brand name. This is most appropriate when the brand name is well established. Major sport codes will advertise the league, sport or competition rather than the specific clubs. The Australian Football League (AFL), Australian Rugby League (ARL), National Basketball Association (NBA) and National Football League (NFL) all use umbrella advertising to promote the sports of Aussie Rules, rugby league, US basketball or American football respectively. They are secure in their knowledge that umbrella advertising will promote consumption of their specific products. However, organisations such as the Women's National Basketball League may find it better to advertise its product, women's basketball, through individual teams such as the Sydney Flames or the Adelaide Lightning rather than the league itself.

Honest twist advertising relies on surprising the intended recipient and is often associated with humour. A recent soft drink advertisement suggested that consumption of its product will not make you play basketball like NBA star Grant Hill, but it may quench your thirst.

Demonstration advertising shows the product in use. This is applicable when potential consumers may be unfamiliar with the product or how to use it. While the obvious example is the myriad of celebrity-endorsed home fitness equipment that appears during late night 'infomercials', it also has applicability to sporting events. Demonstration games can both inform and persuade consumers, especially if associated with lifestyle. The rapid growth of beach volleyball from a summer sand activity to an Olympic sport is a good example of how demonstration advertising can evolve.

Testimonial advertising involves an actual user of the product serving as a spokesperson. Past athletes are often used to promote sport and related products by organisations that believe that former champions strike an accord with older market segments. This in turn may encourage them to consume the current offering. While this may lend a perceived credibility to the product and its use, the 'reality' touch does have its downside. Former New York Jets quarterback Joe Namath regularly appeared in advertisements for a liniment company, suggesting that its application was just the thing his aching arthritic knees needed after years of NFL football. Unfortunately, the advertisement still appeared on US television after Namath had had both knees replaced.

Slice-of-life advertising uses some part of daily life as a part of the advertisement. The intent behind this approach is to communicate messages and images to consumers that they can relate to. This approach is probably most appropriate when it connects fans with their past, usually their youth. While this belief is a fundamental underpinning of Major League Baseball (MLB) in North America, it has real relevance in most sport settings. Hence, when cricket advertisements feature children in backyards hitting 'sixes' over the neighbour's fence, then transforms that action to the final of a day/night match in front of 90 000 at the Melbourne Cricket Ground, consumers readily see the connection between the two.

Lifestyle advertising operates on the basic tenet that the use of a product or service will result in the user accessing a particular lifestyle. Although this type of advertising has obvious relevance to the health and fitness industry, both horseracing and harness racing have adopted this type of advertising in recent years in an attempt to entice groups to the track. In an increasingly hectic environment, sports that can incorporate family lifestyle in their advertising may find themselves well placed in the sport marketplace.

Announcement advertising provides information about a new brand, product, package, design or formula. The most common examples of this type of advertising happen when sports apparel companies introduce new models into the market. In most instances the release is accompanied by a new advertising campaign. Sporting organisations use announcement advertising when they wish to inform their consumers of changes that they need to be aware of to ensure their enjoyment of the event. Event timing, parking conditions, public transport facilities and member information related to event entrance are just a few of the instances that warrant announcement advertising.

Imitation or symbolic association advertising attempts to associate attractive personal qualities with ownership or use of product. This approach is often connected to celebrity endorsement. In this instance the advertisement suggests that adoption of a particular product or service will infuse the consumer with desirable traits. Gatorade tapped into this advertising vein successfully when it ran the 'I want to be like Mike' advertisements. Canon also tried it with its 'Image is Everything' campaign featuring Andre Agassi, which was less successful. Moreover, this campaign allowed a numbers of other firms to adopt humorous parodies of the Canon approach, which were better than the original. Issues such as these are elaborated on in Chapter 10.

MEDIA STRATEGY

Before establishing guidelines that help decide the advertising strategies and media to be used, it is worth noting a number of general observations about key advertising media.

Media alternatives

Newspapers are current and relatively inexpensive and reach a mass audience. In deciding to advertise using newspapers, sport marketers need to provide copy that is eyecatching and succinct. It is also important to be aware of the section the target audience reads. The business sections of daily newspapers are increasingly becoming a repository for sport advertising.

Magazines invite leisure readership as invariably they lie around the house or business for an extended period. Similarly, the one issue is often read, or at least browsed through, by potentially quite different consumer groups. In this instance appearance and layout designs are of paramount importance. Sport-specific magazines such as *Inside Sport* or *Sports Illustrated* provide obvious examples of sport advertising.

Outdoor advertising, in the form of billboards or fence signage, involves the presentation of an uncomplicated message. Usually just a logo or a few words predominate, which hopefully for the advertiser can trigger recognition of a much more complicated message. Signage advertising major sport events such as the Australian Tennis Open, the Formula 1 Grand Prix and the 500 Motorcycle Grand Prix regularly appears at the appropriate time on central-business-district buildings and freeway billboards. Such displays usually feature the major slogan or logo, event date and ticket availability. This information is then reinforced and elaborated on in other media.

Radio advertising relies on recall in a heavily cluttered marketplace, so frequency is critical. Radio's advertising advantage lies in the fact that, given its lack of visual images, the imagination of the listener may be stimulated by suggestive advertising. As a result, event promoters can create advertising around the sounds of the ski slope, the beach and summer or the city, while at the same time creating an element of mystery.

Television advertising exists in an extremely cluttered marketplace, although there is little doubt that television advertising reaches the largest possible audience. Moreover, the use of visuals plus sound provides the most effective mechanism for presenting specific information. One problem facing television advertisers is how to stand out in an increasingly crowded marketplace. Humour and celebrity advertising are usually effective, as is 'black-and-white' or retro advertising. The AFL 'I'd like to see that' series of advertisements over the 1994–96 seasons is a good example of effective sport advertising using humour and celebrity endorsement. Other television advertisements that appear to captivate audiences are those presented in the form of an unfolding tale. An interesting clothing firm advertisement in 1995 incorporated visuals *without* sound. When this advertisement played, detached viewers paid attention to their television thinking that there was something amiss with their equipment. The relationship between sport, advertising and television will be discussed at length in the next chapter.

Brochures, flyers and *posters* usually combine the features of billboards plus newspaper and magazine advertising. The advantage of this type of advertising is that it can segment the market very well.

The *Internet*, especially the World Wide Web (WWW), has become a major source of information and opportunities for both organisations and individuals. While business, government and educational institutions are the major users of such technology, sporting organisations are increasingly turning to the Internet to conduct their business. Comprehensive websites have been established by the Australian Sports Commission, Tennis Australia, the AFL and the Sydney Organising Committee for the Olympic Games. However a myriad of unofficial home pages also exists. Lee (1996) contends that organisations:

> . . . are seeing the promotional and marketing value of being on the net. Not only does it provide up-to-date information for followers of a particular sport here and abroad, there is the potential to capture the interest of children and others tapping into the web. (p. 86)

Other advantages of the Internet include the ability of sponsors to use the home page of a particular sport or organisation to provide a link to the sponsor's site, where further information can be gathered regarding the sponsor's products and services. There is little doubt that this expanding technology is providing information to organisations on a scale that was previously not possible. Moreover, through the use of e-mail and bulletin boards the isolation previously experienced by sport managers of small organisations is no longer a problem.

Timing and cost

Two additional factors that need to be considered, irrespective of the media alternatives, are timing and cost. The dual questions related to *timing* are how soon the advertising goals need to be achieved and how the advertising mix is established to gain optimal support and recognition. Cost is usually determined as cost-per-thousand or CPM. In this instance it needs to be ascertained how much it will cost to make impressions on 1000 people. The formula is:

$$CPM = \frac{Cost}{Reach} \times 1000$$

For example, a radio commercial costs \$200 and is estimated to reach 175 000 listeners; the CPM is \$1.14.

Media selection

The criteria for media selection depend on the factors previously discussed. Elements such as budget, sales or communication objectives, and target audience are, in the main, internal to the organisation. However, there are a number of qualitative and quantitative media factors that need to be considered.

While television advertising can be strong in terms of its total population reach, uniform coverage, emotional stimulation, and ability to use slice-of-life and humour, it is rather weak with respect to upscale selectivity, positioning and the predictability of audience levels. Marginal sports such as polo would be better advertised in other media, such as magazines, whereas television is a perfect outlet for the various traditional summer and winter sports.

Radio's advertising strength lies in its young adult selectivity, its CPM, and its ability to exploit time-of-day factors and to stimulate the imagination. The downside of radio is its lack of uniform coverage, its lack of depth in demographics and its inability to conduct product demonstrations or exploit attention-seeking devices. Demographic-specific activities that have been appropriated by identifiable consumer markets would be well served by using radio. An upcoming skateboard exhibition, surfing contest or harness race meeting could be better served by advertising on a niche market radio station than television.

The potency of newspaper advertising lies in its capacity to select local markets, to exploit day-of-week factors, and to convey detail and information. The downside of newspaper advertising relates to its lack of national coverage (except for national newspapers), its general inability to negotiate rates and its inadequate ability to intrude. For sport marketers, newspapers are best used for providing fixture information and updates.

Finally, magazine advertising is appropriate if market selectivity, frequency control, advertisement positioning and prestige of the medium are important. It is difficult to stimulate emotion or imagination, negotiate rates, use slice-of-life or, once again, be intrusive when using this medium. Noting magazines' strength, sport advertisers would be well served by advertising in their sport-specific magazine.

MEASURING ADVERTISING EFFECTIVENESS

The components of a successful advertising-testing program are many and varied. The successful advertising campaign must not only be clear and objective and aid in the decision-making process; it must also offer good value and be valid and reliable as well as practical and defensible. Finally, it should produce understandable results.

The sport marketer should expect that the organisation's advertising is both seen and heard, communicates messages and/or creates impressions, associates brands with images, is persuasive and sells. To ensure that this is the case the organisation needs to engage in *copy testing*. This action has the potential to minimise risks and marketing mistakes, maximise budget efficiency and move the product or service ahead in the marketplace.

The two major testing programs are recall and recognition. *Recall* requires respondents to remember a particular advertisement (aided) or an advertisement within a product category (unaided). *Recognition* involves showing the respondents the advertisement. Chapter 10 develops the concepts of recognition and recall in detail.

The current industry trend in advertisement testing uses the recall method. The philosophy behind this methodology is that, if people can remember a commercial, its intended message and the brand name, there is a better chance that persuasion will occur and the brand will sell. The most common recall-testing method used in television is the *day-after-recall (DAR) interview*, which is conducted within 24 hours of the advertisement's display. This interview establishes respondent type, programs viewed, whether or not the respondent recalls the advertisement and the components recalled. With respect to the print media, the *Starch Readership Test* also examines recall. Less than 17% related recall is regarded as low and anything above 32% as high. It should be ascertained through additional questioning what the respondent was doing during the advertising period and what media they were attending to.

To perform well in a test of recall a commercial must cut through the clutter of the medium and the apathy of viewers in order to gain attention, which in turn maximises the audience for the message to follow. This has had the tendency to lead to loud and flamboyant commercials. The AFL, the National Basketball League (NBL) and World Series Cricket have adopted stunning visuals, usually augmented by rock'n'roll, to advertise their respective products.

Although there is no guaranteed formula for success, effective advertisements usually exhibit the following traits:

- They identify the brand early.
- They are simple, yet interesting and involving.
- They adopt audio and visual reinforcement.
- They link the brand with the image created.

Once an advertising campaign has been tested, the results obtained can give rise to different courses of action. An organisation may:

- give an unreserved green light to the campaign,
- alter the media mix,
- alter timing based on demographic information, or
- if the advertisement is not communicating the intended message to the correct demographics, decide to start the process again.

SUMMARY

Sport advertising is now a multibillion dollar industry and has as its prime purpose the influencing of consumers to respond positively to products or services. The foundation of successful advertising is the ability to communicate, and this can be conducted through various media using vastly different strategies. Newspapers are current and relatively inexpensive and reach a mass audience, while magazines invite leisure readership. Radio can bring the imagination into play, while television unquestionably reaches the largest possible audience. Outdoor advertising involves the presentation of an uncomplicated message, while brochures, flyers and posters effectively segment the market. The Internet is increasingly being used to provide information and links to sponsors' home pages and to conduct sport business. Two additional factors that need to be considered, irrespective of the media alternatives, are timing and cost.

Media selection depends on elements such as objectives, whether they be sales or communication, budget and target audience. However, there are a number of qualitative and quantitative media factors that need to be considered. The successful advertising campaign must not only be clear and objective and aid in the decision-making process; it must also offer good value, be valid and reliable as well as practical and defensible, and produce understandable results.

Advertising services is different from advertising goods. However, through advertising to employees, realising the value of word-of-mouth, providing tangible clues, making the service comprehensible, ensuring continuity in advertising themes and images and, most importantly, only promising that which can be delivered with total certainty, the potential impact of intangibles on service can be reduced and, to a lesser extent, controlled.

Recognising that creativity in advertising is very much a matter of individual choice and perception, this chapter has focused on the strategies that can be adopted to inform the creative underpinnings of sport advertising.

A thorough understanding of the objectives of, and the budget allocated to, a sport advertising campaign will in part dictate the type of campaign to be run and the media to be used. Once these decisions have been made, the creative component can be established within a well-defined structure. Through the ongoing monitoring of the advertising campaign, a clear indication of the effectiveness of the strategies can be obtained.

<table>
<tr><td>CASE
STUDY</td><td></td></tr>
</table>

THE AUSTRALIAN MOTORCYCLE GRAND PRIX

'I am delighted to say that the Fosters Australian Grand Prix has been voted the best GP in the world by riders, managers, the media and others,' said the NSW Minister for Sport and Recreation Chris Downy in a media release on 8 December 1993. Speaking at the launch of the 1994 Grand Prix, Mr Downy further suggested that a 1991 study of the economic impact of the Grand Prix at Eastern Creek showed that visitors had spent almost $13 million at the event.

The 1994 Fosters Grand Prix, promoted under the banner 'Come on feel the noise', offered 37 hours of action and entertainment, which included 500 cc, 250 cc and 125 cc bike races, rock concerts, and four support-class races with Big Bangers and Harley Davidson twin sports. Footraces, the RAAF Roulettes, the Red Beret parachute team, a motorcycle stunt team, the Bridgestone Holden Precision Driving Team, a Touring Car grudge match and activities for children were all part of the day's entertainment. However, the hoped-for numbers of spectators were never achieved.

When Barry Sheene took over the running of the 1995 Grand Prix for IMG he became the third promoter in five years for the event. His charming, affable manner was ever present in all the television advertisements as he asked the question 'But are you going to be there?', but little changed in 1995. Although spectator attendances increased slightly each year, not enough spectators attended to make the race an economic windfall. By 1996 attendance had subsided and the event was headed for its previous home at Phillip Island in Victoria in 1997.

Potential consumers were targeted through a variety of advertising media, but in the main they failed to hit the mark. Radio advertisements on Triple M, and television advertising featuring the lead riders, spectacular crashes and loud noise, appeared regularly in the days and weeks leading up to the event, especially on Channel Nine sport programs. Similar advertisements were played in Sydney cinemas. Newspapers, magazines and billboards on Parramatta Road all advertised the upcoming Grand Prix. However, in most instances the impact was minimal.

The results from a survey conducted for the 1994 race indicated that, although nearly 20% of respondents found out about the Grand Prix from either television or via word-of-mouth, cinema, newspapers and radio appeared to have minimal reach. While word-of-mouth was the main source of Grand Prix information for women, the print media had a greater reach with older respondents and the electronic media with younger. It was also found that advertising had a greater impact on purchases of single-day tickets as opposed to three-day passes.

The results from a survey conducted for the 1995 race indicated the following rates of exposure:

- Channel Nine15.67%
- Triple M 3.23%
- AMEN 2.53%
- Advertisements/billboards 1.76%
- *Two Wheels* 1.67%
- *Telegraph Mirror* 1.18%

In both years the category 'word-of-mouth' was significant.

Source: Adjusted from Quick (1994, 1995).

Questions

1 What are some additional creative twists that could be used?
2 Which media would you use with which target markets, and what would be the communication message?
3 How would you rectify the lack of response to radio, newspaper, cinema and magazine advertising?
4 When conducting research on advertising, how do we resolve the 'word-of-mouth' issue?
5 What advice would you give future promoters of the Grand Prix in terms of advertising?

REFERENCES

Bragg, R. (1996). 'The adman's Olympics', *The Age*, 20 June, B2.
Brian Sweeney (1994). *Australians and Sport*, Annual Survey of Sporting Participation, Attendance, TV Viewing and Sponsorship Awareness, 3, Brian Sweeney & Associates, Melbourne, pp. 22–37.
George, W. and Berry, L. (1981). 'Guidelines for advertising services', *Business Horizons*, 24 (4), pp. 52–6.
Hertz Walpole (1990). *The Impact of Tina Turner on Rugby League* (videorecording), The Tape Business, Sydney.
Jones, M. (1996). '$200 m race for gold at Atlanta', *The Age*, 26 March, p. B1.
Lee, J. A. (1996). 'Sites for sore eyes', *The Bulletin*, 7 May, p. 86.
Marketing News (1988). 'Clients now insist that their ads actually sell products', collegiate edn, January, p. 3.
McCanndo (1996). 'Capitalising on a unique opportunity', June, p. 2.
Mullin, B., Hardy, S. and Sutton, W. A. (1993). *Sport Marketing*, Human Kinetics, Champaign, Ill.

Newton, R. (1996). 'Pepsi and Coke pop cork on high-stakes cola battle', *The Age*, 2 April, p. B3.

O'Hara, B. and Weese, W. J. (1994). 'Advertising theory applied to the intramural—recreation sports environment', *Sport Marketing Quarterly*, 3 (1), pp. 9–14.

Quick, S. (1994). *Fan Survey Report to IMG* (Australian Motorcycle Grand Prix), Unpublished technical report.

——(1995). *Fan Survey Report to ACU* (Australian Motorcycle Grand Prix), Unpublished technical report.

Shoebridge, N. (1993). *The Secrets of Successful Marketing*, Text Publishing, Melbourne.

——(1996). 'The sprint to Atlanta becomes a marathon to Sydney', *Business Review Weekly*, 29 April, p. 75.

Stanton, W., Miller, K. and Layton, R. (1995). *Fundamentals of Marketing*, McGraw-Hill, Sydney.

Sutherland, M. (1993). *Advertising and the Mind of the Consumer*, Allen & Unwin, Sydney.

9

Sport and television

CHAPTER OUTLINE

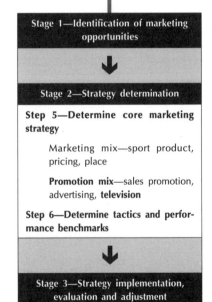

Stage 1—Identification of marketing
opportunities

Stage 2—Strategy determination

**Step 5—Determine core marketing
strategy**

    Marketing mix—sport product,
    pricing, place

    Promotion mix—sales promotion,
    advertising, **television**

**Step 6—Determine tactics and perfor-
mance benchmarks**

Stage 3—Strategy implementation,
evaluation and adjustment

CHAPTER OBJECTIVES

Chapter 9 examines the television–sport nexus. Specifically, it describes how television generates its principal source of revenue through advertising and how this revenue determines the level of television rights paid to sporting organisations. This chapter also describes how program popularity is measured, and the link between this system of measurement and how advertisers assess the value of their advertising investment. Pay-television also is discussed in this chapter.

After studying this chapter you should be able to:

1 Identify the nature of the sport–business–television relationship.
2 Understand the commercial basis on which television operates.
3 Identify why sport programming is so attractive to television networks.
4 Understand and apply the terminology used to measure television audiences.
5 Recognise issues associated with determining advertising effectiveness.
6 Explain the new dimension that pay-television brings to the sport–television relationship.
7 Calculate advertising revenue generated from sport programming.
8 Convert advertising revenues to the relative worth of sport television rights.

HEADLINE STORY

TELEVISION RIGHTS TO THE OLYMPIC GAMES

Lausanne, December 12, 1995. The International Olympic Committee (IOC) has decided to grant National Broadcasting Company Inc. (NBC) the exclusive television rights in the United States of America for the 2004 Olympic Games (Summer), the 2006 Olympic Winter Games and the 2008 Olympic Games (Summer) for a total sum of approximately $US2.3 billion not including further revenue sharing.

Lausanne, 17 January, 1996. The IOC has reached agreement with the Seven Network Limited to grant exclusive broadcast rights to four successive Olympic Games. The rights fees for each Games have been affixed as follows:

2002 Olympic Winter Games	$US11,750,000
2004 Olympic Summer Games	$US50,500,000
2006 Olympic Winter Games	$US14,825,000
2008 Olympic Summer Games	$US63,750,000

Lausanne, 30 January, 1996. The IOC has decided to grant to the European Broadcasting Union (EBU) the exclusive rights for the 2000 Games in Sydney for the amount of $US350 million, and for the Winter Games in 2002 in Salt Lake City for the amount of $US120 million. It also decided to grant the EBU the rights for the 2004 Games ($US308 million), the Olympic Winter Games in 2006 ($US135 million) and the 2008 Games for $US443 million.

(International Olympic Committee 1996a)

In an unprecedented rush to secure the television rights to a succession of Olympic Games, the television networks of the world are signalling the importance of the Games as a source of competitive advantage:

> Long term deals such as these have taken Olympic broadcasting relationships beyond merely commercial links to generate airtime sales. They have changed the dynamics between the IOC and broadcasters from a traditional 16 day commercial advertising/sales platform into a joint partnership with a mutual interest to promote the Olympic movement on an ongoing basis. (International Olympic Committee 1996b, p. 1)

For the broadcaster, it is simply good business. Each broadcaster anticipates recouping its investment through strong advertising and sponsorship sales during Olympic programming. The Summer Olympics in particular provides two weeks of premier programming during which the networks will sell advertising inventory at peak rates. In addition, inventory will be available through lead-up and profile programming before each Olympic Games. Finally, for the networks, programming of this profile provides the opportunity for pre-emptive promotion of forthcoming station programs to a large and captive audience. In essence, the networks capitalise on the opportunity to boost the ratings of future programs, further enhancing the value of Olympic Games programming.

TELEVISION AND SPORT MARKETING

The purpose of this chapter is to explore the sport–television relationship. Clearly, it is a business relationship and one that has throughout the world increased in importance for many sports. For many sports, including the National Basketball Association (NBA) and National Football League (NFL) in the United States, cricket and the Australian Football League (AFL) in Australia, and soccer, golf and tennis worldwide, television rights revenues provide a substantial source of revenue. (A summary of some of the world's major professional-sport television rights is shown in Appendix A.) As a consequence, television networks now demand more from their right to broadcast than merely existing as a passive business partner with various sports. To ensure that networks maximise their revenue and profits, program directors and television executives are increasingly influencing the scheduling of games and events. The balance between playing at times conducive to optimum athletic performance and playing at times best suited to optimum ratings is one aspect of the sport–television relationship that creates tension. This tension has the potential to upset the mutually beneficial relationship currently in existence.

Figure 9.1 displays the principal players in the sport television business. Fundamentally, the business of the commercial television industry is the sale of airtime to advertisers. The price at which commercial television airtime is sold is a function of a number of factors, the most important of which are: the number of television viewers, and the price and availability of advertising

FIGURE 9.1

**The
sport–business–
television
relationship**

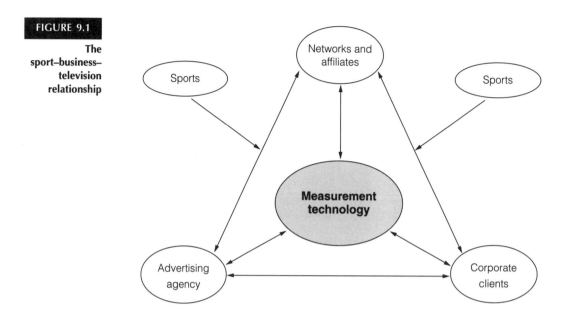

space on suitable alternative media. Commercial television uses programming to influence the size and profile of its viewing audience, which is measured by independent ratings:

> The principal profit equation for commercial television is to ensure that the revenue generating capacity of a schedule of programming sufficiently exceeds both its cost of production or acquisition as well as associated overheads, to produce a reasonable return on investment for the broadcaster. (ANZ McCaughan 1993, p. 9)

To achieve a reasonable return on investment the networks rely on programming that has the ability to capture and captivate an audience.

The series of relationships shown in Figure 9.1 is driven by the middle circle: the system of measuring the number of people watching specific programs. The currency used to measure the success of television programming is a *rating point*. These rating points, as will be shown later in this chapter, determine the success or failure of programs, and as a consequence network profitability.

The advertising agency shown in Figure 9.1 acts as a broker or 'middleman' between corporate clients purchasing advertising time and the networks. In general, advertising agencies form *buying groups*, allowing them to obtain discounts on advertising rates from the networks. These discounts are obtained due to the high volume of advertising inventory purchased by the advertising agency, a volume that corporations individually cannot match. Corporate clients at times also negotiate directly with networks, although this is less common as a consequence of the ability of the advertising agency to negotiate more favourable rates due to the volume of inventory being purchased.

Advertising agencies also offer expertise in recommending the most efficient forms of advertising or media buys for a particular product. A *media buy* refers to the range of advertising spots purchased across a variety of networks and programs. In its broadest sense, a media buy also includes other avenues for advertising such as radio, newspapers, magazines and outdoor billboards. A *spot* refers to the purchase of advertising inventory on television, usually in the form of a 15-, 30- or 60-second placement of an advertisement during a program. The costs to purchase these spots during sport programming will be considered later in this chapter.

SPORT PROGRAMMING

The importance and significance of the sport–television relationship is indicated by the rapid increase in sport programming in Australia since the inception of television in 1956. In Sydney in 1958 just over twelve hours of sport programming went to air during the week commencing 1 September. Ten years later during the week commencing 31 August, four stations showed a total of 22 hours of sport programming. Channels Seven and Nine covered Australian Rules and rugby league, with ten one-hour boxing and wrestling programs shown also. By 1978, in the week commencing 2 September, 33 hours of sport programming were shown in Sydney, and by 1988 five channels showed 43 hours of sport during the week beginning 15 August (Jarratt, 1988). In Melbourne during the week beginning 26 May 1996, sport programming had escalated to 79 hours. These 1996 results do not include pay-television sport programming, which would add a considerable number of hours.

These results suggest that sport programming is a ratings winner. Networks would not schedule so much sport programming if it were not profitable to do so. Why then is sport programming so attractive? Klattell and Marcus (1988) summarise the intrinsic value of sport programming to television:

> At its best, television sports is the finest programming television can offer. In many respects, sports may be the quintessential television program format, taking fullest advantage of the role TV plays in our daily lives. Sports on TV have visually attractive elements—splashy colours, attractive locations, motion and movement galore. They have expansive vistas, exquisite details, and larger-than-life images . . . There is drama, tension, suspense, raw emotion, real anger, unvarnished joy, and a host of other responses. Most of all you are watching real people compete for real, as unsure of the outcome as the viewer. In sports TV the 'bad guy' of the script often wins, unexpected things happen, virtue doesn't necessarily triumph, and goodness is not always rewarded. (p. 4)

The features of sport programming described by Klattell and Marcus underpin the reasons why sport is so attractive to television. They also explain why the networks are prepared to pay large fees to obtain the exclusive rights to broadcast a competition such as the AFL or cricket, or a major event such as the Olympic Games. The Olympic Games, as shown in the introduction to this chapter, are able to command extremely high rights fees.

How is the IOC able to command these fees, and how do sports such as cricket, rugby union and tennis command significant revenues from the sale of these exclusive rights? Calculation of fees is based on the projected advertising sales and profit derived from the exclusive broadcasting of an event such as the Olympic Games. The value of advertising is determined by the system of measurement used to determine the popularity of programs or, more specifically, how many people watch. Measuring the success of television programs is the focus of the next section.

MEASURING THE TELEVISION AUDIENCE

The size and composition of television audiences are measured by ratings services. Ratings are collected by using the *people meter*, an electronic measuring device that records what programs are being watched. This device also has the capacity to record *who* is watching, which provides important demographic information to networks and advertisers.

Measurements made

The following terminology is used in relation to measuring television audiences.

Homes using television
Homes using television (HUT) is the number of homes where at least one television set is switched on at any point in time. For example, in January 1994, there were 1.26 million households (HH) in Sydney and 1.12 households in Melbourne. In excess of 3.8 million households use a television in Sydney, Melbourne, Brisbane, Adelaide and Perth.

Program ratings
Program ratings are the percentage of households that are tuned to a particular station at a particular time. For example, the top-rating shows in Melbourne for the week ending 21 July 1996 are shown in Table 9.1. Rating points for those programs were derived using the following formula. One rating point is equal to approximately 35 000 people in households tuned to a program.

$$\text{Rating} = \frac{\text{HH tuned to program}}{\text{Total HH}}$$

Audience share
Audience share is the percentage of total viewing audience in a given period tuned to a particular station. This is an important figure because it considers the number of televisions actually in use, and the total size of the potential audience. The number of televisions in use is likely to be less than the total

Program	Average audience	Average rating	Peak audience	Peak rating	TABLE 9.1
1 Olympics Opening Ceremony	971 200	27.7	1 058 600	30.2	**Top ten**
2 The Footy Show (AFL)	797 200	22.8	852 600	24.4	**programs,**
3 Better Homes and Gardens	749 700	21.4	774 200	22.1	**week ending**
4 Blue Heelers	732 900	20.9	752 900	21.5	**21 July 1996**
5 Great Outdoors	705 200	20.1	716 200	20.5	
6 Our House	681 100	19.5	699 700	20.0	
7 E.R.	637 100	18.2	686 200	19.6	
8 Sixty Minutes	604 100	17.3	671 900	19.2	
9 Burke's Backyard	581 100	16.6	623 700	17.8	
10 National Nine News (Sat.)	569 700	16.3	595 100	17.0	

Source: The Age Green Guide, 25 July 1996.

number of households with televisions. Audience share is calculated by dividing the number of households watching a program by the number of households using televisions.

$$\text{Share} = \frac{\text{HH tuned to program}}{\text{HUT}}$$

Target audience rating points

Target audience rating points (TARPs) are the audience at a given point in time expressed as a percentage of the potential audience available. Table 9.2 illustrates the cumulative nature of TARPs in relation to 1992 Sunday night NSW Rugby League (NSWRL) telecasts. Also shown are the various demographic groups typically used in the analysis by advertisers, networks, corporations and sporting organisations. Corporations are often more interested in the detailed demographic data, as they relate to the groups most likely to purchase the firm's product. In other words, if Coca-Cola advertised during the rugby league telecast, the company might be more interested in the number of people in the 16–24 age group watching Sunday night matches, as this might represent an important buying group. The cost of a 30-second spot during the 1993 telecast times shown in Table 9.2 ranged between $6000 and $6500 for Sydney and Brisbane. Table 9.2 shows 1992 ratings figures, which formed the basis of the cost of advertising in 1993.

Gross rating points

Gross rating points (GRPs) are another cumulative measure representing the sum of TARPs for a given schedule, often referred to as *total TARPs.* Cumulative ratings such as GRPs and TARPs are usually calculated for a week or month and, as noted by Buzzard (1992), are often 'used as a comparison to circulation figures in the print media. It measures the station's overall effectiveness, or the total number of different people who saw a program or commercial' (p. 40). *Reach* is a measure of the number of different people watching, and *frequency* is the number of times a person or household watches the same program, commercial or station. A total television buy of 240 GRPs could be calculated as follows:

$$\text{GRPs} \quad \text{Reach} \quad \text{Frequency}$$
$$240 \quad = \quad 80 \quad \times \quad 3$$

Average audience
Average audience is the estimated audience over a stated period, usually 15 minutes. This figure is usually expressed in thousands. Examples are shown in Table 9.2.

People meters

The method used to collect ratings data changed during the last decade. Up until 1991 the *diary* was used. This required randomly selected households to fill in their viewing patterns during a two-week period, usually referred to as the *ratings period*. At the end of the two weeks, the diaries were collected and analysed to determine program ratings. The method by which this information was collected, collated and interpreted was rather slow and cumbersome, compared to the use of the people meter.

TABLE 9.2 Sunday night NSWRL ratings 1992		TCN 9 Sydney		QTQ 9 Brisbane		
	Reach	Average homes rating		Reach	Average homes rating	
	Over 14 weeks	6.30 – 7.30pm 24 weeks		Over 14 weeks	6.30 – 7.30 pm 24 weeks	
		000	TARPs		000	TARPs
Homes	72.2	284	23	68.7	138	22
All people	59.2	542	15	61.1	268	14
Children 5–12	48.1	40	10	50.1	20	9
Teens 13–17	53.8	27	11	53.7	18	13
All people 18+	60.6	450	16	63.5	223	16
Men 18+	65.3	262	19	68.5	131	20
16–24	54.6	33	13	55.2	18	13
25–39	64.2	78	18	74.7	37	18
40–54	73.2	77	21	62.6	40	22
55–64	70.5	39	25	66.0	16	21
65+	57.5	46	25	62.4	25	26
Women 18+	56.1	189	14	59.0	91	13
16–24	36.0	19	8	46.0	11	8
25–39	63.2	53	12	65.7	27	12
40–54	58.9	44	13	52.5	25	14
55–64	54.6	26	17	59.2	10	13
65+	55.5	50	19	61.0	20	16
Grocery buyers	62.0	189	15	62.3	88	14
Socio ec. AB	60.8	60.	16	51.8	15	10

Source: GTV Nine (1993).

In 1989 the first trials began using A. C. Nielsen's *people meter*. The most significant change as a result of using the people meter was that data could be collected for 52 weeks of the year, thereby removing the tendency of networks to schedule major programs during known ratings periods. A major advantage of the people meter technology is its capacity to download the results of the previous day's viewing by nine o'clock the next morning, allowing television executives to receive immediate feedback on the success of their programs. What then is the people meter, and how does it work?

The A. C. Nielsen people meter is a small eight-button unit placed on top of the television set. Each member of the household is assigned a button number, and their name is printed above their assigned button number. There is a set of red and green lights on the front of the unit to indicate whether selected people are in the viewing audience. Green indicates viewing; red indicates no viewing. Each household member indicates their viewing by pushing their assigned button on either the people meter or the remote control, changing their light from red to green. There is a button labelled OK that must be pressed when all viewing entries have been made. When a household member leaves the room, they must again press their button to indicate no viewing and press the OK button to signify a change in audience. When a visitor comes into the room, they must indicate their presence by pushing a visitor button on the unit placed on the television. The visitor will be asked their sex and age.

Data collected from people meters are downloaded to a central computer, and it is from here that the various rating figures are generated. As can be seen from the need for visitors to input their basic demographic information, detailed reports are possible for every program. Indeed, detailed reports are possible for every minute of the day for every program. Typically, data are reported in fifteen-minute blocks.

People meters are an improvement on the diary system where the accuracy of data reported by households was often suspect. Household members often forgot to complete the diary daily, relying on their memory to fill it in at a later date. People meters rely on household members diligently turning their green and red lights on and off as they cycle in and out of watching television.

The other major weakness of the people meter is that it cannot detect whether household members are actually watching the television, even though they are recorded as being in the room. Remember, this is important because the advertisers assume that people recorded as being in the room actually watch the program and register or acknowledge the advertisements shown. Whether this is the case will be examined later in this chapter.

Audience sampling

People meters are not installed in every house using a television. This would be too costly and time consuming. To obtain reliable data a *random sample* of the population is taken. The objective of the sample is to install meters in a random, representative and projectable sample of households for the defined market. To ensure that regional populations are proportionally represented in the sample, a two-stage sample design is used. In the first instance, Collection Districts (CD) are randomly chosen in proportion to the population. For example, if 10% of the population lives in Queensland's Gold Coast region, 10% of the sample must be in this region. The second stage requires all private dwellings to be enumerated. Households are then randomly selected. Households not eligible for the sample include:

- non-private dwellings—hospitals, prisons, schools, etc.;
- households without a television;
- households of people working in the television, market research or advertising industries;
- households moving within the next three months; and
- households occupied for less than nine months a year.

In Australia a total of 1900 households are randomly selected, including 440 from Sydney and Melbourne, and 340 from Brisbane, Adelaide and Perth. These 1900 homes determine the success and failure of television programs and in turn the value of advertising.

ADVERTISING DURING SPORT PROGRAMMING

Super Bowl XXVII between the Dallas Cowboys and the Buffalo Bills sold out advertising inventory three weeks before the game despite record rates of between $US850 000 and $US900 000 per 30-second spot. A total of 52 half-minute spots were sold (Elliott 1993). The 1995 AFL Grand Final, one of the biggest television watching days of the year in Australia, attracted advertisers at $25 000 in the Melbourne market, dropping to $4000 in Brisbane. In total, the Seven network, the national broadcaster of AFL games, had 1327 30-second spots to sell during the 1995 season. The potential income from the sale of this inventory, as reported by the Seven network, was $2 455 300. In the 1994/95 summer of cricket, advertising rates peaked at $10 000 for the first and second one-day finals played in Sydney and Melbourne. Test Matches played against England in 1994/95 attracted advertising rates of $2600, and one-day matches played during the day in Melbourne cost advertisers between $2250 and $2600. Day/night matches advertising escalated to $7500.

An example of the strategy used to sell advertising inventory by the networks is seen in Figure 9.2. Sales data for the 1993 Australian Formula 1 Grand Prix in Adelaide are shown in Figure 9.2, which includes ratings data for 1992, telecast schedules for 1993, the cost of television sponsorships of the event and the cost of 30-second spot packages. National sponsorships of such sporting events usually offer more to the corporation than traditional spot advertising.

Wide World of Sports Telecast Guide for the Australian Formula 1 Grand Prix, Adelaide 1993   FIGURE 9.2

The Formula One Grand Prix season terminates at the best Grand Prix of them all—Adelaide.

By November 1993 all the technology which will have been developed in response to the new 1993 rules such as the narrower tyres and uniform fuel will have been optimised to provide the closest F1 racing for years.

Not that the lack of close racing in recent years has in anyway handicapped the Adelaide Grand Prix; for some reason it doesn't affect Adelaide success.

The whole city of Adelaide changes for the race.

The track through the parklands and the city perimeter is considered by the drivers as one of the safest and best they race on and they obviously enjoy it and give their best.

The whole weekend is magic filled with the full gamut of motor racing involvement including the fantastic F1 practice sessions.

Touring cars, Australian Drivers Championship races, celebrity races, displays and almost constant events make for an unsurpassed weekend of motor racing entertainment culminating in Australian F1 Grand Prix.

Whatever it is that makes Adelaide special—it works. Crowds flock regardless of weather and the carnival goes on. The television audience likewise is drawn each year to this marvelous event.

The Adelaide Grand Prix is unquestionably the best F1 Grand Prix telecast in the world.

It is also the best motor racing telecast in Australia.

It is watched by at least half of all homes in each city and by a lot more in some cities such as 61% of homes in Melbourne and a phenomenal 77% of homes in Adelaide.

The telecast reached the following % of homes:

TCN-9 Sydney	53%
GTV-9 Melbourne	61%
QTQ-9 Brisbane	51%
NWS-9 Adelaide	77%
STW-9 Perth	51%

1992 RATINGS SUMMARY

The peak audience for the race was outstanding for a daytime telecast. Adelaide had half of the homes tuned to the race while elsewhere audiences peaked at approx one quarter of all homes.

PEAK AUDIENCE	All People 000	Homes Rating
TCN-9	453	25
GTV-9	485	28
QTQ-9	231	23
NWS-9	384	50
STW-9	163	22

As expected, the audience for the actual race was massive in each city, but the average audience for the whole of Sunday was also large.

This indicates a big audience for the hours before and after the race.

	Race Average		All Day (Sunday)	
	000	Homes Rating	000	Homes Rating
TCN-9	435	23	313	18
GTV-9	440	25	345	20
QTQ-9	222	22	172	17
NWS-9	370	49	268	36
STW-9	145	21	89	14

Demographically the audience for the whole telecast was particularly strong in men and socio economic group AB although the youth and female audience was also very healthy.

AVERAGE RATING FOR SUNDAY 8TH NOVEMBER, 1992

	TCN-9 Sydney	GTV-9 Melbourne	QTQ-9 Brisbane	NWS-9 Adelaide	STW-9 Perth
Homes	18	20	17	36	14
All people	9	10	9	22	7
Child 5–12	5	6	4	11	4
Teens 13–17	9	8	6	19	4
All people 18+	9	11	11	26	8
Men 18+	13	15	15	28	12
Men 18–24	14	21	16	23	14
Men 25–39	12	13	13	26	15
Men 40–54	16	15	18	32	12
Men 55–60	7	11	18	30	6
Men 65+	14	16	10	29	5
Women 18+	6	8	7	23	5
Women 18–24	5	9	6	15	6
Women 25–39	5	8	6	22	4
Women 40–54	7	6	7	27	4
Women 55–64	2	10	9	33	7
Women 65+	9	8	11	22	5
Grocery Buyers	8	9	7	26	5
SE AB	11	7	10	28	8

The audience on Saturday was considerably higher than normal Wide World of Sports ratings and the late night ratings on Friday 6th November, 1992 were also strong.

A full Homes Rating summary is as follows:

	TCN-9 Sydney		GTV-9 Melbourne		QTQ-9 Brisbane		NWS-9 Adelaide		STW-9 Perth	
	Peak	Ave	Peak	Ave	Peak	Ave	Peak	Ave	Peak	Ave
Friday 6 Nov 92 Latenight	6	5	6	5	5	4	10	8	4	3
Saturday 7 Nov 92 Noon to 6pm (ESST)	14	11	11	7	12	10	20	16	13	9
Sunday 8 Nov 92 11am to 6pm (ESST)	25	18	28	20	23	17	50	36	23	14
The Race 8 Nov 92 2.30pm to 4.30pm (ESST)	25	23	28	25	23	22	50	49	22	21

1993 TELECAST SCHEDULE

	FRI 5 NOV 93	SAT 6 NOV 93	SUN 7 NOV 93
TCN-9 Sydney GTV-9 Melbourne QTQ-9 Brisbane	1 HOUR HIGHLIGHTS FROM 11.30PM	12.00MD–6.00PM	11.00AM–6.00PM
NWS-9 Adelaide	1 HOUR HIGHLIGHTS 10.30PM–11.30PM	11.30AM–5.30PM	10.30AM–5.30PM
STW-9 Perth	1 HOUR HIGHLIGHTS FROM 11.30PM	9.00AM–3.00PM	8.00AM–3.00PM

Details of telecast times are subject to confirmation by each Network station.

TELEVISION SPONSORSHIP

National Sponsorship of the telecasts of the Adelaide Grand Prix is available and provides association with this unique sporting event.

Sponsorship benefits include:

- Specially produced opening and closing billboards on shared basis.
- Sponsor identification placed strategically during the telecasts on Saturday and Sunday.
- Pullthroughs through all "live" telecasts on the Saturday and Sunday on a rotational basis.
- 15 × 30 second spots spread through all telecasts on all Nine Network stations. Only sponsors receive commercials placed in the telecast of the actual Grand Prix race.
- Sponsors' identification on all telecast promotion.

The price of this National Sponsorship is:

TCN-9 Sydney	51000
GTV-9 Melbourne	47000
QTQ-9 Brisbane	21000
NWS-9 Adelaide	38000
STW-9 Perth	18000
NETWORK	**175000**
AFFILIATED STATIONS	
WINTV — Queensland	6500
NBN — Northern NSW	8000
WINTV — Southern NSW	7500
VICTV — Victoria	7500
TASTV — Hobart	5000
NTD-8 — Darwin	TBA

SPOT PACKAGES

Spots can be purchased through all telecasts on all stations or in any specific telecast on individual stations or in any combination.

	FRI 5 NOV 93 LATENIGHT HIGHLIGHTS	SAT 6 NOV 93 12.00MD–6.00PM (EXCLUDING RACE)	SUN 7 NOV 93 11.00AM–6.00PM
TCN-9 Sydney	1000	1400	3300
GTV-9 Melbourne	1000	1000	3300
QTQ-9 Brisbane	500	750	1100
NWS-9 Adelaide	1000	1200	2250
STW-9 Perth	500	500	1100
NETWORK	**4000**	**4850**	**11050**
AFFILIATED STATIONS			
WINTV — Queensland	180	180	350
NBN — Northern NSW	165	250	450
WINTV — Southern NSW	180	180	350
VICTV — Victoria	200	200	200
TASTV — Hobart	160	170	200
NTD-8 — Darwin	TBA	TBA	TBA

Source: GTV Nine (1993).

In this example, television sponsorship benefits included:

- specially produced opening and closing billboards on a shared basis;
- sponsor identification placed strategically during the telecast on Saturday and Sunday;
- *pullthroughs* (advertisements across the bottom of the screen during telecast) through all live telecasts on Saturday and Sunday;
- fifteen 30-second spots spread through all telecasts on all Nine network stations;
- restriction to sponsors only of commercials placed during the telecast of the actual Grand Prix race; and
- sponsor's identification on all telecast promotion.

Sponsoring an event like the Grand Prix is obviously more expensive than simply purchasing a series of 30-second spots, as is indicated in Figure 9.2. Most coverage of major sporting events includes television sponsorship opportunities. Sales of advertising time and television sponsorships are the precursor to determining the worth of television rights purchased by networks. It is important for sport managers to value the potential revenue to networks of televising their sport. Sportview 9.1 illustrates how revenue generated from advertising during sport programming can be calculated. It is this calculation that leads to determining the television rights paid by networks for exclusive broadcasting of sporting events.

| SPORTVIEW 9.1 | CALCULATING THE WORTH OF AFL TELEVISION RIGHTS |

The first live telecast of Australian football occurred in 1957. The popularity of these broadcasts resulted in the Victorian Football League (VFL) charging £500 per station to televise football in 1958. The television station that has remained most closely aligned with football is the Channel Seven network. In 1976, Channel Seven paid $3 million over five years. Channel Seven has retained the rights throughout except season 1987. In 1988, the Seven network paid $30 million for the seasons 1988 to 1992. In 1991, the Seven network renegotiated the rights for $47 million for three years to the end of the 1995 season. A further $10 million in free advertising was also negotiated during this contract period (Linnell 1991). In 1993, the AFL again renegotiated the rights deal with the Seven network for a figure reported to be $90 million for the three years 1996 to 1998. Another new contract was established for the period 1999 to 2001 and was negotiated in 1995. This latest deal also included an agreement between the Seven network and pay-television operator Optus Vision to telecast all AFL games during the 1996 season. Mostly, these games were replays, with a handful shown live.

Data collected during the 1995 season showed how much revenue advertising during AFL programming on the Seven network generated. The information shown in this sportview was collected during telecasts of

Rounds 21 and 22 and the first final round of the 1995 season. Content analysis of the sport programming shown in Melbourne revealed 860 minutes of AFL programming shown during Round 21, 870 minutes in Round 22 and 570 minutes during the first week of the finals. The purpose of this investigation was to determine the worth of advertising during these matches to the Seven network. The table below shows the amount of actual football shown (F), advertising time (Ad) and time given to station promotions (Ch 7).

AFL programming on the Seven network, Melbourne, 1995 (minutes)

	Round 21			Round 22			First week finals		
	F	Ad	Ch 7	F	Ad	Ch 7	F	Ad	Ch 7
Friday night	132.7	22.2	5.0	146.5	30.0	3.5	155.5	20.5	4.0
Saturday replay	69.75	17.25	3.0	69.5	17.5	3.0	68.0	19.0	3.0
Saturday night	153.0	33.0	4.0	146.5	29.75	3.75	153.0	22.0	5.0
Sunday gameday	46.0	12.0	2.0	46.0	12.0	2.0	45.25	12.75	2.0
Sunday live	297.5	55.0	7.5	294.0	59.5	6.5	46.0	12.0	2.0
Total	699.0	139.5	21.5	702.5	148.7	18.75	467.5	86.25	16.0
Percent	81.3	16.2	2.5	80.7	17.1	2.2	82.1	15.1	2.8

On average, 81.6% of telecast time was devoted to football. The remaining 18.4% of the telecast featured non-program material of which 15.9% was devoted to advertising and 2.5% to Seven network promotions. The total potential revenue generated through sale of advertising was determined by multiplying the rate for a 30-second commercial by the number of advertisements that appeared throughout the telecast. A 60-second advertisement was simply credited with two commercial placements and a 15-second advertisement, with half a commercial placement. The cost to advertise (30-second spot) ranged from $1500 for Sunday gameday to $4000 for Saturday night replay, Saturday and Sunday night live, and $4800 for Friday night.

From calculating the worth of time dedicated to advertising, revenue to the Seven network during each weekend of the broadcasts was worth in excess of $1.2 million. Over the three weekends $3 854 000 million of advertising inventory was available. Actual revenue generated was $3 307 850, which represents inventory available minus Seven network promotions.

The Seven network paid approximately $13.5 million for the rights to the 1995 season. Based on a 22-week home and away season, and three rounds of finals (total 25 weeks), there was a capacity to generate advertising revenue in excess of $32 million (averaged over 25 weeks at $1 284 700 per week) in the Melbourne market. Other special events during the season included State-of-Origin, the Brownlow Medal count and the Grand Final, which would generate significantly more advertising revenue and value to the advertiser.

Numerous methods exist enabling advertisers to measure the cost efficiency of their advertising in terms of number of people reached. These methods utilise the value of gross rating points, total audience rating points, cost per rating point and cost per thousand. To obtain a measure reflecting the needs of advertisers, the cost per thousand (CPM) was used to determine advertising effectiveness (i.e. homes reached). CPM is defined as 'how much it costs to advertise to reach 1,000 homes or viewers' (Buzzard 1992, p. 42). The formula for determining CPM is the cost of the buy divided by the average households or persons reached, per average minute or quarter-hour, multiplied by 1000.

Average household ratings for each segment were obtained for each telecast and converted into the total number of Melbourne households (1 118 000) tuned to the telecast. The cost to reach 1000 Melbourne homes ranged from $14 to $29 over the review period of the telecast. The range in Round 21 was $15 to $22, in Round 22 $14 to $19 and in the first week of the finals $14 to $29. Using the Friday night Round 21 fixture as an example, the calculation of the CPM is obtained by taking the advertising rate of $4800 and dividing by the average homes viewing (220 000, rating 18.9). This figure is then divided by 1000, providing a resultant figure of 22, indicating that it cost the advertisers $22 to reach every 1000 Melbourne homes during the Round 21 Friday night game. These figures indicate a good return on investment to advertisers in terms of audience reach. In essence it cost advertisers 22 cents per home.

Results achieved from this study indicate that the Seven network seems to be performing extremely well in recouping its investment in football. Revenue exceeding $1 million each weekend for 10–15 hours of telecast equates to in excess of $27 million for the season, solely from the Melbourne market. These figures are achieved despite the Seven network forgoing $4.5 million of potential revenue each season in order to promote its own programs.

The Seven network incurs production costs as well as its outlay to the AFL for the rights, and these production costs reduce the revenue generated from sale of advertising time. Production costs usually assume approximately 20% of the network's total outlay. Considering the cost of the rights paid to the AFL ($500 000 per weekend) and including costs of production (assuming costs in the region of $100 000 per weekend), the revenue obtained from the Melbourne market appears to indicate a very healthy return on investment. Income exceeding $1.1 million each weekend, minus expenditures of $600 000 for production and station promotions, provides a weekly profit in excess of $500 000. Over a 25-week period this represents profits exceeding $25 million.

Lawrence (1995) indicates that in 1994 the rights fees were worth between $15 million and $17 million and the revenue generated from sales of advertising was worth $35 million. Based on the figures obtained from the analysis of three rounds of AFL extrapolated over 25 weeks, it would seem that a large proportion of this $35 million would be generated through the Melbourne market alone, highlighting the strategic significance of the Melbourne television audience to both the AFL and Seven network.

Source: Adjusted from Turner and Shilbury (1997).

ADVERTISING EFFECTIVENESS

Nakra (1991) notes that:

> . . . commercial avoidance and audience erosion are two interrelated problems that marketing executives and media planners have been aware of for more than 30 years. With the rapid advancement of technology the problem of 'zapping' has become even more predominant. (p. 217)

Zapping involves viewers rapidly changing channels in order to avoid commercials. It also involves video-recorded programs where viewers simply fast-forward past the advertisements. Zapping therefore represents a fundamental challenge to the basis of the television advertising formula, which assumes, as indicated earlier in this chapter, that viewers recorded as watching a program also watch and acknowledge advertisements. A difference can exist between exposure to the program and exposure to the commercial messages. It is likely that further advances in technology will increase the ability of the viewer to zap commercials.

Central to this issue of zapping is the cost effectiveness of advertising. The most well-known method for establishing the cost efficiencies between program buys is *cost per thousand* (CPM). An example of the use of CPM was shown in Sportview 9.1. This method has been widely used to show 'audience or target size counts, which may or may not accurately represent the number of people viewing the program, segments of it, or the commercials' (Lloyd & Clancy 1991, p. 34). Lloyd and Clancy (1991) posit three questions in relation to their suggestion for the use of a measure known as *cost per thousand involved* (CPMI):

■ Do individual programs differ in their ability to involve viewers?
■ Just how closely related are CPM and CPMI for the same set of programs?
■ In other words, would media planners and buyers make the same or different media buys if the decision were based on CPM versus CPMI?

The answers to these questions are based on the extent to which the media environment affects, tempers or moderates the nature of advertising response.

Two hypotheses have emerged from research investigating these questions. The *first hypothesis* asserts that the more involved viewers are in a program and the more they like it and are engaged by it, the weaker will be the advertising response. Proponents of this hypothesis maintain that commercial breaks represent an unnecessary intrusive element into an otherwise enjoyable viewing experience. As a consequence, the advertisements are filtered out, perceived negatively or simply avoided. The *second hypothesis* adopts the opposite view. It suggests that characteristics of the program, as subjectively perceived by the involved viewer, produce efforts to minimise surrounding distractions and cause an enhanced orientation towards the program and source of the stimulus (Lloyd & Clancy 1991). Enhanced involvement prompts the viewer to remain activated, producing a more positive impact on advertising effectiveness. Implications of these hypotheses are:

■ to develop appropriate ratings indexes to determine program involvement, and
■ to factor these indexes into CPMI measures.

At present, no research is available indicating the level of involvement sport programming generates. In terms of zapping, however, sport programming such as cricket, where only one short commercial can be shown between overs, may have an advantage in ensuring that viewers watch and acknowledge the commercial. Australian Rules football may also have a similar advantage, as commercials are shown after a goal is scored and are typically of 30 seconds duration before play recommences. Sports such as golf, basketball and car racing may provide viewers with the opportunity to leave the room knowing that a series of four to five commercials will be shown.

This also raises the question of advertisement placing in programs. Typically, first-in and last-out commercials are considered more valuable, as viewers see the first before leaving the room and the last when returning after the commercial break. Interestingly, networks often use the first or last advertisement for their own station program promotion purposes.

All of these factors impinge on the effectiveness of advertising during sport programming. Little research has been conducted on sport programming to shed more light on the answers to the questions raised in this section. There is little doubt, however, that these issues all form the basis on which networks set advertising rates and, as a consequence, the amount of television rights they are prepared to pay sporting organisations.

PAY-TELEVISION

Another player has recently entered the sport–business–television relationship. Pay-television was introduced to Australia in 1995. Slowly, it is becoming available worldwide, contributing to the globalised economy and in particular the familiarity of sport.

The business basis on which pay-television is predicated is fundamentally different from that of the free-to-air networks previously described in this chapter. So far we have described how free-to-air networks rely on advertising as their primary source of revenue and profit. Free-to-air networks are in the business of reaching the widest possible audience, hence the term *broadcasting*. Free-to-air television is popular and in general taken for granted as an everyday part of life. Pay-television, on the other hand, requires the payment of subscription fees to receive programming. The basic operating premise on which pay-television exists is known as *narrowcasting*, and its revenue base is sourced from subscription fees. Unlike with the free-to-air networks, advertising is not the predominant revenue source.

Pay-television in Australia at present is not as freely accessible as the free-to-air networks. Over time it is assumed that this market will expand. Initially, advertising on pay-television was banned for a period of five years, although in mid-1997 advertising became legal, diversifying revenue opportunities and more closely aligning pay-television with the free-to-air networks. Logically, this will intensify competition for advertising revenue in the television industry.

Legislation governing the introduction of pay-television in Australia prevents major sporting events being shown solely on pay-television. For example, the AFL Grand Final, Melbourne Cup, major golf and tennis events, and the Olympic Games are subject to anti-siphoning laws designed to ensure that the majority of the population retains the ability to see these sporting events. Pay-television represents further opportunities for sports with their marketing, promotion and revenue-generating strategies. The sport channels, in concert with the movie channels, are pay-television's greatest strength in terms of attracting subscribers. The opportunity therefore presents itself to an increasing range of sports to obtain some exposure via pay-television.

In terms of extracting rights revenue from pay-television operators, the same principle applies as for free-to-air operators: to determine how much revenue the sport contributes to the network. The difference, however, is that it is not so easy to calculate this contribution. Free-to-air networks, as shown earlier in this chapter, can simply calculate the total advertising time in dollar terms, thereby determining how much direct value sport programming represents. It is more difficult to determine how many subscribers subscribe solely or predominantly because a specific sport is shown on a pay-television channel. In some cases, major sports such as cricket, the AFL and rugby league clearly add to the likelihood that subscriptions will increase due to their availability on a pay-television channel. The AFL, for example, has a dedicated channel on Optus Vision at a cost of an extra $6 per month. Rugby league is shown extensively on Optus Vision's 'Sports Australia', exemplifying the impact of the major sports as a strategic source of programming.

Fundamentally, sports not already receiving extensive free-to-air coverage will wish to obtain exposure on pay-television. In the end, for some of these sports, the benefits may be the exposure via programming rather than any financial gains via television rights for exclusive coverage. This highlights the important role of television in the overall marketing and promotion of sport. Some sports, as demonstrated in this chapter, have the capacity to gain financially from television broadcasts; others do not have this capacity. For some sports, the opportunity to gain exposure through programming without receiving any financial incentive is also an important consideration when developing promotion mix decisions. It is also possible that some sports will have to pay to have their sport shown on either pay-television or free-to-air television. In this case, the decision to spend money will come from the promotion mix budget. Television therefore is an important consideration when framing promotion mix decisions.

Another question that arises is what sport managers need to do to increase the attractiveness of a sport for television. There is no easy answer to this question. Some sports have used rule changes to make the game more attractive; other sports have changed the uniforms worn by players to make them more attractive and appealing; and other sports have simply paid for airtime until their sport has become well recognised and people want to watch it on a regular basis. Whether it is pay-television or free-to-air television, the formula does not change. Television executives will want to know how much revenue and subsequent profit the sport will attract for the network before they agree to show it on television. It is possible that pay-television offers slightly greater opportunities in the early years, as there will be pressure to fill programming, particularly on all-sport channels.

One thing is certain: the complexity of the sport–business–television relationship is increasing and intensifying in terms of attracting revenue sources and viewers. What has not changed is that programming is designed to capture a market of viewers, to either expose them to advertising or to get them to subscribe to a pay-television operator's range of channels.

SUMMARY

This chapter has attempted to demystify the sport–business–television relationship. Television rights to sporting events are one of the most visible and talked-about components of sport marketing. The networks of the world pay exorbitant sums for the exclusive rights to broadcast sporting events such as the Olympic Games and World Cup in soccer. These sums merely recognise the number of people watching such events. Sporting events at varying levels, some worldwide, some nationally, deliver audiences to advertisers via programming, which in turn delivers revenues to sport in the form of rights fees and profits to television networks via the sale of advertising inventory.

The people meter is the electronic device used to measure the success of television programs. The people meter collects ratings, which measure how may people with televisions are watching a particular program. Audience share and TARPs also measure the success of television programs, providing detailed and specific information about who is watching. It is not enough to simply identify how many people with televisions are watching a program; it is also important to know more about the demographic profile of these viewers. Advertising rates are based on rating figures and the income derived from advertising determines what rights fees be paid for the exclusive broadcast rights to sporting events.

Some sporting organisations have been slow to awaken to the value of their product. In marketing terms, many sports have not maximised their revenue opportunities through television, primarily because of not understanding how the worth of television rights is calculated. As the sport sector professionalises, this is changing. Evidence of this is shown in the escalation of rights fees during the last decade.

The other major marketing benefit to be gained from television is exposure. Indirectly, televised sport has the potential to attract viewers to the live event, thereby contributing to the revenue generated via gate receipts. In many ways this is a vicious circle. Televised sporting events can contribute to reduced attendances, explaining why sport programming is often 'blacked out' in the city where the event is being staged. Television therefore is an important consideration when framing marketing and promotion mix decisions.

Pay-television contributes to the exposure sporting organisations may gain from television. The relatively recent introduction of pay-television to Australia has meant exposure for sports not normally shown on television. Pay-television does not offer a huge amount of exposure at present because the subscriber base is still rather small. Therefore, only the major professional sports have demonstrated the capacity to attract revenue from pay-television providers. Over a period of time, however, it might also offer some revenue-generating potential for smaller sports. This chapter has shown that the principal source of revenue for pay-television operators comes from individual household subscriptions. During the next few years, pay-television operators will be allowed to show advertisements, thereby diversifying sources of revenue. This revenue source is not anticipated to be large in the short term.

The various business relationships described in this chapter are not mysterious nor surprising once the commercial basis on which television operates is understood. What is interesting is the complex set of relationships developing between sport and television as both endeavour to maximise the revenues and profits from their respective product offerings.

MURDOCH ADDS FOOTBALL TO LIST OF GLOBAL AMBITIONS

CASE STUDY

'Hail Mary. That's what some sideline spectators initially thought of Rupert Murdoch's NFL pass. They saw the $1.6 billion bid to acquire four years of National Football Conference coverage as an act of desperation, necessitated by two seasons of declining prime-time ratings and a lack of overall momentum at Fox. But with less than two months before Fox Sports kicks off its first NFL season, Mr. Murdoch's pricey gamble looks more like a touchdown drive that will take his burgeoning media enterprise past the U.S. end zone and into a playing field of global proportions. "I think football will be a key element in the globalization of Murdoch's media holdings," said Arnie Semsky, exec VP-worldwide media director at BBDO Worldwide, New York.

'In 1986, BBDO negotiated what was billed as the first-ever global media buy for client Gillette Co., a package including the fledgling Fox network in the U.S., British Sky Broadcasting in Europe and Murdoch's network in Australia. "It worked very well for us," Mr. Semsky said. "One of the main reasons we did it was to show that it could be done and to foreshadow the things that would come—global media, global advertising and global advertising agencies." NFL President Neal Austrian said the league commands more than $1 billion a year in rights fees in the U.S. but only about $10 million from other countries. "The deal with Fox was just for domestic rights," Mr. Austrian said, "but clearly by partnering with Rupert, we see an opportunity to grow the NFL in the international marketplace because of the reach and prominence of his global media resources."

'Earlier this year, Fox became an equity partner in the NFL's relaunch of the World League. Fox's 49% stake is unprecedented. No U.S. media outlet has ever owned as significant a stake in a professional sports league. Fox executives last week were believed to be negotiating details with the NFL on international distribution rights for the World League. It's assumed Mr. Murdoch's TV outlets in the U.K., Asia and Latin America will be given first choice of carrying the games. "We certainly see great [NFL] opportunities in Europe, and we'll start there first," Mr. Murdoch said in an interview. "But I think it's going to take a long time to get the NFL as a major sport in every country in the world in the way that soccer already is."

'Meanwhile, Twentieth Century Television, the TV syndication arm of Fox Inc., has cut a deal with NFL Films to be its marketing and distribution partner. In a very little time, News Corp. and the NFL have become closer perhaps than any media company has ever bonded to a sports league. Whether the partnership comes at the expense of the NFL's other global media partners— Capital Cities/ABC's ABC plus ESPN, NBC and Turner Broadcasting System—remains to be seen. But one thing is clear: Mr. Murdoch's NFL bid was no act of desperation but part of a expansionistic global game plan.

'The top media executive at a major multinational football advertiser said the NFL tried, but failed, before to expand internationally. "This time, they are doing it with a media partner that brings not only credibility but strong existing outlets throughout the world," the executive said. George Krieger, exec VP at Fox Sports and one of Mr. Murdoch's key NFL strategists, said News Corp. wants to market football as "a year-round sport." Fox's $395 million annual NFL payment exceeds comparable investments in its entire prime-time schedule.

'Whether that makes sense depends on whom you ask. "[CBS Inc. Chairman-CEO] Larry Tisch does something like that, and everybody said he was a jerk. Rupert does it, and everybody says he's a genius," said Paine Webber analyst Alan Gottesman. Fox will lose money, but the deal has already paid off in other ways. Since acquiring NFL rights, Fox has picked up enough affiliates to increase coverage to about 96% of U.S. TV homes from about 93%. News Corp.'s recent deal with New World Communications Group boosts that coverage even higher. The NFL is projected to double Fox's supply of gross rating points during the critical fourth quarter. Fox executives project football will average the 13.8 rating that CBS' regular-season coverage averaged last year, nearly twice Fox's 7.3 prime-time rating and a powerful advertiser lure.

'At nearly $120,000 per 30-second spot, Fox is expected to gross nearly

$250 million annually from football, not including about $25 million in NFL-related programming and revenue to Fox-owned stations. Fox will also derive as much as $75 million from the sale of ad time in Super Bowl XXXI in 1997, further cutting losses. During the 1994–95 upfront football season, Fox cut deals with General Motors Corp., Ford Motor Co., Chrysler Corp., American Honda Motor Co. and Toyota Motor Sales USA, as well as major beer marketers. Under a four-year, $40 million deal with McDonald's Corp. announced last week, the two will team for a major, fourth-quarter integrated marketing effort. The cross-promotion deal will use a watch-and-win game that will give away hundreds of thousands of dollars in prizes, intended to drive tune-in to the NFL on Fox. McDonald's will back the effort with an ad campaign from Leo Burnett USA, Chicago, and will feature the promotion in its 9,400 U.S. restaurants.

'Fox also has its own promotional and ad blitz planned. "We are going to make sure all the viewers who were used to watching the NFL on CBS know that almost half the NFL schedule is now on Fox," said Tony Seiniger, president of Seiniger Advertising, Beverly Hills, Calif., named last week as Fox's agency for all creative work on the NFL. Mr. Seiniger, whose agency has worked primarily for movie companies, said Fox will take an unconventional approach. "We are going to find ways of taking the helmets off of the players and showing that there are living, breathing personalities under there. We want to develop the personalities behind the sport, the way the NBA did with basketball," he said. "[CBS] sold it like it was a videogame. It didn't have any personality."

'Still, convention has its place, even at Fox. The network was quick to hire veteran CBS analysts John Madden and Terry Bradshaw, and also put former Dallas Cowboys coach Jimmy Johnson on its roster. Fox Sports isn't stopping with football. Executives are already waging a clandestine campaign to shake baseball rights away from the Baseball Network, a fledgling partnership of ABC, NBC and Major League Baseball. Though the joint venture is a six-year deal, it's believed team owners have options to cancel if the venture doesn't deliver on certain revenue goals.

'But Fox Sports isn't pinning all its hopes on baseball. The network expects to play in every major sport that comes up, even basketball, when the NBA's contract with NBC comes due. The jewel Fox Sports is angling toward is the 2000 Summer Olympics in Mr. Murdoch's native Sydney.'

Source: Reprinted from Mandese (1994, pp. 66–7).

Questions

1 Describe why the rights to televise the NFL will assist Murdoch's plans to globalise the Fox Network.
2 What is the significance of the media buy by Gillette Co. in the development of the fledgling Fox Network?

3   What is the significance of the Fox Network's decision to become an equity partner in World League?

4   Based on the evidence from the case study, is Fox likely to recoup its investment from the NFL rights?

5   Discuss the role of 'convention' as it is used in this case study.

REFERENCES

ANZ McCaughan (1993). *Broadcasting Bounces Back: A Financial Evaluation of Australian Commercial Metropolitan Television, Part 1 Industry Overview*, ANZ McCaughan, Melbourne.

Buzzard, K. (1992). *Electronic Media Ratings: Turning Dollars into Sense*, Focal Press, Boston, Mass.

Elliott, S. (1993). 'Despite record ad rates, the Super Bowl is a hot ticket again', *New York Times,* 26 January.

GTV Nine (1993). *Wide World of Sports Telecast Guide*, Melbourne.

HSV Seven Network (1995). *Seven Network Major Sponsorship of the 1995 AFL Season*, Seven Network, Melbourne.

International Olympic Committee (1996a). Press releases, World Wide Web page.

——(1996b). *Marketing Matters: The Olympic Marketing Newsletter*, 8, Spring, Lausanne.

Jarratt, P. (1988). 'A nation of Norms', *The Bulletin*, 4 October, pp. 56–8/92.

Klattell, D. A. and Marcus, N. (1988). *Sports for Sale*, Oxford University Press, New York.

Lawrence, M. (1995). 'High stakes keep growing and there can only be one winner', *The Age*, 8 April, 17.

Linnell, S. (1991). 'How Channel Seven scored the rights to TV football', *The Age*, 25 September, pp. 3/29.

Lloyd, D. C. and Clancy, K. J. (1991). 'CPMs versus CPMIs: implications for media planning', *Journal of Advertising Research*, August/September, pp. 34–43.

Mandese, J. (1994). 'Murdoch adds football to list of global ambitions', *Advertising Age*, 65 (25), p. 13.

Nakra, P. (1991). 'Zapping nonsense: should television media planners lose sleep over it?', *International Journal of Advertising*, 10, pp. 217–22.

Nine Network (1993). *Wide World of Sports: Australian Grand Prix Adelaide 1993*, Nine Network.

Turner, P. and Shilbury, D. (1997). 'Sport on television: a study of the Australian Football League television rights', *Sport Marketing Quarterly*, 6 (3), pp. 55–62.

USA Today (1994). 'TV pays the way', 21 October.

Warneke, R. (1996). 'How they rated', *The Age Green Guide*, 25 July, p. 6.

APPENDIX: WORLDWIDE TELEVISION RIGHTS

US professional sports

NFL	$US million	Network	Baseball	$US million	Network
1981	142	ABC, CBS, NBC	1980–83	46	ABC, NBC, USA
1982–86	378	ABC, CBS, NBC	1984–89	183	ABC, NBC
1987–89	417	ABC, CBS, NBC	1990–93	365	CBS, ESPN
1990–93	912	ABC, CBS, NBC, ESPN, TNT	1994	85	The Baseball Network (joint venture ABC, NBC), ESPN
1994–98	1100	ABC, Fox, NBC, ESPN, TNT			

NBA	$US million	Network	NHL (in USA)	$US million	Network
1982–86	27	CBS, TBS, USA	1987–88	8	ESPN
1986–90	66	CBS, TBS	1988–89	15.9	SportsChannel
1990–94	219	NBC, Turner	1989–90	16.8	SportsChannel
1994–98	275.5	NBC, Turner	1990–92	23.3	SportsChannel
			1992–94	29.5	ESPN
			1994–99	47	Fox, ESPN

Source: *USA Today* (1994).

Olympic Games

USA Summer	$US million	Venue	Network	USA Winter	$US million	Venue	Network
1980	85	Moscow	NBC	1980	15.5	Lake Placid	ABC
1984	225.6	Los Angeles	ABC	1984	91.6	Sarajevo	ABC
1988	300	Seoul	NBC	1988	309	Calgary	ABC
1992	401	Barcelona	NBC	1992	243	Albertville	CBS
1996	456[a]	Atlanta	NBC	1994	295	Lillehammer	CBS
2000	705	Sydney	NBC	1998	375	Nagarno	CBS
2004	793[a]	Athens	NBC	2002	545[a]	Salt Lake City	NBC
2008	894[a]	?	NBC	2006	613[a]	?	NBC

Australia Summer	$US million	Venue	Network	Australia Winter	$US million	Venue	Network
1984	10.6	Los Angeles	10	1984	1	Sarajevo	7
1988	7.4	Seoul	10	1988	1.1	Calgary	7
1992	34	Barcelona	7	1992	8.5	Albertville	9
1996	30	Atlanta	7	1994	5	Lillehammer	9
2000	45	Sydney	7	1998	9.3	Nagano	7
2004	50.5	Athens	7	2002	11.8	Salt Lake City	7
2008	63.8	?	7	2006	14.8	?	7

Olympic Games (continued)

Europe Summer	$US million	Venue	Network	Europe Winter	$US million	Venue	Network
1980	7.1	Moscow	EBU[b]	1980	4	Lake Placid	EBU[b]
1984	22	Los Angeles	EBU	1984	5.6	Sarajevo	EBU
1988	30.2	Seoul	EBU	1988	6.9	Calgary	EBU
1992	94.5	Barcelona	EBU	1992	20.3	Albertville	EBU
1996	247.5	Atlanta	EBU	1994	26.3	Lillehammer	EBU
2000	350[a]	Sydney	EBU	1998	72	Nagano	EBU
2004	394[a]	Athens	EBU	2002	120[a]	Salt Lake City	EBU
2008	443[a]	?	EBU	2006	135[a]	?	EBU

Notes: [a] Includes profit sharing.
[b] EBU = European Broadcasting Union.

Source: International Olympic Committee (1996b).

10

Sponsorship

CHAPTER OUTLINE

Headline story: Increasing sales, raising awareness or philanthropy?

What is sponsorship?
    The market for sponsors
    Sponsorship goals: advertising or public relations?
    Advantages and disadvantages of sport sponsorship

Creating win-win situations

Sponsoring individual athletes and celebrity marketing
    Credibility and attractiveness
    Considerations when using athlete celebrities
    Sportview 10.1: Marketing Michael

The integrated marketing approach
    Sponsorship support activities
    Sponsoring (inter)nationally but making it work locally

Measuring sponsorship effectiveness
    Ambush marketing
    Sportview 10.2: Ambush marketing at the Olympics

Summary

Case study: Attracting a naming sponsor for the local badminton club

References

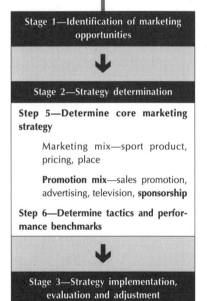

Stage 1—Identification of marketing opportunities

⬇

Stage 2—Strategy determination

Step 5—Determine core marketing strategy

Marketing mix—sport product, pricing, place

Promotion mix—sales promotion, advertising, television, **sponsorship**

Step 6—Determine tactics and performance benchmarks

⬇

Stage 3—Strategy implementation, evaluation and adjustment

CHAPTER
OBJECTIVES
Chapter 10 examines the concept of sponsorship. Sponsorship is one of the most visible elements of the sport promotion mix. In this chapter, a framework for how to create win-win relationships is presented. Celebrity and ambush marketing as special issues in sport sponsorship are also discussed.

After studying this chapter you should be able to:

1   Describe sponsorship as a distinctive element of the promotion mix.
2   Create a win-win relationship between a sponsor and a sponsee.
3   Describe different methods of measuring sponsorship effectiveness.

HEADLINE
STORY

INCREASING SALES, RAISING AWARENESS OR PHILANTHROPY?

I was always very conscious of the fact that we weren't able to offer our sponsors anything specific in return for their support . . . The obvious way of raising money by doing deals was just not available to us. I wanted to make sure that the Sydney bid was never criticised if we lost; that no-one could say we didn't look after the people who had given us money. So I worked hard at trying to give all our sponsors value for their money. (McGeoch & Korporaal 1994, p. 114)

In these few lines, Rod McGeoch, chairman of the Sydney 2000 bid committee, succinctly described the sponsorship dilemma. One organisation needs sponsorship to reach its goals; another expects to benefit from sponsoring an organisation or individual. How can sponsorship be made to work? When is the sponsor satisfied? Can the effectiveness of the sponsorship be measured? Is sponsorship more effective than, for example, advertising? These questions only can be answered if a clear understanding of the goals of the sponsoring organisation exists. Does it want to increase sales or raise awareness, or is the chief executive officer simply a philanthropic follower of the team or sporting code?

The first part of this chapter will define and discuss the concept of sponsorship from both the sponsor's and the sporting organisation's points of view. It is important to understand which other organisations are competing with sporting organisations for limited sponsorship dollars; so a brief overview of the market for sponsors is provided. Sponsorship as an advertising and public relations tool will be discussed when goals of sponsorship are considered, followed by the advantages and disadvantages of sport sponsorship. The second part of the chapter presents a sponsorship framework and discusses how to create win-win situations. Win-win situations are created when all parties entering into an agreement benefit from it. Sponsoring individual athletes, as an area of special interest in the sport industry, will be considered next. The benefits for both the sponsor and sponsee should be taken into consideration when wanting to create a balanced win-win situation.

The third part of the chapter takes us beyond the basics of sponsorship.

To really take an integrated marketing approach, sponsorship support activities and tie-in promotions need to be initiated. When the complete sponsorship program is put into action, it is important for both the sponsor and sponsee to measure sponsorship effectiveness. Effectiveness, however, can be diminished by the practice of ambush marketing, the final topic to be discussed.

WHAT IS SPONSORSHIP?

Historically, sponsorship has often been associated with charity and altruism. The *Penguin Pocket English Dictionary* still defines *sponsorship* as 'somebody who pays for a project or activity'. In today's (sport) business environment, however, nothing is less true. As an important marketing tool for many organisations, sponsorship involves a *reciprocal relationship*. One party puts something in and the other party returns the favour. Sleight (1989), in his definition of sponsorship, acknowledges the importance of the reciprocal relationship. This definition will be used in the remainder of this book:

> Sponsorship is a business relationship between a provider of funds, resources or services and an individual, event or organisation which offers in return some rights and association that may be used for commercial advantage. (p. 4)

In marketing it is common to look at the different marketing tools, like sponsorship, from an applied point of view. In other words, how can we use this tool (i.e. *spend* money, resources or services) to reach sales-related goals? This is the *sponsoring* organisation. From the sporting organisation's point of view, the main goal of sponsorship is not sales related. Sporting organisations or athletes mainly use sponsorship to *accumulate* funds, resources or services. These funds, resources or services are then used to run the operations of the organisation. This is the *sponsored* organisation. We will further discuss the business relationship between the sponsor and sponsee later in this chapter.

Application of the sponsorship tool is not limited to sporting organisations, as will be shown in the next section.

The market for sponsors

A *market*, as a collection of buyers, consists of all those organisations and individuals in need of something. The collection of organisations and individuals in competition for sponsors (funds, resources or services) therefore makes up the market for sponsors. Expenditure in this market, worldwide, was estimated to top $11.7 billion in 1995. Of this, $4.7 billion would be spent on sponsorship in the United States, of which 65–70% would be sport related (Kyriakopoulos 1995, p. 76). According to the Sydney-based Sponsorship

Market Group, $510 million was spent in Australia in 1994, estimated to reach $650 million in 1995. Broadcast sponsorship and back-up promotions would push this figure over the $1 billion mark (Richardson 1994). It was estimated that in 1993 in the United Kingdom, total spending on sponsorship topped £350 million (Wilmshurst 1993, p. 373).

Although these figures are only estimates, it can be argued this is a huge pool of potential funds for sporting organisations. There are two major trends that have to be taken into consideration before we arrive at a final conclusion about available funds:

- the move to big event sponsorship, and
- the increasing competition for sponsorship dollars.

The move to big event sponsorship is exemplified by the Sydney Olympic Games in the year 2000. It is estimated that the Sydney 2000 Games need to attract close to $500 million in sponsorship. Around $300 million will be accounted for by local sponsors; the worldwide International Olympic Committee (IOC) TOP sponsors will contribute the rest. Towards the year 2000, local (Australian) companies will have to redirect their sponsorship dollars from local, regional or national sporting organisations to the Olympic Games. This will put a drain on the sponsorship budgets of Australian sporting organisations. This is the same for other, media-attractive events (e.g. Grand Prix events, World Swimming Championship) that are able to attract mass television audiences. In other words, a relatively large amount of sponsorship funds goes to relatively few organisations.

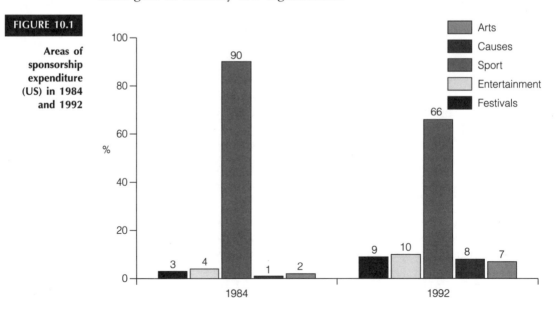

FIGURE 10.1

Areas of sponsorship expenditure (US) in 1984 and 1992

Legend: Arts, Causes, Sport, Entertainment, Festivals

1984: 3, 4, 90, 1, 2
1992: 9, 10, 66, 8, 7

Source: Lyall (1995).

In the market for sponsors, competition is also increasing. The US figures presented in Figure 10.1 indicate for the worldwide trend towards an increase in sponsorship in other areas than sport.

Although expenditure on sponsorship is still growing, the increasing dominance of big sporting events and powerful sporting organisations, and increasing competition from organisations other than sport, are making it more difficult for many sporting organisations to attract funds, resources or services through sponsorship.

Sponsorship goals: advertising or public relations?

The sponsorship tool can be seen as a derivative of either advertising or public relations, as elements of the promotion mix, or a combination of the two.

In Chapter 7 *advertising* was defined as a non-personal communication by an identified sponsor. From the sponsor's point of view, the difference between sponsorship and advertising is the actual message communicated, and how the message is communicated. In advertising, the content of the message and the moments of communication are determined by the paying organisation. When using sponsorship, however, the sponsor provides financial or material support for what often are independent organisations, individuals or activities. Less control can be exercised over the communication through these entities, and the timing of communication cannot be controlled. Although indirect (through the sponsored organisation), the actual message is often communicated at a more personal level (e.g. towards people visiting an event). These points will be returned to when discussing the advantages and disadvantages of sport sponsorship.

Public relations goals like 'earning understanding and acceptance' and 'creating goodwill' can be sponsorship goals as well. The fact that the organisation has to pay for the association with the sponsored organisation, and that communication takes place through an independent organisation, distinguish sponsorship from pure public relations. The sponsored organisation is used as the means of communication, which in effect can make sponsorship a public relations tool, and sponsorship therefore is a subset of public relations.

A general goal of sponsorship is described by Wilmshurst (1993). Elements of both advertising and public relations can be found in this goal, which reads:

> . . . sponsorship is usually undertaken to encourage more favourable attitudes towards the sponsoring company or its products within a relevant target audience, such as consumers, trade customers, employees or the community in which it operates. (p. 377)

Earlier in this chapter we described the difference in goal orientation between the sponsoring organisation (sponsor) and sponsored organisation (sponsee).

Because the sporting organisation most of the time is the sponsee, both advertising and public relations goals do not seem to fit! In order to obtain sponsors, it is important to know about the sponsor's goals, but sponsee goals often are different. Table 10.1 presents an overview of different sponsor and sponsee goals—goals that have to be matched when a sponsorship framework is created.

TABLE 10.1	Sponsor goals	Sponsee goals
Sport sponsor and sponsee goals	Image creation or improvement	Obtaining *funds*
	Business relationship marketing	Obtaining *resources* (goods)
	Media relationship marketing	Obtaining *services*
	Employee relationship marketing	Raising awareness
	Community relationship marketing	Brand positioning
	Business development	Raising credibility
	Increasing sales	Image creation or improvement
	Brand positioning	
	Raising awareness	
	Corporate responsibility	
	Targeting new market segments	
	Develop new distribution channels	

Advantages and disadvantages of sport sponsorship

In the previous section it was shown that sponsorship has distinctly different characteristics from other elements of the promotion mix like advertising and public relations. Sponsorship in a sport context allows the sponsor to communicate more directly and intimately with its target market (in this case the people interested in the sporting organisation and its products).

In Chapter 1 some unique characteristics of the sport product were listed. Some of these are applicable when discussing the advantages of sport sponsorship. First, sport consumers tend to identify themselves personally with the sport, which creates opportunities for increasing brand loyalty in products linked to the sport. Sport evokes personal attachment, and with this the sponsor can be linked to the excitement, energy and emotion of the sporting contest. In other words, sport has the potential to deliver a clear message. Sport has universal appeal and pervades all elements of life (geographically, demographically and socioculturally). This characteristic presents the opportunity to cross difficult cultural and language borders in communication, enabling the sponsor to talk to a (global) mass audience. At the same time the variety in sports available makes it possible to create distinct market segments with which to communicate separately. The universal appeal and high interest in sport give sport a high media exposure, resulting in free publicity. Free publicity can make a sponsorship deal very cost effective. Thousands of dollars in advertising expenditure can be saved when a sporting organisation or athlete attracts a lot of media attention. This makes many organisations want to be associated with sport. Also, because of the clear linkage of the sponsor to a sporting organisation or athlete, sponsorship stands out from the clutter, contrary to mainstream advertising, in which people are bombarded with hundreds of messages each day.

With so many advantages, why do organisations not simply spend their complete promotional budget on sponsorship? There are, however, some disadvantages to be considered before entering into a sponsorship agreement. In ambush marketing (discussed at the end of this chapter), non-sponsors take advantage of the efforts of real sponsors in that they try to be associated with the sponsored organisation, event, product or athlete. The lack of control over media coverage is another disadvantage of sport sponsorship. Also, the media sometimes are reluctant to recognise the sponsor's name when reporting on events or the achievements of athletes. Achievements of teams or athletes are another area that cannot be controlled. A non-performing team or athlete will have direct influence on the perception of the public about the sponsor. The implications of this on the sponsorship of individual athletes will be considered later in this chapter.

The first part of this chapter discussed the concept of sponsorship. The second part deals with the creation of *win-win situations*—situations in which both the sponsor and sponsee benefit from the cooperation.

CREATING WIN-WIN SITUATIONS

If both the sponsor and sponsee have to benefit from a cooperation, certain goals of both need to be satisfied. The main question that sponsor and sponsee have to ask themselves is: How can we successfully reach *our own* goals by assisting the sponsor/sponsee to reach *their* goals? The sponsorship framework in which win-win situations are created is conceptually quite simple. This framework is presented in Figure 10.2.

The assumption in the framework is that certain benefits will satisfy certain goals. Those benefits can only be delivered by an entity other than the organisation. If two entities, both in search of benefits to satisfy their own goals, are able to deliver the benefits needed by the other entity, they can become engaged in an *exchange of benefits*. By exchanging benefits, both organisations 'benefit' from the cooperation; therefore a win-win situation is created.

It must be noticed though that in today's sporting environment it often is not enough to 'create' a win-win situation and leave it at that. It is rapidly becoming common practice for sponsor and sponsee executives to organise

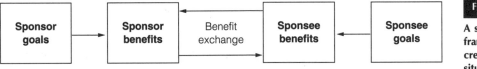

FIGURE 10.2

A sponsorship framework to create win-win situations

regular strategic-planning meetings, in order to maximise the effectiveness of the sponsorship. During these meetings it is evaluated whether the goals of both the sponsor and sponsee are being reached and whether any new insights and ideas can increase the effectiveness of the sponsorship. More and more, executives discuss new business opportunities beyond the scope of the (current) sponsorship through which the actual sponsorship can lead into a strategic alliance. A *strategic alliance* is a commitment and relationship between two organisations from which both organisations hope to benefit.

It is now time to examine the conceptual sponsorship framework in practice. Table 10.1 presented possible sponsor and sponsee goals. Table 10.2 expands on this to include the operationalised benefits needed to reach the listed goals and provides an example. The goals of a sponsor (beer brewer Heineken) and a sponsee (a sporting organisation) are shown in bold type. The benefits needed by both organisations to reach their goals are shown in bold type as well. If both organisations are willing and able to provide the benefits needed by the other organisation, a win-win situation can be created. The example is summarised at the bottom of the table.

	Sponsor goals	Sponsor benefits	Sponsee benefits	Sponsee goals
TABLE 10.2 **Exchanging benefits to satisfy goals of sponsor and sponsee**	Image creation or improvement Business relationship marketing Media relationship marketing Employee relationship marketing Community relationship marketing Business development Increasing sales **Brand positioning** Raising awareness Corporate responsibility Targeting new market segments Develop new distribution channels	**Television exposure** **Print media exposure** Access to sporting organisation's mailouts Naming rights Logo use Signage **Advertising rights** Merchandising rights Product exclusivity Sampling opportunities Athlete use **Hospitality opportunities** Access to database (addresses etc.)	**Dollars** Goods **Services** Exposure Affiliation	**Obtaining funds** **Obtaining resources** (goods) **Obtaining services** (Raising awareness) (Brand positioning) (Raising credibility) (Image creation or improvement)

Heineken Beer Breweries goal	Heineken Beer Breweries benefits	Sporting organisation benefits	Sporting organisation goals
Brand positioning	Television exposure Print media exposure Advertising rights Hospitality opportunities	$25 000 Fully-catered party for sporting organisation members	Obtaining funds Obtaining services

There are a variety of issues to consider before a deal can be closed and a win-win situation is created. How to write a sponsorship proposal and how to increase the value of a sponsorship are covered in the concluding case study of this chapter. Now we take a closer look at a typical sport industry sponsee: the individual athlete.

SPONSORING INDIVIDUAL ATHLETES AND CELEBRITY MARKETING

Belch and Belch (1995) suggest that when communicating a message the credibility and attractiveness of the source are of particular importance. Credibility and attractiveness are therefore the concepts to consider when organisations choose to use athletes as their source of communication. Consider the following example:

> General Motors Holden's trump card has been its use of Greg Norman as an advertising icon. After only three years, according to the Sweeney survey, 15 percent of consumers identify Holden and golf as partners, largely due to Norman's high profile. They are now aiming to make the link even stronger having signed up female golf champion Karrie Webb as part of its stable. (Lynch 1996, p. C2)

Credibility and attractiveness

Why is Greg Norman so successful in conveying the Holden message? Why is he such a powerful source? Are there limitations to the credibility and attractiveness of sporting celebrities like Greg Norman? To answer these questions, it is first necessary to elaborate on the concepts of credibility and attractiveness. A simplified model of the communication process, including these concepts, is presented in Figure 10.3. The model shows that, when a source is credible and attractive, the message will become more powerful and will have a higher impact on the receiver of the message. This in turn will lead to a positive association with the source and message, eventually leading to a planned change in the perception, awareness or buying behaviour of the receiver. If the source is not credible and attractive, the opposite is more likely to happen.

According to Belch and Belch (1995), a source is *credible* when it has *expertise* about the message. When Michael Jordan endorses the sport drink Gatorade, he is a more credible source than golfer John Daly endorsing basketball shoes. It is more likely that Jordan has expertise about the sport drink than Daly about the shoes. A source becomes also more credible when it is *trustworthy*. Brazilian soccer star Romario will probably be more honest and believable in supporting the well-being of the Amazon rainforest than in endorsing the benefits of being a member of the Turkish Automobile Club. Information from credible sources will influence the receiver in that the

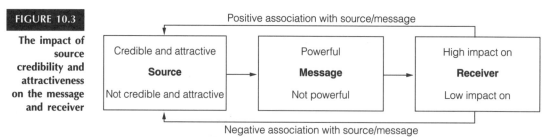

FIGURE 10.3

The impact of
source
credibility and
attractiveness
on the message
and receiver

message communicated will become the opinion of the receiver. This opinion will have an influence on the (buying) behaviour of the receiver.

A source becomes more *attractive* when there is a *similarity* between the source and the receiver. The more similarities a person can (or wants!) to identify between the athlete and themselves, the more likely that person is to be influenced by the message of the athlete. Many juniors aspire 'to be like Mike'. Linking this message to drinking Gatorade, Michael Jordan successfully influences the buying behaviour of many juniors around the world. *Likeability* is another determinant of attractiveness. Sporting celebrities are admired for their performances and become well known to the public, given the high visibility and hence media coverage of sport. Rather than a plain advertisement, General Motors Holden uses Greg Norman to draw attention to its message, in order to stand out in the very cluttered advertising media.

Credibility and attractiveness, however, are influenced by other factors when using an athlete celebrity.

Considerations when using athlete celebrities

Using a single athlete, as opposed to a sporting organisation, team or event, brings with it advantages and disadvantages.

The single athlete can stand out in a myriad of advertising messages, especially when *performance* is high. Nike athletes like Andre Agassi and Richard Krajicek, both considered to be huge tennis talents, did not perform up to the expectations of the general public over the longer period. Agassi's world ranking fell to as low as 30, and Krajicek never seemed to perform when it really mattered (in Grand Slam tournaments). Nike even considered discontinuing the agreement until Agassi, with a new coach, became number 1 in the world and Krajicek won Wimbledon in 1996. The performance of athletes cannot be controlled but can heavily influence their credibility.

Another uncontrollable factor is the *personality* of the star athlete. Athletes who find it hard to control themselves when they lose, say things to the press they regret later, or always seem to run into trouble, are risky investments for organisations trying to build a consistent image or sell more products.

Organisations also have to realise that young people are more likely to be influenced by athlete celebrities than older people. Therefore the *target*

publics that organisations want to communicate with by using athlete celebrities have to be carefully selected.

When using high profile celebrities, organisations run the risk that the
message or product they want endorsed will be *overshadowed* by the celebrity.

Because high profile celebrities are attractive to a mass audience, many
organisations want them to endorse their messages. This easily can lead to
overexposure of the athlete, which will make the messages they communicate
less credible. Overexposure is noted when it becomes too obvious that the
celebrities are being paid to endorse the message, and the public can become
very sceptical.

Sportview 10.1 gives examples of these considerations.

MARKETING MICHAEL

SPORTVIEW
10.1

According to *Forbes* magazine, in 1995 Michael Jordan received more than
$US40 million for endorsing such products as Nike basketball shoes, Big Macs,
Gatorade, cars for Chicago-area Chevy dealers, basketballs for Wilson, lottery
tickets for the state of Illinois, calendars, school supplies and greeting cards
for Cleo, underwear for Hanes and Oakley sunglasses (part of this deal with
Oakley was a seat on the board). 'His alignment with Wheaties is so strong
that the cereal's manufacturer, General Foods, has printed a special edition
Wheaties box with Jordan and the Chicago Bulls on the cover. When the Bulls
won the NBA title in June 1996, Michael Jordan Wheaties boxes were in
supermarkets within hours. It seems Wheaties needs Jordan more than he needs
the cereal. Its share of the US$7.9 billion ready-to-eat cereal market is only
1.6%. The idea of having to do without Jordan is a nightmare for General
Foods. Jordan's endorsement power, which barely waned during his two
seasons of retirement, continues to grow. "Forbes" estimates that since 1990,
when he started getting major product endorsements, he has earned $170
million as a "pitch man".' (Hay 1996, p. 18)

'David Falk, Jordan's marketing agent from ProServ says, "we haven't
packaged Michael Jordan, we have done a good job exposing who he is and
what he is to corporate decision makers. Once they saw what he was firsthand,
the rest flowed from there". It was clear from the beginning that Jordan was a
made-for-the-media athlete. He had natural ability to communicate, to provide
intelligent answers to questions, to delicately handle the tough questions. The
1984 Olympic gold medal enhanced Jordan's image as an all-American kid,
and unlike other Olympic heroes, his star only has risen from there. His
visibility was a key factor in reversing the declining fortunes of the NBA in the
1980s and when Nike and Jordan developed the first Air Jordan basketball
shoes, Jordan told his former roommate at the University of North Carolina to
"better get some Nike stock; they are going to make a shoe for me, these Air
Jordans, and someday it's going to be worth a lot of money". At Nike the
director of design, after releasing the Air Jordan No. 6 says, "one of the things

about Michael Jordan is we can take incredible risks in the product because his wearing them validates it. The fact that Michael Jordan is wearing this plain-toed shoe will make it all right for a lot of people".

'Jordan's fame presents him with a range of moral dilemmas. In 1989, kids began murdering one another for the $115 sneakers that bore his name. Jordan was first informed about sneaker violence by Sports Illustrated reporter Rick Telander, whose May 14, 1990, cover story "senseless" helped focus attention and sharpen debate on the issue. "I thought I'd be helping out others and everything would be positive", a visibly shaken Jordan told Telander. "I thought people would try to emulate the good things I do, they'd try to achieve, to do better. Nothing bad. It is kind of ironic, though, that the press builds people like me up to be a role model and then blames us for the unfortunate crimes kids are committing".

'Although Jordan's image has suffered some minor damage in 1993, when rumours regarding selfishness, aloofness and serious gambling problems surfaced, David Falk remains confident his client will remain among the few celebrity legends, who will not lose their public appeal. Although Michael will lose the principal platform from which he addresses the public, he will not fade into obscurity. "It is assumed that when you stop playing the impact dramatically goes away. Quickly because you are not in the public eye. In his case I don't think that is going to be the situation at all. I think he is going to be very much before the public eye, and he is still going to be doing Nike commercials and other commercials".' (Naughton 1992, pp. 11–29)

Sources: Excerpts from Hay (1996, p. 18) and Naughton (1992, pp. 11–29).

THE INTEGRATED MARKETING APPROACH

Earlier in this chapter we presented figures on sport sponsorship expenditure, estimated to reach $650 million in 1995. Broadcast sponsorship and back-up promotions pushed this figure over the $1 billion mark. In other words, over 30% of the total expenditure on sport sponsorship is spent on broadcast and back-up promotions! *Sponsorship support activities* complement the sponsor's goals. Given the sponsorship framework, the sponsee can either supply support activities or participate in support activities in order to increase the value of the sponsorship for the sponsor. Examples of different sponsorship support activities are given below. Fuji Xerox Australia, as an Olympic sponsor, will serve as a case example, presented from the sponsor's point of view.

Sponsorship support activities

A personal letter *(direct mail)* notified business relations that on 5 September 1995 Fuji Xerox Australia would host a special Olympic *event* in the central business district of Melbourne. The media were informed through a press release *(publicity)*, and around 400 general managers and marketing managers of a variety of organisations were invited to the Victorian Arts Centre to witness and participate in Fuji Xerox's Olympic sponsorship launch. A well-organised introductory show, in which the Olympic flame was lit, led into a *video presentation* of Australia's Olympic achievements throughout the years. The motivator of the Australian Olympic team, Mr Laurie Lawrence, followed the video presentation and entertained the crowd with sport stories in which the importance of teamwork was stressed. Fuji Xerox's marketing manager then highlighted his organisation's commitment to the Olympic team, enabling Australian athletes to represent their country. Four Olympic athletes were honoured and awarded before a variety of new Fuji Xerox products were introduced. Guests were invited to take drinks and food after the formal presentation and to see the new products in action in the different demonstration areas *(personal selling)*. Different Olympic prizes were given away by the present Olympic athletes, and every guest deciding to buy Fuji Xerox products in the following weeks automatically entered the draw for a trip to the Atlanta Games in 1996 *(sales promotion)*. Opportunities for interviews and photo sessions were given after the event *(public relations)*. In the months following the Olympic launch several *television commercials* and newspaper *advertisements* backed up the Olympic sponsor involvement of Fuji Xerox.

Sponsoring (inter)nationally but making it work locally

Cousens and Slack (1996) state that sport sponsorship can be a very effective tool to enhance corporate image at the (inter)national level. However, consumer awareness of the fact that McDonald's was the sponsor of the 1994 World Cup of the World Soccer Federation (FIFA) might not have been enough to strengthen consumer demand at the local level. McDonald's franchisees needed to have the opportunity to leverage the sponsorship to make it work in their local store. For example, McDonald's, as the sole retail sponsor of the World Cup, was able to feature the games in its restaurants. It organised local franchise-backed soccer tournaments and hosted local McKicks mobile soccer clinics. Although optional for franchisees, these local tie-in promotions proved to be very successful in increasing sales, developing relationships with the local community and targeting new market segments. Smaller sponsorships (e.g. the local bakery sponsoring the local hockey club) can be leveraged according to the same principle, tie-in promotions making customers aware of the association between sponsor and sponsee.

The above examples show the importance of leveraging the sponsorship through support activities and tie-in promotions. If sponsorship is seen as a single, separate tool, benefits resulting from it will be much less. Leveraging the sponsorship is as much in the interest of the sporting organisation as it is in the interest of the sponsor. An unsuccessful sponsorship deal is less likely to be renewed, leaving the sporting organisation without a sponsor.

When the sporting organisation is able to supply or participate in support activities, sponsorship will more successfully operate as part of the total promotion and marketing plan. This ultimately will lead to a win-win situation.

To distinguish a win situation from a not-win situation, it is important for the sport marketer to measure the effectiveness of sponsorship.

MEASURING SPONSORSHIP EFFECTIVENESS

How effective a sponsorship is or has been depends on the goals the sponsor and sponsee have set before they enter the sponsorship agreement. The Ford Motor Company has different goals sponsoring the Australian Open Tennis Championships, compared to sponsoring Formula 1 races. The first goal is awareness related, whereas the second goal is more related to direct sales. How the publics perceive the association between the sponsor and sponsee determines what can be measured as the effect of the sponsorship. If, for example, the public only links the name of the sponsor to the event, and do not change their buying behaviour, it makes little sense to measure after-sponsorship sales. In this section, it is assumed that the overall effectiveness of the sponsorship is based on the achievement of the sponsor's goals. Achievement of sponsee goals are partly met at the agreement of the sponsorship (i.e. receiving funds, goods or services). Other goals, like brand positioning, can be measured in a similar fashion to the sponsor's goals.

Hansen and Scotwin (1995) identify four levels of measuring sponsorship effectiveness:

- exposure,
- attention,
- cognition, and
- behaviour.

Exposure is the broadest measure of sponsorship effectiveness. It measures how many times (in seconds on television, or number of columns and photographs in print media) an organisation or brand is observable. Television exposure, for example, is measured by multiplying seconds by the number of viewers; hence exposure is expressed in 'exposure per 1000 viewers in 30 seconds'. Exposure value can be compared with advertising value by multiplying seconds (30) by advertising rates for 30-second commercials. The resulting value presents the sponsor with the money figure that would have been paid had the sponsor invested the money in 30-second commercials.

Attention to a brand or an organisation can be measured in terms of changes in recall or recognition by individual target-market members. Recall is the more powerful measure of effectiveness in that research subjects are not aided in recalling sponsors' names. In recognition, subjects are asked to choose from a list of possible sponsors. The benchmark for attention measures has to be the recall or recognition measure *before* entering the sponsorship agreement. Otherwise, changes in recall or recognition cannot be measured.

Cognitive effects also can be measured in individuals who are part of the target market(s) of the sponsor. The association between a car manufacturer and a car-racing event evokes a stronger cognitive effect than the association between a car manufacturer and a tennis event. The *car* manufacturer—*car* race link is logical and requires little explanation. The car manufacturer-tennis event link is expected to evoke a more general association and tries to link the image of the event to the image of the car. Both effects are often measured in associative tests. In the example given, the Australian Open, the question 'Which sponsors do you associate with this event?' can be asked.

The most direct measure of sponsorship effectiveness is buying *behaviour.* What are the effects of the sponsorship on the sales figures or turnover of the organisation, or the sales figures of certain product lines? In this case, the benchmark for measurement has to be set *before* the sponsorship. Behavioural measurement of sponsorship has often been criticised because of the difficulties in isolating the effects of sponsorship on sales and turnover from those of other promotion mix tools.

Measurement of sponsorship effectiveness is a difficult issue. How effectiveness is measured strongly depends on the goals of the sponsor, and even then many variables can influence effectiveness. One of the most important variables to influence sponsorship effectiveness is ambush marketing.

Ambush marketing

The Australian Trade Practices Act defines *ambush marketing* under Section 53 as follows: 'Ambush marketing occurs where a business markets its goods or services in a way which suggests that the business has a connection with a team, event or a competition, where there is in fact no connection.'

Ambush marketing is a problem for the sponsor in that funds or services are invested in an association with a sporting organisation of which non-investing organisations reap the benefits. Ambush marketing is a problem for the sponsee in that the effectiveness of the sponsorship will diminish and a prolonged business relationship with the sponsor will be put in jeopardy. More and more, sponsors are demanding that sponsees take precautions to prevent ambush marketing. In servicing the sponsor, sponsees should therefore take a *proactive* stance in preparing for potential 'ambushers'.

A proactive strategy can consist of the following actions:

- identification of potential ambushers (they often are potential sponsors the sporting organisation did not sign up);
- identification of the commercial value of the sponsorship (which benefits can the sponsee deliver, and how can potential ambushers obtain these benefits without being involved as an official sponsor);
- detailed contracts (including exclusivity rights, detailed descriptions of

what is being considered as conflicting signage/advertising, sponsor/sponsee obligations to prevent ambush marketing); and

■ joint sponsor/sponsee counteract strategies (which determine how sponsor and sponsee will react in terms of public relations, advertising or public appearances when commenting on an ambusher's actions).

This is a limited and certainly not complete list of actions to prevent ambushers from taking advantage of a sponsorship relationship. Although ambush marketing never can be eliminated, solid preparation can assist the sport marketer in servicing the sponsor to the best of their ability.

Sportview 10.2 is an example of ambush marketing during the 1988 Winter Olympics in Calgary, Canada.

<table>
<tr><td>SPORTVIEW
10.2</td><td>**AMBUSH MARKETING AT THE OLYMPICS**</td></tr>
</table>

'The Olympic Games attract global interest and can deliver tremendous exposure. Billions of spectators watched the combined 1988 Summer and Winter Olympics and many corporations would therefore like to benefit from the exposure of being associated directly or indirectly with the Olympic Games.

'Research evaluating the effectiveness of sponsorship and ambush marketing at the 1988 Olympic Winter Games investigated the recall and recognition of official sponsors, ambushers and other organisations. The large drawing power of the Olympics was evidenced by the fact that 82 percent of the people surveyed watched some part of the Olympic telecast. Of the respondents, 41.4 percent were light viewers (watched 1 to 4 days), 27.2 percent were moderate viewers (5 to 9 days) and 31.3 percent were heavy viewers (10 to 16 days).

'Overall, 20 percent of the respondents correctly recalled the official sponsors, with recall varying by product category: from 50 percent correct for credit cards to 7 percent for airlines. Recognition (choosing from a list with names) of sponsors was higher, with 39 percent of respondents correctly recognising official sponsors. Recognition also varied by product category, from a high of 59 percent for fast foods to 25 percent for hotels.

'To determine the effect of viewing the Olympic telecast on consumer perceptions, the three viewer groups were used to analyse sponsor awareness. The ability to both recognise and recall sponsors varied directly with viewership: light viewers averaged 18.9 percent correct recall, moderate viewers 33.5 percent and heavy viewers 37.5 percent. For recognition, the numbers ranged from 37 percent to 46 percent to 52.2 percent.

'Ambush marketers attempt to avoid the up-front high investment of sponsorship while gaining the glamour and benefits of an Olympic tie-in; their hope is that consumers associate their products with the Olympic Games and thus weaken any major advantage of their competitors who paid for official sponsorship. To determine the effect that ambushers had on sponsorship awareness, the number of correct sponsor identifications were compared with the number of ambushers as sponsors. Seven product categories, each with one official sponsor and one major ambusher, were chosen. The results for recall and recognition were aggregated. Across the overall sample an average of 2.57 official sponsors were correctly identified (out of possible 7). In comparison, on average 1.43 ambushers were identified as official sponsors. Ambushers were significantly less recognised as official sponsors.

'A closer look at these data by product category, however, leads to some interesting cautions for advertisers. In only four out of seven product categories studied were the correct official sponsors identified more than the non-sponsors (ambushers and others). In the other three cases the sponsor was not number one when it came to sponsor identification; in two of these three cases the official sponsors, while engaging in other promotional activities, were not major advertisers on the Olympic telecast, and in the third case (cars), the ambushers were engaged in very heavy advertising (Ford and Chrysler bought all available advertising time for domestic cars). This might indicate that to achieve any benefits from being a sponsor it is necessary not only for a company to sponsor an event such as the Olympics but to heavily advertise the fact that they are *official* sponsors. Buying the right to be an "official sponsor" may, in reality, only be buying a license to spend more money!'

Source: Excerpts from Sandler and Shani (1989, pp. 9–14).

SUMMARY

In this chapter, the strategic importance of sponsorship for sport organisations was shown. For both the sponsor and sponsee, sponsorship can be used to satisfy multiple goals, particularly advertising and public relations related for the sponsor and fundraising related for the sponsee. The relationship between the goals of the sponsor and sponsee were shown in the sponsorship framework for how to create win-win situations. Relationships between sponsor and sponsee can even lead to a strategic alliance between the two organisations. Sponsorship as a tool of the promotion mix is still increasing in popularity because it generally is seen as a cost-effective manner of achieving the sponsor's communication goals.

Because of the high visibility and attractiveness of sport as a communication medium, many sporting organisations tend to overemphasise the importance of sponsorship as a potential source of income. Sporting organisations should be aware that this 'sponsorship myopia' can lead to an under-usage of the other elements of the marketing mix in developing a broad-based marketing program. From the sponsor's point of view, sponsorship alone will not satisfy the communication goals set. A comprehensive set of sponsorship support activities and tie-in promotions is required to optimise the sponsorship effort and make the sponsorship as successful as possible in the overall marketing effort.

Sponsoring individual athletes has distinct advantages and disadvantages. The sponsor–athlete relationship is similar to the sponsor–sporting organisation relationship in that both involve mutual commitment and obligations. Sponsorship support activities need to be considered in both relationships, and even ambush-marketing practices are applicable to both the sponsored sporting organisation and the sponsored individual athlete.

CASE STUDY

ATTRACTING A NAMING SPONSOR FOR THE LOCAL BADMINTON CLUB

This case study is purely fictional. The persons and organisations in the case are non-existent.

Simon Huttle, president of the local badminton club, was enjoying an after-the-match mineral water with his fellow board member, Robert Acket. Simon was particularly pleased with himself, because he had won the match against his ten-years-younger treasurer.

Robert, being quite embarrassed about his loss, tried to direct the conversation away from their game, asking Simon, 'What's the state of affairs in renewing the contract with our current naming sponsor, Simon?'

Simon's smile disappeared. 'Two weeks ago I got the news that they're not willing to renew. They'll cease the agreement at the end of this financial year. I wanted to wait till our board meeting tomorrow night to tell you this, but now you're asking . . .'

'Why?' Robert responded in a sudden state of shock. 'We've done everything we can to make them happy. Their name is on the racquets, we tell our members to fill up their cars with their fuel, and we invited their local employees to our general assembly. And how can we possibly field a team in the regional competition without the support of a naming sponsor?'

'Well, I was going to ask you that question, Rob. You're the treasurer. You should be able to answer that question better than me. But for your information, a friend of mine is in the advertising business. His name is Jim Beam and his company has been involved in sport sponsorship as well. I've asked him to prepare an outline for a sponsorship proposal. He'll present it tomorrow night.'

Disappointed with this news on top of his earlier loss, Robert drank his water and grabbed his gear. 'Well, catch you tomorrow night then,' he said and went home.

Question 1: Given your knowledge of sponsorship after reading this chapter, can you detect any information explaining why the sponsor decided to cease the agreement?

When Robert drove home, he tried to think of reasons why an affluent sponsor like theirs would choose not to continue the very pleasant relationship they had built through the years. He decided to prepare some questions to ask Jim during the board meeting tomorrow night.

When Robert arrived at the board meeting the next night, his colleagues and Jim Beam were already there. Simon welcomed Robert and started the meeting.

'Welcome, fellow board members. As you can see I've invited a guest tonight. I'd like to welcome Jim Beam from A. M. Bush Advertising. I have a special reason for inviting him. Two weeks ago our sponsor for five years gave me a call to tell me that unfortunately they were not in the position to continue their association with our club.'

'What!' Pamela Rush, the secretary, cried out. 'They can't do that. And by the way, why didn't you tell us earlier, Simon?'

Simon ignored her second question and continued introducing Jim. 'I've asked Jim to prepare an outline for a sponsorship proposal, in order to prepare ourselves as soon as possible and find a new sponsor for the new season.'

'You still haven't answered my question, Simon,' Pamela interrupted. She rephrased her second question.

Question 2: By telling the other board members earlier, could they have done other things before calling in the advertising expert?

'I don't know, Pamela,' Simon responded, slightly irritated, 'but the fact is that we have a problem, and I took the liberty to initiate action to solve it!'

Robert came to Simon's rescue by asking Jim what he thought of the situation. Simon looked gratefully in Robert's direction for a moment and finished his introduction of Jim. 'Can you present us your suggested sponsorship proposal outline Jim?'

'Yes, thank you, Simon, for your kind words and your invitation . . . Dear board members, the outline I will present to you is very brief. I deliberately left blank spaces in order to give you the opportunity to actively contribute. Every heading of the outline is accompanied by one example,' Jim said.

Question 3: Contribute examples and possibilities in the context of your organisation for every heading in Jim's outline:

Suggested sponsorship proposal outline

- Executive summary.
- Organisation/event/athlete history and present situation
  — achievements of the club in the competition they played in.
- Target audiences (for sponsor and sponsee)
  — sponsee target audience: families with young children.
- Sponsorship track record
  — five years of successful sponsorship with last sponsor.
- Period of association for the proposed sponsorship
  — a period of three years with annual options to renew after that.

■ Benefits on offer
   — sponsor's name on the racquet.
■ Benefit valuation (capitalisation)
   — sponsor's name on the racquet of all teams: $1000.
■ Packages
   — signage package: court 1, 2 signage, sponsor's name on first-team shirts.
■ Sponsorship support activities
   — local paper advertising.
■ Ambush prevention strategy
   — exclusive sponsor rights.
■ Effectiveness measurement
   — recall measurement among members.

Question 4: Are there any elements missing in this outline? Are the listed elements presented in the right order?

Robert decided that it was about time he asked one of the questions he had prepared on the way home yesterday. He was wondering how they could avoid contracting a sponsor with whom there obviously wasn't a 'fit'. He still could not figure out why the current sponsorship did not work out.

'Jim, why do you think our sponsor wasn't interested in continuing the relationship?' Robert asked.

'That's a good and vital question, Robert. I think we are dealing with a classic case of incongruity of goals.'

'Can you explain that in plain English?' Robert responded.

'Of course. Both the sponsor and the badminton club have certain goals they want to achieve with the sponsorship, right? Well, in this particular case, it's likely that the sponsor was able to satisfy your goal, which was supplying you with an amount of money, but the club wasn't able to let the sponsor effectively communicate with their potential clients', Jim said.

'Effectively, in that other organisations or events were more related to their products?' Pamela contributed.

'Exactly!' Jim said. Pamela smiled in Simon's direction and Jim continued. 'By linking the sponsor goals to tangible benefits, you, as an organisation looking for sponsors, can identify whether you're in the position to supply the desired benefits. If this is the case you have prepared a potential "fit" between your organisation and the sponsor. In other words, you need to do a bit of work before you send out proposals!'

'But Jim, if we go through all of this, and we actually have a sponsor, how can we make sure we hang on to that sponsor?' Sandy Mash, the vice president of the club, involved herself in the discussion.

'You mean, how can we increase the value of the sponsorship?' Jim replied. Sandy nodded and Jim grabbed an overhead and put it on the projector. 'Here are a few hints how you can do this, Sandy. The list is not complete, but it is a helpful tool in intensifying the relation with your sponsor.'

The overhead showed the following list:

How to increase the value of a sponsorship

- Keep the sponsor informed.
- Remain informed about the sponsor.
- Promote the sponsor in the organisation and develop a sponsor culture.
- Create media alliances and involve the sponsor in them.
- Offer exclusivity.
- Maintain personal contact with the sponsor.
- Deliver *more* than promised.
- Acknowledge the sponsor in all communication.

'I want to suggest the following,' Jim Beam said to the board members. 'I've given you some information now.'

Question 5: Follow Jim's suggestions and take some time to prepare a draft proposal for your club, directed to a sponsor that fits your organisation.

'I think that's a good idea, Jim,' Simon said. 'Let's close the meeting here. I invite you all for drinks, and to meet again next week to discuss our proposals.'

The rest of the meeting agreed, and after thanking Jim Beam, they went off to the bar to enjoy a good whisky.

REFERENCES

Belch, G. E. and Belch, M. A. (1995). *Introduction to Advertising and Promotion: an Integrated Marketing Communications Perspective*, Irwin, Homewood, Ill.

Cousens, L. and Slack, T. (1996). 'Using sport sponsorship to penetrate local markets: the case of the fast food industry', *Journal of Sport Management*, 10 (2), pp. 169–87.

Hansen, F. and Scotwin, L. (1995). 'An experimental inquiry into sponsoring: what effects can be measured?', in *Advertising, Sponsorship and Promotions: Understanding and Measuring the Effectiveness of Commercial Communication*, ESOMAR, Amsterdam, pp. 65–82.

Hay, D. (1996). 'Jordan plays the money game', *Sunday Age*, 26 May, p. 18.

Kyriakopoulos, V. (1995). 'Big players pay the game', *The Bulletin*, 27 June, pp. 76–7.

Lyall, S. (1995). 'Cause and effect', *Sponsorship and Events News*, May, p. 24.

Lynch, M. (1996). 'Advertisers take $600m sports punt', *The Age*, 8 July.

McGeoch, R. and Korporaal, G. (1994). *The Bid: How Australia Won the 2000 Games*, William Heinemann, Melbourne.

Naughton, J. (1992). 'Marketing Michael: the making of a commercial superstar', *Washington Post Magazine*, 9 February, pp. 11–29.

Richardson, N. (1994). 'Sport's great sell out', *The Bulletin*, 11 October, pp. 100–3.

Sandler, D. M. and Shani, D. (1989). 'Olympic sponsorship vs. "Ambush" marketing: who gets the gold?', *Journal of Advertising Research*, August/September, pp. 9–14.

Sleight, S. (1989). *Sponsorship: What Is It and How to Use It*, McGraw-Hill, Sydney.

Wilmshurst, J. (1993). *Below-the-line Promotion*, Butterworth/Heinemann, Oxford.

11

Public relations

CHAPTER OUTLINE

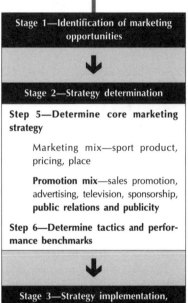

Stage 1—Identification of marketing opportunities

⬇

Stage 2—Strategy determination

Step 5—Determine core marketing strategy

Marketing mix—sport product, pricing, place

Promotion mix—sales promotion, advertising, television, sponsorship, **public relations and publicity**

Step 6—Determine tactics and performance benchmarks

⬇

Stage 3—Strategy implementation, evaluation and adjustment

Chapter 11 introduces public relations as an element of the sport promotion mix. The public relations process, applied both proactively and reactively, is examined in this chapter. This chapter notes how sporting organisations have been required to take a more active role in managing their public relations. How to execute a public relations program is discussed by examining the various stages of communicating with different media. Special attention is paid to publicity as an important component of the overall public relations strategy.

After studying this chapter you should be able to:

1   Identify critical activities of the public relations process.
2   Create an extensive list of sporting organisation publics.
3   Distinguish between proactive and reactive public relations strategies.
4   Link the public relations strategy to the promotion and marketing strategy.
5   Develop a comprehensive set of public relations actions in order to generate publicity.

SOLVING THE CRISIS?

Australia's favourite sportswoman, Samantha Riley, faces the ruin of her international swimming career today after giving a positive drug test late last year. Australian Swimming confirmed last night that world breaststroke champion Riley, 22, took a headache tablet which contained a banned drug, dextropropoxyphene, two days before she competed at the world short course championships in Brazil last December. (Jeffery 1996a, p. 1)

Almost daily, news like this appears in the papers or is broadcast on television or radio. Sporting organisations or athletes without problems are rare. Perhaps sporting organisations have more problems than other organisations, but more likely the reason is their high visibility in society. This chapter deals with the management function of public relations, showing how public relations can be helpful in solving a crisis, such as the Samantha Riley example. It will also be shown that public relations can be used in a planned and positive way.

As introduced in Chapters 1 and 7, public relations is one element of the promotion mix. Many people show considerable interest in the fortunes of sporting organisations and their athletes. A high interest results in a high visibility, and therefore sporting organisations have relations with many publics. A *public* is a group of people who share an evaluation about specific problems or issues. This justifies special attention to public relations in the context of the sport industry. Being part of the promotion mix, public relations deals with communicating with the target audiences, or better, publics of the organisation. To understand better how, when and with whom to communicate, it is first necessary to define the concept.

DEFINING PUBLIC RELATIONS

Griswold (1995) defines *public relations* as:

> . . . the management function which evaluates public attitudes, identifies the policies and procedures of an individual or an organisation with the public interest, and plans and executes a program of action to earn public understanding and acceptance. (p. 7)

Three critical activities can be derived from this definition:

- evaluating public attitudes;
- identifying the policies and procedures of an individual or an organisation with the public interest; and
- planning and executing a program of action.

These three activities will form the basis for this chapter.

EVALUATING PUBLIC ATTITUDES

In Chapter 4 we discussed the process of *marketing research*. Marketing research techniques are also used in identifying and evaluating the attitudes that publics have about the sporting organisation, its products and its employees (often the athletes). In order to communicate effectively, however, it is important not only to identify public attitudes, but also to convey these attitudes to management of the organisation. Management can then adjust organisational strategies to more effectively influence publics attitudes. If, for example, the local soccer club is suddenly losing members, attitudinal research might find that members and supporters did not understand why the club decided to sell the league's top scorer to a rival club and therefore decided to cease their memberships. With this information, management of the soccer club could put public relations strategies in place to increase members' understanding pertaining to this decision.

Public relations objectives and their relationship to promotion and marketing objectives

Because public relations is part of the promotion mix, and the promotion mix part of the marketing mix, it is obvious that marketing objectives are the basis for both promotion and public relations objectives. Returning to the soccer example, one of the club's marketing objectives might be to increase memberships by 10% in the next year. A promotion objective to support the marketing objective could be to sign up at least fifteen new youth members during a weekend shopping-mall promotion. This objective could more easily be achieved if the club has a favourable image over three other soccer clubs in the area. A public relations objective therefore could be to become the preferred soccer club in the area with 75% of the population. If this percentage were not reached (e.g. as a result of selling the top scorer), a public relations program of action could help the promotion and marketing activities to become more successful.

In general, the following broad public relations objectives can be formulated to support promotion and marketing objectives:

- earning understanding and acceptance for organisational activities;
- explaining certain behaviour;
- educating and informing publics;
- raising awareness for the organisation or new products;
- creating trust (in the organisation or its products); and
- creating goodwill.

These objectives show that most public relations objectives, and hence activities, will not be aimed directly at increasing sales or, in the soccer example, increasing memberships. Linked with the other marketing functions in the organisation, public relations becomes part of an integrated marketing approach. This integrated approach should lead to a more efficient and effective achievement of overall marketing objectives.

To know where to start, the organisation needs to be aware of public opinion about the organisation and its product range.

Public opinion

Evaluating public attitudes has been defined above as one of the critical activities of the public relations function. Seitel (1995) defines an *attitude* as 'an evaluation people make about specific problems or issues' (p. 52). A *public* then is a group of people who share an evaluation about specific problems or issues. When certain group attitudes become important and strong enough, they turn into *opinions*. Opinions about certain issues can lead to *behaviour*. It is the opinion of the larger public that influences the buying behaviour of target markets.

Consider the following example by Rhoden (1993):

> By the summer of 1993, Michael Jordan, the most widely recognised athlete in the world had begun to develop serious public opinion problems. After leading the U.S. Dream Team to an Olympic victory and then his Chicago Bulls to an unprecedented third straight National Basketball Association title, Jordan was the focus of nasty rumours regarding selfishness, aloofness, and serious gambling problems. Then, late in the summer of 1993, tragedy struck. Jordan's father, James, was found murdered in his car. The nation mourned with Michael. Scarcely two months later, in the midst of major league baseball's playoffs, Michael Jordan stunned the world by announcing his retirement from basketball. The news was so jarring that President Clinton even took time out to address a statement of support to Michael. In the space of one traumatic quarter of the year, Michael Jordan's public opinion ratings had rebounded from questionable to sky high. (p. B11)

It was in the commercial interest of the multiple organisations that Michael Jordan was associated with to turn around the negative public opinion. Not many people in cities other than Chicago will become season ticket holders of the Chicago Bulls (they are a public, not a target market), but their opinion about Jordan and hence the Chicago Bulls will influence Chicago citizens to affiliate with the Bulls. Not many senior citizens will consider drinking Gatorade (a sport drink endorsed by Jordan) because Jordan does (they are a public, not a target market), but their opinion about Jordan will influence young people in their decision to drink Gatorade.

In other words, public opinion highly influences the buying behaviour of target markets and therefore becomes one of the primary areas of public relations activity. Reinforcing existing positive public opinions and changing negative public opinions are the underlying aims of all public relations strategies. Depending on marketing objectives and public opinion, certain publics will become the target audience for public relations activities.

Publics of sporting organisations

In previous chapters the term *target market* was used to define the group of people towards whom marketing activities are directed. Target market implies a focus on exchange between the sporting organisation and its customers. It was shown in the previous section that publics have a much wider scope. The Michael Jordan example showed that the public at large can be the target audience of public relations activities, without being a target market. In other cases, such as a product recall after a manufacturing mistake, the target market may be the target audience as well. Often, public relations activities will go beyond direct communication with the target market, aiming to influence positively the wider public opinion.

Jefkins (1994, p. 97) lists the following basic publics that apply to most organisations:

- the community,
- potential employees,
- employees,
- suppliers of services and materials,
- the money market,
- distributors,
- consumers and users,
- opinion leaders.

Jefkins shows that the public at large, organisational members, organisational stakeholders and customers of the organisation are all potential target audiences of the public relations function. These four headings are used in Table 11.1 to identify a range of more specific publics, most common for sporting organisations. Table 11.1 expands on Figure 2.4 in Chapter 2, where the publics of a professional sport club were identified.

TABLE 11.1	Public at large	Organisational members	Organisational stakeholders	Customers
Publics of sporting organisations	Television representatives Radio representatives Written media representatives Local community National community Global community Educators Schoolchildren	Voting members Voluntary workforce Voluntary board Professional administrative workforce Professional playing workforce Coaches Recruiting officers	Investors, lenders Sponsors Licensees Sport-governing bodies Local government National government Grassroots sporting organisations	Spectating members Sponsors Fan club members Merchandise customers Corporate guests Casual visitors Television audience Radio audience Newspaper audience

When the publics of a sporting organisation are identified, and the sport marketer has knowledge about their opinions, the policies and procedures of the organisation can be linked to the public interest.

LINKING POLICIES AND PROCEDURES WITH THE PUBLIC INTEREST

How can an organisation create a fit between what it does and what its publics are interested in? If people are not interested in buying an organisation's products, can it at least make sure that they have a favourable perception of the organisation? These are questions that need to be answered when trying to act, in a positive way, as perceived by the publics. The organisation can do this in a planned, proactive way but sometimes is forced to do this in a reactive way. Examples of both are given in the following sections. How far an organisation can go in manipulating public opinion is discussed under ethics, and then media relations, as one of the most important relationships to foster, are considered.

Proactive public relations: Why do we do the things we do?

Proactive public relations can be defined as the planned effort to influence public attitudes in order to create favourable opinions. Creating favourable opinions in order to increase sales, to enhance an image or to raise awareness for the organisation can all be the broad objectives of proactive public relations. Sportview 11.1 is an example of a proactive public relations campaign in which raising awareness for a new product was the aim of the campaign, supporting the marketing goal of increasing sales of the product. The product launch is a good example of proactive public relations. As an integrated part of the overall marketing efforts of an organisation, it supports the achievement of marketing objectives.

Sport, however, is much more familiar with reactive public relations.

THE GREAT DUNLOP SQUASH RACQUET

'One good example of pro-active product public relations is the launch of the Dunlop MAX 550G squash racquet in the autumn of 1985. It was the latest in the Dunlop range of racquets—of which there were a dozen or so—and, consequently, it had to be made to stand out from the rest as well as from the competition, especially to justify its premium pricing position.

'All the usual advertising and point-of-sale activities were planned with a substantial launch budget. This was all fine as far as it went. However, it was important to address the large body of keen squash players (there are about two million players in the UK alone) who would not necessarily be exposed to this campaign. So we decided to mount a regional press launch, partly because local papers are a great place to sell consumer goods and partly because the specialist squash media is very restricted.

'The problem here was that there was very little reason for regional newspapers to write about a new squash racquet which had little local or national news interest. Somebody introduces new racquets every five minutes and they all look much the same—and play in much the same way as well—true "me too" products.

'So, we decided to use the services of Dunlop Slazenger's best-known retained squash player, Jonah Barrington, to host a series of press launches at prestigious squash clubs throughout the UK—Canons in London, the Priory in Birmingham and the Village in Manchester. By this means we were able to invite literally hundreds of journalists all within a couple of hours travel of the venues.

'The evening began with a brief (five minutes) presentation on the background to the squash racquet market so that the journalists were given the context in which the product was being launched and the strength of the Dunlop brand in that market (over 40 per cent).

'The squash manager then described the properties of the MAX 550G and especially the benefits of the high technology design with its hollow, carbon fibre frame. He introduced a seven minute video—also featuring Jonah—illustrating these properties. After this, journalists had the opportunity to ask questions and discuss the main issues before Jonah gave one of his famous clinics.

'In this, he talked very entertainingly about squash in general for about an hour, illustrating some of his points with a hapless, volunteer guinea pig player (who received a free racquet for his pains). Then Jonah rounded off the evening with an exhibition match against a well-known local player, usually the unfortunate local squash club professional (Jonah likes to win his exhibition matches). A buffet gave further opportunity for discussion until the small hours.

'The venues were packed at each session and the resulting regional coverage was very satisfactory. Much of the expenditure was being incurred in any case (the video was produced for clubs and retailers, for instance), but the entire cost was not more than a fraction of the launch advertising and promotional budgets. It was a drop in the ocean for a product which became by far the best selling squash racquet in the UK with three months of launch.

'The cost (which was less than £3,000 for each occasion) included all the press releases and photographs, invitations, hospitality and catering, hire of venues, Jonah's fee, travel and subsistence as well as a few free racquets. The evenings were enjoyable and successful and helped to forge stronger links with the clubs and the public as well as the press. It was a classic example of the product launch.'

Source: Excerpt from Greener (1990, pp. 6–8).

Reactive public relations: Why have we done the things we've done?

Reactive public relations actions are put in place when unplanned events occur that negatively influence the attitudes of the organisation's publics. Preventing the problem is always better than fixing the problem, but sometimes even careful planning does not prevent things from happening. Sporting organisations and their athletes receive high attention from the media and hence are more likely than other organisations or persons to become involved in crisis situations. This chapter's opening example presented the news of the positive drug test of Australian swimming star Samantha Riley. Sportview 11.2 is an example of reactive public relations by this athlete, her coach and her legal adviser. Notice the support they seek from powerful organisations in their efforts to change around their fortunes.

SPORTVIEW 11.2

RILEY FACING DRUGS BAN

Australia's best gold medal hope Samantha Riley may be suspended for the Atlanta Olympic Games after giving a positive drug test. World record holder Riley tested positive at the world short course championships in Rio de Janeiro, Brazil last December for a banned drug contained in a headache tablet. The punishment could range from a warning to a two-year ban. And her coach Scott Volkers could also be suspended, which would leave the country's swimming squad in disarray. Riley, a four-time world champion is understood to be devastated by the incident, which casts a pall over her stellar international career. She is expected to make a public statement today. (Jeffery 1996b, p. 24)

Riley, who believed she had taken a Panadol containing no banned substances, commented that she could not think of anything worse than being banned for two years.

Riley's coach, Scott Volkers said that in the 'biggest error of my career', he gave Riley a tablet that had been in the bottom of his bag for three years, that had previously been prescribed to his wife for headaches. 'Sam had had seven days of headaches and we had exhausted all avenues'. (Magnay 1996, p. B12)

Riley was accompanied by her coach and her lawyer, Peter Baston, when she spoke at a news conference in Brisbane:

> 'Obviously I'm devastated. I support FINA (the international swimming body) 100 per cent in their fight to eradicate drugs . . . it's getting harder to get the cheats. But on the other hand I am not a cheat and I have never cheated. I hope I have a fair trial and that they will see that what has happened to me is an innocent mistake. It is not a performance enhancing drug at all. I've been outspoken, my opinion on steroids hasn't changed . . . I still want to do everything I can to fight steroids. My drug is not performance enhancing. I think two years is not fair for a headache tablet.' (Jeffery 1996b, p. 24)

> It was commented by Baston after he met the FINA executive in Berlin, that the more time it took the executive to decide, the better it would be for Riley. He also said that the Australian Olympic Committee and the IOC had been sympathetic to Riley's case and had given him access to files of three unreported cases of innocent doping.
>
> About swimming in the Atlanta Olympics, Riley said: 'it's my view I deserve to be there and I have proved myself over the past few years'. (Magnay 1996, p. B12)

It can be argued that a crisis, like a positive drug test, can be expected and prepared for. During major events like the Olympic Games, national sporting bodies know that the chances of athletes being caught using banned drugs are much higher. How can a sporting organisation employ a proactive public relations strategy in preparing for a crisis situation? The case study at the end of this chapter describes an organisation preparing for a crisis. Sporting organisations cannot always prevent a crisis from happening, but anticipation and preparation will reduce the damage.

Ethics

Seitel (1995) defines an individual's or organisation's *ethics* as the 'standards that are followed in relationships with others—the real integrity of the individual or organisation' (p. 121). If one of the most important goals of the public relations function is to enhance public trust in an organisation, clearly the public relations professional must act in an honest and trustworthy manner. Linking the policies and procedures of the organisation to the public interest means that no other organisation or individual should be harmed by the actions of the organisation. Spreading rumours about rival athletes or clubs not based on facts, to enhance one's own image is therefore unethical behaviour. Bribing the media to report favourably on important issues is also unethical behaviour. Much can be written about this topic. The bottom line is that, in the interest of the publics and the organisation, honest information and genuine procedures will benefit most in both the short and long run.

Media relations

Earlier in this chapter it was shown that public opinion is one of the most important forces influencing the buying behaviour of publics of sporting organisations. It is the task of the sport marketer to influence the public opinion in order to create a favourable image of the sporting organisation. In this decade of globalisation and booming communications technology, the media, communicating to a global mass audience, are unequivocally the most powerful means of influencing the public opinion. This is both good and bad for sporting organisations: good because, as we will discuss later in this chapter, sporting organisations receive a lot of free publicity; bad because the content and timing of this free publicity cannot be controlled. This makes sporting organisations dependent on the media.

This dependency, however, can be managed to a certain extent. This is done through fostering media relations. To create and maintain favourable media relations, three actions are important to consider:

- form,
- inform,
- informal.

Depending on the type of sporting organisation and its strategies, certain media channels are more important than others. The local tennis club, for example, will benefit more from local newspaper coverage and local radio, whereas a Grand Slam tennis tournament will need global television and newspaper coverage to satisfy sponsor needs. That is why a comprehensive *form* of potential media outlets has to be put together. This form, or media database, will enable the sport marketer to *inform* the media. This is done through formal channels, but communication may also be successful if *informal* communication can be developed with media representatives. Different ways of how to form, inform and be informal are now discussed.

PLANNING AND EXECUTING A PROGRAM OF ACTION

Once the sport marketer has identified the attitudes of the sporting organisation's publics, and thought of ways of linking their interest with the activities of the organisation, it is time to develop a program of action. With the media as one of the sport marketer's most powerful means of communication, a large part of this section will be devoted to public relations communication through the media. To start this process, it is first necessary to know which media are available and how to get in contact with them.

Form—the media database

Helitzer (1995) lists three main sources that have to be included in the sporting organisation media database:

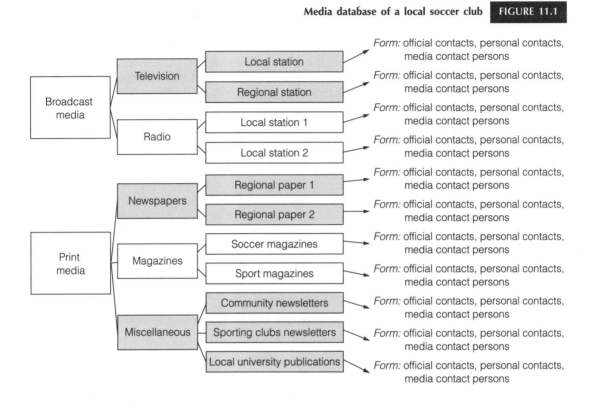

Media database of a local soccer club   FIGURE 11.1

- the media that routinely cover sport,
- personal contacts, and
- media directories.

These sources have to be categorised in a logical order. This is, the media outlets and contacts must be ordered according to the most relevant publics for individual sporting organisations. Contact persons and addresses are vital and should be updated regularly. A simple example of a media database of a small professional soccer club is presented in Figure 11.1. The different forms per media outlet can range from one or two contacts to several hundred!

Form—the communications plan

Planning communications is nothing more (and nothing less!) than putting together a plan of *what* to tell *which* media *when*. As previously discussed, proactive public relations communications should support the promotion and marketing goals of the sporting organisation. In relation to setting goals for the organisation, public relations action plans can be put together and, with the help of the database, distribution of information can be planned. Returning to the soccer example cited earlier in this chapter, when aiming to become the preferred soccer club in the area with 75% of the population, the local television station, regional newspaper 1 and community newsletters can be selected as the preferred media outlets. The local television station is targeted (once) for the finals at the end of the season, regional newspaper 1 is approached every week in relation to the weekend's results, and the community newsletters are targeted at least twice during the season in every suburb, with information about youth activities at the club. Simple planning boards can be used to create a comprehensive annual overview of planned communications.

Inform—the press release

Press releases, as a means of informing the media, can be used for long-term proactive, short-term proactive and reactive public relations. Many organisations issue press releases on any topic of interest for one or more of their publics. The main goal of the press release is to inform the publics through the media in the way the organisation wants. Hopefully, it will generate positive publicity for the sporting organisation or sport persons. An example of a press release is seen in Sportview 11.3.

A few standard rules apply to the format of press releases:

- Use a catching and informative short title.
- Present the backbone information in the first paragraphs. Answer the questions who, what, when, where, why and how.
- Put facts first. Give accurate information. Use correct grammar.
- Include the name and address of a contact person.
- Use current media contacts and addresses when sending the press release.
- State the source of the press release, and date it.

The major causes of rejection of some press releases are:

- limited reader interest;
- poorly written;
- conflicts with media outlet policies;
- hard to distinguish from advertising;
- material obviously faked or exaggerated;
- apparent inaccuracies in story;
- duplicates story previously used.

If an issue is important enough to create widespread media attention, a press release can be used to announce a press conference.

Inform—the press conference

A press conference presents the sporting organisation with the opportunity to inform all present media at once. Also, when media representatives consider the issue of the conference important enough to attend, it is very likely that

SHANE KELLY PRESS RELEASE

SPORTVIEW
11.3

WOODHOUSE MANAGEMENT PTY LTD
EVENT & SPORTS MANAGEMENT CONSULTANCY

9 August 1996
CYCLIST SHANE KELLY LAUNCHES FIVE YEAR SPONSORSHIP DEAL

World champion cyclist Shane Kelly, the man who tragically didn't get past the starting line in his gold medal race in Atlanta exactly two weeks ago, today launched a five year endorsement deal with Headgear Bicycle Helmets.

Kelly, the reigning world champion and world record holder in the kilometre time trial, was an unbackable favourite to take gold in the event which earned him a silver medal four years earlier in Barcelona.

Kelly's left foot slipped from the pedal as he started in Atlanta, effectively robbing him of what many believed was certain gold. To his credit, Kelly congratulated the winners, accepted all the blame for his mistake and earned the respect of all Australians with his dignified behaviour after the event.

Headgear managing director, Mr Dan Taylor, said Kelly displayed all the qualities that Australians love to identify with in his post race attitude.

'Shane is a quiet achiever, modest in victory and gracious in defeat,' said Taylor. 'While his Atlanta experience was nothing short of a tragedy, the way Shane carried himself in those minutes after the race showed what a great role model he is to all Australians. Shane has all the qualities we look for and that's why we want him involved with our company.'

Headgear today officially launched the first of a signature range of Shane Kelly bicycle helmets, with a unique head holster to ensure super fit and security.

Kelly leaves our shores again next Friday, flying to Manchester, England to defend his world title. While a win in England won't compare to an Olympic gold medal, Kelly sees the world championships as the start of his preparation for Sydney in 2000.

'I have unfinished business as far as the Olympic Games are concerned,' Kelly said.

For further enquiries, please contact Rob Woodhouse on (03) 2555 9999.

54 SPORT STREET, COLLINGWOOD, VICTORIA 3066, AUSTRALIA
TEL: 61 3 2555 9999 FAX: 61 3 2555 9998 MOBILE: 019 666 333

Source: Reprinted from Woodhouse Management (1996).

some kind of publicity will be the result. When the media attend, they often use the provided information. Conference organisers should realise that, besides printed publicity, photographs and audiovisual information also will be collected by the media. This has implications for who the spokesperson will be, how they will dress, and how and where the names and logos of sponsors and the organisation will be presented.

Helitzer (1995, pp. 180–1) states eleven reasons for sporting organisations to call a press conference:

- a major change in personnel;
- a major change in the status of a star player;
- an important event scheduled;
- a major investigation (e.g. into illegal drug use);
- a change in a major facility;
- award presentations;
- crisis developments;
- post-game interviews;
- the sport banquet speaker;
- the introduction of a new product;
- a new rule that is complex or controversial.

A press conference should only be called when the general public or specific publics of the sporting organisation are interested enough to be informed. One of the above reasons might be applicable to a sporting organisation. If, however, the people or issues involved are still insignificant to the public, the media will not show up and the unsuccessful press conference will only damage the reputation of the organisation.

Inform and informal—interviews

Both a press release and a press conference can serve as an invitation for interviews. Interviews are one-on-one contact opportunities in which disseminated information can be best controlled. The interviewee has the opportunity to tell only what they want to tell. However, conducting an interview and taking part in an interview are both skills in their own right. Poor preparation or failing to recognise an interviewer's leading questions can turn the opportunity into disaster for the organisation.

Helitzer (1995, p. 273) provides a list of the do's and don'ts of interviews:

- Don't permit off-the-record statements. Don't try to become a major part of the interview.
- Don't assume that every fact will be used.
- Don't complain if the result is not totally satisfactory.
- Do pick the best spokesperson.
- Do try to limit the subject to areas where your spokesperson is an authority.
- Do provide suggested quotes, anecdotes and statistics that can be used.

■   Do rehearse fully!
■   Do select the site where the spokesperson will be most comfortable.
■   Do provide the press with full background.
■   Do keep every promise to supply supplementary information.
■   Do show your appreciation in a letter. It's even better than a call.

The interview presents the experienced sport marketer with an opportunity to use their personal media contacts, and disseminate information in an informal way. Informal contacts do not imply less care when supplying the information! The opportunity to talk informally with media representatives should not be turned into a disadvantage by accidentally releasing confidential information.

Form, inform and informal—publicity

Publicity, according to Belch and Belch (1995), refers to 'the generation of news about a person, product, service [or organisation] that appears in broadcast or print media [at no cost for the organisation]' (p. 533). Although not every public relations effort necessarily has to result in news appearing in broadcast or print media, it can be an effective and efficient means of public relations communication. As a subset of the overall public relations exercise, planning and executing a program of action (press release, press conference, interview) often lead to the generation of publicity. Mullin et al. (1993) state that:

> . . . sport is the most interesting specimen examined by the media . . . and it prospered because it received at no cost reams of publicity in daily and Sunday papers . . . This coverage, for which any other business would have had to pay, was given freely because of its entertainment value and because a newspaper that contained information about sport would sell more copies, creating both higher circulation and higher advertising rates. (p. 260)

Publicity is generated when the information has news value. Because the sporting organisation does not pay for the publicity, content is very hard to control. Also, when to release information and the accuracy of information are hard to control. Because the sporting organisation is not the direct source of information (other than in advertising or sales promotions), positive publicity can, however, become very powerful and credible. Negative publicity then has the opposite extreme effect. Samantha Riley generated a lot of negative publicity when she tested positive for performance-enhancing drugs. This negative publicity affected herself, her coach, Swimming Australia, her sponsors and FINA, the international swimming governing body. Sportview 11.1, on the other hand, showed that the launch of the Dunlop MAX 550G squash racquet generated a lot of positive publicity, benefiting Dunlop, squash centres, squash players and the sport as a whole.

In an integrated public relations strategy, the content, timing and generation of publicity are as much as possible controlled in the proactive strategy, and as much as possible prepared for in the reactive strategy.

ADVANTAGES AND DISADVANTAGES OF PUBLIC RELATIONS

At the beginning of this chapter, public relations was introduced as one element of the promotion mix. Similar to other elements, public relations has some distinct advantages over other elements when applied under certain conditions. Belch and Belch (1995, pp. 529–31) list the following advantages:

- *Credibility*—contrary to advertising, the source of the public relations message is often not the organisation itself, which makes the message more credible to the receiver.
- *Cost*—apart from the public relations personnel cost, few other expenditures have to be incurred.
- *Avoidance of clutter*—because many public relations efforts lead to news generation, information will stand apart from, for example, advertising or sales promotions.
- *Lead generation*—for example, when John Daly—the longest driver on the Professional Golf Association Tour—was seen playing in the internationally televised Skins Game using a Cobra golf club, the club manufacturer received enquiries from all over the United States, Europe and Japan.
- *Ability to reach specific groups*.
- *Image building*—effective public relations programs lead to the development of a strong image, one that can resist negative publicity for a while as well.

The main disadvantage of public relations is the *uncontrollability of publicity*. When proactive or reactive public relations results in negative publicity, all potential advantages of public relations turn into disadvantages. Negative information will impact more powerfully, and cost will be high to repair the damage. The avoidance of clutter, lead generation and ability to reach specific groups will now work against the organisation, and the favourable image will be damaged.

SUMMARY

This chapter described and discussed the promotion mix tool, public relations. This is an important tool for the sport marketer because of the high visibility and attractiveness of the sport product. Three critical activities were derived from a public relations definition in order to describe the main public relations activities:

- evaluating public attitudes;
- identifying the policies and procedures of an individual or organisation with the public interest; and
- planning and executing a program of action.

It is important for the sport marketer to know how the sporting organisation's publics perceive the organisation and its product range. Knowledge of public opinion and how to influence opinion is vital in order to create proactive public relations strategies. Therefore public attitudes need to be evaluated. Proactive strategies enable the sport marketer to 'control and adjust' public opinion, whereas reactive strategies always require changing negative public opinions. Prevention is better than repairing damage.

As a very influential public of many sporting organisations, relations with the media were considered, and the public relations tools of press release, press conference and interviews were introduced. There are basically three things that need to be considered when communicating with the media. The sport marketer has to know with whom to communicate, what information to supply and how to maintain excellent relationships with media representatives. In sport marketing special attention needs to be given to the concept of publicity as it is probably the most important means (and opportunity) of conveying information in the sport industry.

RACISM—NEW RULE

CASE STUDY

'On the cover and page 4 of this week's *Football Record*, the focus of our attention is on the new rule dealing with racial and religious vilification which has been adopted by the Australian Football League Commission. The new rule is part of a broader strategy designed to educate the football industry and wider community about why racial abuse is simply not acceptable and the important role played by various ethnic communities as well as Aboriginal and Torres Strait Islander athletes in our game.

'Our other initiatives include:

- A cross-cultural diversity program for AFL staff and senior AFL club officials. This program has been developed by the Victorian Aboriginal Education Association and will be held during late July. We will also be encouraging clubs to follow the lead of the West Coast Eagles and Footscray to run their own programs.
- Developing a proposal for consideration by the Federal Government for funding to assist the employment of Aboriginal development and liaison officers in each State. This would be similar to the employment of Gilbert McAdam as a development officer with the Queensland Australian Football League whose job is jointly funded by the AFL and the Department of Employment, Education and Training.
- Developing a public education program, initially utilising a television

commercial, to change the attitude and behaviour of spectators. The television commercial is being produced this week by our advertising agency, the Campaign Palace, and is expected to be on-air within two weeks. It will carry the tag line "Racism: the Game Is Up".

■ In conjunction with the Australian Football Foundation, review the extent of football being played in Aboriginal communities throughout the country, what funding is currently available and how further junior development programs can be implemented in those communities. This is part of an overall review of football development around Australia.

■ In conjunction with the Directorate of School Education in Victoria, the AFL has agreed to participate in a program designed to help combat racism in Victorian Government Schools. The program will involve Aboriginal players and other high profile athletes visiting schools to educate youngsters and talk about racism in sport.

■ Each AFL coach has also received a letter from the AFL this week reinforcing the role they can play in stamping out on-field racial abuse which in turn will set an example for supporters off the field.

'The AFL Commission believes racial and religious vilification must not be tolerated and urges everyone associated with football to do all in their power to stamp it out of our game.

Signed,
Ross Oakley, Chief Executive Officer, Australian Football League

Source: Excerpts from Oakley (1996).

Questions

1   Use Table 11.1 to identify the different publics with which the AFL aims to communicate.
2   Identify the public relations goals the AFL is aiming to satisfy.
3   Are the new rules and resulting strategy a form of reactive or proactive public relations? Justify your answer.
4   Can you think of marketing goals, other than public relations, that can benefit from this strategy?
5   Write a one-page media release announcing this program of action.

REFERENCES

Belch, G. E. and Belch, M. A. (1995). *Introduction to Advertising and Promotion: an Integrated Marketing Communications Perspective*, Irwin, Homewood, Ill.
Jeffery, N. (1996a). 'Riley's career on the line', *The Australian*, 13 February, p. 1.
——(1996b). 'Riley facing drugs ban', *The Australian*, 13 February, p. 24.
Jefkins, F. (1994). *Public Relations Techniques*, Butterworth/Heinemann, Oxford.

Greener, T. (1990). *The Secrets of Successful Public Relations and Image-making*, Butterworth/Heinemann, Oxford.

Griswold, D. (1995). In *The Practice of Public Relations*, F. P. Seitel, Prentice-Hall, Englewood Cliffs, NJ.

Helitzer, M. (1995). *The Dream Job: Sports Publicity, Promotion and Marketing*, University Sports Press, Athens, Ohio.

Magnay, J. (1996). 'IOC steps in over Riley ban', *The Age*, 14 February, p. B12.

Mullin, B. J., Hardy, S. and Sutton, W. A. (1993). *Sport Marketing*, Human Kinetics, Champaign, Ill.

Oakley, R. (1996). 'Racism: new rule', *Football Record*, Round 13, 30 June – 2 July, pp. 3/9.

Rhoden, W. C. (1993). 'High stakes: low sense of values', *New York Times*, 21 July, p. B11.

Seitel, F. P. (1995). *The Practice of Public Relations*, Prentice-Hall, Englewood Cliffs, NJ.

Woodhouse Management (1996). 'Cyclist Shane Kelly launches five year sponsorship deal', Press release, 9 August.

12

Promotional licensing

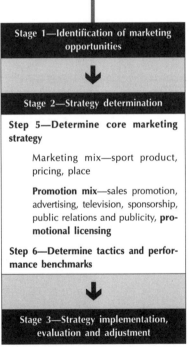

Stage 1—Identification of marketing opportunities

Stage 2—Strategy determination

Step 5—Determine core marketing strategy

Marketing mix—sport product, pricing, place

Promotion mix—sales promotion, advertising, television, sponsorship, public relations and publicity, **promotional licensing**

Step 6—Determine tactics and performance benchmarks

Stage 3—Strategy implementation, evaluation and adjustment

CHAPTER
OBJECTIVES
Chapter 12 deals with promotional licensing as an element of the sport promotion mix. Promotional licensing involves developing a relationship between a licensor and licensee with respect to the right to use the name or logo of the sporting organisation. Terms such as licensor, licensee, royalty and trademark are introduced in this chapter. Related issues, including the role of licensing in raising revenues and branding, are also discussed.

After studying this chapter you should be able to:

1 Understand the importance of the (registered) trademark.
2 Identify the different steps in building a sport licensing program.
3 Identity licensor and licensee goals.
4 Describe the central role of branding in the sport licensing program.

**HEADLINE
STORY**

LICENSING, BIG PROFITS AND SOMEBODY ELSE IS DOING THE WORK . . .

'This will be the biggest advertisement Malaysia's ever had,' says Hashim Ali, the executive chairman of Sukom 98—the private company that will organise, promote and market the Commonwealth Games, scheduled for 1998 . . . Sukom 98 hopes to recoup its investment through sponsorships, licensing arrangements, merchandising and the sale of television rights . . . Nine private companies have been licensed to sell official Games memorabilia—from T-shirts to licence plates—and money is already rolling in. (Jayasankaran 1996, p. 50)

The chairman of Sukom 98, the organiser of the forthcoming Commonwealth Games in Kuala Lumpur, Malaysia, presents a very positive view of the licensing opportunities that will arise as a result of the Games.

Although the income from licensed merchandise for sporting organisations worldwide has increased enormously throughout the last twenty years, it has never been easy to put together a solid licensing program. How to build a sporting organisation's licensing program will be discussed in the second part of this chapter. The first part will discuss the different elements of the licensing concept. The different parties involved and terminology employed will be defined and, where possible, placed in a sport context.

Licensing, as an activity, involves a *licence*, a *licensor* and a *licensee*. 'A licence is first and foremost the granting of an intellectual property right from the licensor to the licensee' (Wilkof 1995, p. 5). This means that the *intellectual property right* of a licensor must be valuable enough for a licensee to use and pay a royalty fee for. A *royalty* is a fee paid for usage of the intellectual property and is often calculated as a percentage of the sales of licensed products.

As implied in the title of this chapter, *promotional licensing* can be seen as an element of the promotion mix. In the context of the sport industry it basically serves two purposes:

- promotion of the sporting organisation, and
- promotion of a third party or its products through use of the sporting organisation's name or logo.

In the latter case, the sporting organisation will derive royalty income from licensing the third party with the name or logo usage.

In the sport industry we are most familiar with the usage of names and/or logos (as the *licensed property*) of sporting teams or organisations printed on apparel (e.g. baseball caps, T-shirts) or other merchandise (e.g. pens, mugs, umbrellas). Names and logos of sporting organisations are intellectual properties representing a certain or potential value. This value is built into the name or logo as a result of the organisation's sporting achievements and hence popularity, but also through (monetary) investment in the name or logo through the promotion efforts of the sporting organisation.

Not all sporting organisations, however, are in the position to license their name, logo or other properties to third parties. The name of the sporting organisation, or more broadly the *brand*, must be strong enough to generate interest and attention. Many sporting organisations set up licensing programs to receive royalties from the sale of licensed merchandise. However, without a strong brand name this makes little sense. Potential licensees are only interested if the name or logo can generate extra interest in, and demand for, the products that the name or logo is attached to.

A sporting organisation without a strong brand name can still become involved in a *licensing strategy*. The main aim of the licensing strategy is to increase awareness in the sporting organisation and indeed in its brand. The licensee, in turn, can use already strong sport brands in its own branding strategies, attaching the brand to newly introduced products, or products with a questionable image. The Australian Football League (AFL) in 1991, for example, attached its brand name to the products of 53 companies. On those products, the AFL logo and an 'approved product' sign were printed.

Branding will be discussed in the third part of this chapter. Before turning to this, it is necessary to discuss the basis for licensing in the sport industry: trademark licensing.

TRADEMARK LICENSING

The Australian Trade Marks Act 1995 defines a *trademark* as 'a sign used, or intended to be used, to "distinguish" goods or services of the plaintiff from those of any other person' (Section 17). A *sign* then includes the following, or any combination of the following: any letter; word; name; signature; numeral; device (i.e. symbol or logo); brand; heading; label; ticket; aspect of packaging; shape; colour; sound; or scent.

Trademark licensing is a multibillion dollar industry and is defined by

Wilkof (1995) as 'an arrangement by which one party consents to the use of its trade mark in accordance with specified terms and conditions' (p. 1). It is used in many industries for different purposes, which can be appreciated by considering the following examples:

- using the Calvin Klein clothing trademark to sell perfume (using the established brand/trademark to sell new products);
- Coca-Cola using an overseas franchisee to sell in new markets (using the established brand/trademark to sell in new markets);
- McDonald's using the Olympic rings to sell more hamburgers (using the established brand/trademark to increase sales);
- licensing the sporting organisation's logo to an apparel manufacturer (building brand/trademark awareness and raising funds).

For a trademark to become the property of an organisation, it needs to be *registered*. When a trademark is registered, the owner will have the exclusive rights to:

- use the trademark, and
- authorise other persons to use the trademark (Section 20(1)).

Registration of the trademark is of extreme importance for the sporting organisation. Without this registration the original owner of the trademark has little legal protection when other organisations use the trademark in one way or the other. This point is reinforced by the Australian Olympic Committee's (AOC) decision to seek additional protection for its insignia. The Olympic Insignia Act came into force in 1987 to enable the AOC to regulate the use of the Olympic symbol and other nominated Olympic designs. The Sydney Olympic Organising Committee also sought added protection via the proclamation of the Sydney 2000 (Indicia and Images) Act 1996.

Use of a trademark is important for an organisation in many ways. Some of the reasons will be discussed in the next section.

Functions of a trademark

Wilkof (1995) identifies six different functions of trademarks. These functions developed over time, and hence the merchandising function incorporates elements of all other, earlier developed functions. The functions are:

- identification,
- physical source,
- anonymous source,
- quality,
- advertising,
- merchandising.

Identification

The most obvious function of the trademark is to identify ownership or who is responsible for producing the product. When Juventus played Ajax in the European Champions League final, for example, soccer consumers knew that the 'black and white' Italians played the 'red and white' Dutchmen.

Physical source

Without being able to witness the production of certain products, the trademark can be seen as the acknowledgement of the physical source of the purchased goods. The trademark serves as a *stamp of approval*. When licensing trademarks, however, the licensee is not the actual source of the goods. T-shirts with National Basketball League (NBL) logos printed on them are not produced by the NBL. Manufacturers are granted a licence to produce merchandise, and hence licensing seems incompatible with this function of the trademark. To reduce this incompatibility, it is important that the sporting organisation put in place stringent quality control procedures to ensure that products will be of a quality that the 'physical source' organisation would deliver itself.

Anonymous source

When the scope of production and marketing of an organisation expands, it becomes less likely that consumers of goods will know the actual name of the producer. The anonymous source function ensures that purchasers of goods or services with a given established trademark know that these goods or services emanate from a source that established those trademarks. In other words, the trademark products have proven their quality, validating their anonymous source. Large consumer good producers like Procter and Gamble and Unilever have hundreds of trademarks validating the 'anonymous source'. Sporting organisations are less likely to use this function of the trademark, although large entertainment companies involved in the sport industry actually do. For instance, the famous Madison Square Garden and its subordinate properties the New York Knicks, New York Rangers, Madison Square Garden Network, Miss Universe, Miss USA and Miss Teen USA are all actually owned by the partnership of the ITT Corporation and the Cablevision Corporation. As the owners of the Garden, ITT and Cablevision also own the names, logos and trademarks. In the case of the two professional teams—the New York Knicks and New York Rangers—there are also licensing restrictions on the use of the logos and names placed by the National Basketball Association (NBA) and National Hockey League (NHL) as part of the franchise agreements.

Quality

Licensing of sport trademarks has become so popular because of the quality function of trademarks. If a trademark has the power to convey a quality perception, surely this perception can be transferred to products or entities linked to the trademark. From a legal perspective this concept changed the position of licensing. Provided that the licensor establishes sufficient quality control measures and procedures, it does not really matter whether the products emanate from the licensor (i.e. owner of the trademark) or another source. The quality level provided to the end consumer by the licensee should be similar to the quality level if the product had been provided by the licensor.

Advertising

Fuji Xerox using the Olympic rings, the Ford Motor Company using Tennis Australia's logo and Coca-Cola using the AFL's logo are all examples of trademark usage that goes beyond the creation of goodwill (as exemplified in the previous functions). Trademarks have become symbols with the power to sell goods and services. Although advertising can be criticised as an effort to manipulate the consumer's mind through slick, high impact campaigns, it does serve as a way to mass-communicate the source and quality of a product through the trademark. It complements the source and quality functions. The positive perception that consumers have of the AFL, Tennis Australia or the Olympic organisation is transferred to the associated organisations and products, stimulating these consumers to drink Coca-Cola, drive a Ford or use Fuji Xerox products.

Merchandising

The trademark becomes a product in itself when it is not serving to sell other goods or services, but serving to sell itself. Examples are the teenage fans of a rockband buying all possible merchandise with the name of the band on it, or football fans buying shirts, mugs, jackets, pens with the name of their team on it. The consumer wants to be identified with the trademark organisation. Which merchandise they buy is secondary. Often, the only criterion is that it is visible to others, showing the consumer's allegiance to the trademark organisation.

Quality control

Quality control is a vital and integral component of trademark licensing. It was shown in the previous section that the legal position of licensing changed when the concept of quality control was included. It was stated that, as long as the licensor establishes sufficient quality control measures and procedures, it does not really matter whether the products emanate from the licensor (i.e. owner of the trademark) or another source. The trademark identifies the source and distinguishes the products from those of others. Standards for quality control are loosely formulated by law in that the owner of the trademark should be capable of exercising control over the users of the trademark.

Wilkof (1995) distinguishes between two types of quality control: contractual and financial. *Contractual control* exists between two unrelated parties whose only mutual interest is the exploitation of the trademark. *Financial control* exists when two parties are related in that one of them has an ownership relation to the other (e.g. a holding or subsidiary relation). Financial control is more stringent because the aims of benefiting from the trademark are more likely to be in line with each other because of the ownership relation between the organisations.

In the sport industry, contractual control is the most frequently used type of quality control. A *contractual specification* of quality control terms and conditions should identify at least the following aspects of quality control:

- specification of standards;
- inspection of products and methods of production;
- supply of samples.

The trademark licensing agreement

The *trademark licensing agreement* sets out the broader relationship between the licensor and licensee. Ownership of the trademark, who can use the trademark as the licensee and how the trademark can be used (contractual, i.e. quality control) are described first. Then the commercial and financial terms and conditions are described. Issues like how merchandise is going to be marketed and which royalties have to be paid by the licensee are described in this part of the agreement.

Sherman (1991, pp. 330–1) describes several key areas that need to be addressed when preparing the trademark licensing agreement. In summary, the key areas are:

- scope of the territorial and product exclusivity;
- assignability and sublicensing rights;
- definition of the property and the licensed products;
- quality control and approval;
- ownership of artwork and designs;
- term renewal rights and termination of the relationship;
- initial licence and ongoing royalty fees;
- performance criteria for the licensee;
- liability insurance;
- indemnification;
- duty to pursue trademark and copyright infringement;
- minimum advertising and promotional requirements;
- accounting and record keeping of the licensee;
- inspection and audit rights of the licensor;
- right of first refusal for expanded or revised characters and images;
- limitations on the licensee's distribution to related or affiliated entities;
- representations and warranties of the licensor with respect to its rights to the property;
- availability of the licensor for technical and promotional assistance; and

- miscellaneous provisions, such as law to govern, inurement of goodwill, nature of the relationship notice, and force majeure.

It goes beyond the scope of this text to specify further the contents of the trademark licensing agreement.

Before taking a closer look at building the sporting organisation's licensing program, the trademark licensing agreement will be briefly outlined from both the licensor's and licensee's perspectives.

Licensor's and licensee's perspectives

The trademark licensing agreement from the licensor's perspective should serve one most important goal. If the trademark is used by the licensee in any other matter than was intended by the licensor when entering the agreement, contractual arrangements must be in place to entitle the licensor to take action. Although this point is of obvious importance to the licensee as well, the focus of the licensee should be on the terms and conditions related to commercial and financial matters. This requires identifiying the commercial possibilities of the trademark usage and how these may translate into a dollar figure. Sportview 12.1, adjusted from Schaaf (1995), exemplifies the licensor's and licensee's perspectives.

<table>
<tr><td>SPORTVIEW
12.1</td><td>**THE RUGBY UNION 'ALL BLACKS/WALLABIES/SPRINGBOKS' VIDEO GAME**</td></tr>
</table>

Sport Excitement Video Games (fictitious name) wants to create a game called 'The All Blacks/Wallabies/Springboks conquer the world'. The game will be marketed in New Zealand, Australia and South Africa. When sold in New Zealand, the game will be marketed as 'The All Blacks conquer the world', in Australia as 'The Wallabies conquer the world' and in South Africa as 'The Springboks conquer the world'.

Sport Excitement has several licensing considerations. The company needs to develop the actual game, which includes writing the software code for graphical display, play options, opponents and voice enhancement features (cost can go up to $400 000). Sport Excitement also needs to pay the New Zealand, Australian and South African national governing bodies of rugby union their licensing fees. In this case all organisations have negotiated a minimum advance fee ($100 000) plus a percentage of sales royalty fee (4%). On top of the licensing fees, Sport Excitement has to undertake the packaging, warehousing and shipping costs. Then it has to obtain the other necessary licences, from either the International Rugby Football Board (IRFB) or the Players Association, to feature identifiable teams and/or players other than the three already identified. Next, Sport Excitement has to decide which game platforms it will develop for (e.g. Sega®, CD-Rom, Nintendo®). Depending on which platform the manufacturer develops, the cartridges will add extra costs.

An analyst calculates the revenue streams and forecasts the potential return on investment. The net revenue per platform for an average game is $32 per game *sold through*, meaning purchased at a retail outlet such as Target. The All Blacks royalty would likely be 4% of that, less the advance. Therefore, if 100 000 units sold through, the All Blacks' royalties would amount to:

$$100\ 000\ (\text{units}) \times (0.04)(\$32) - \$100\ 000 = \$28\ 000$$

In this case, the sporting teams are not the catalyst for the game. The developer seeks a category and the teams are merely the well-known vehicles to differentiate the product. In the competitive video-game development industry, the sophisticated marketplace will weed out poorly conceived games, and they will fail in spite of a fabulous licensor. Licensors, in this case, will help to sell products, if those products are good!

Source: Adjusted from Schaaf (1995).

How the general trademark licensing issues can be linked to a sporting organisation is explored in the next part of this chapter. Sportview 12.2 highlights some of the issues arising in using sport trademarks.

SPORT TEAM LOGOS ARE BIG BUSINESS

SPORTVIEW
12.2

'Have you ever considered using the logo of your favourite professional sports team in a promotional campaign? Did you know it would cost you? Apparently not all marketing professionals realise that sports teams, like other companies that produce products or services, own protectable trademarks that others may not use unless they first obtain the trademark owner's permission and usually pay a licensing fee.

'In a recent case, the California Angels baseball team defended its trademark rights when it sued the Broadway department store after it ran an ad for women's dresses featuring three children wearing Angels uniforms. Broadway had failed to first obtain the requisite permission from the Angels and later refused to pay the Angels' requested licensing fee. Broadway claimed that it did not know it was supposed to pay a licensing fee, even though the Angels uniforms used in the ad contained registered trademark notations.

'Professional sports teams aggressively protect their trademark rights, which include its name and its logos. This is done by demanding licensing fees on other contexts which may, at first glance, appear worlds apart from the department store advertisement case. Recently, Major League Baseball has even cracked down on Little League and amateur adult teams that use major-league nicknames. Because Major League Baseball owns trademark rights in the names of all its teams when they are used in connection with baseball, it can legally require amateur teams using these names to wear only licensed apparel. This can add about $6 to the cost of each uniform.

'Trademark licensing increased the marketing opportunities for many companies. Instead of diversifying directly into a new product line, a trademark proprietor could license an existing producer in another industry to manufacture a line of goods under the licensor's trademark. This became very common, for example, between perfume companies and apparel manufacturers. It is now also common between professional sport organisations and apparel and novelty manufacturers.

'The sport organisation must specify the products on which any licensee is permitted to use the trademark, as well as supervise and control the quality of those products. The public will benefit because it will receive a guarantee that the sport organisation stands behind the goods bearing its trademarks. What would happen if Major League Baseball ignored the Little Leaguers' use of its nicknames? Major League Baseball could lose its trademark rights and that would mean the loss of millions of dollars a year in royalties from its extremely lucrative licensing business.

'Professional sport organisations have much to lose if they do not adequately control the use of their trademarks. In addition, it is safe to say that many consumers want to know that the products they buy are both high quality and "approved".'

Source: Excerpts from Lans (1995, p. 6).

BUILDING THE SPORTING ORGANISATION'S LICENSING PROGRAM

An operational protocol

Irwin and Stotlar (1993) investigated the operational protocol employed by six major US sporting organisations in their sport licensing programs. The six organisations were Major League Baseball (MLB), National Football League (NFL), National Basketball Association (NBA), National Hockey League (NHL), National Collegiate Athletic Association (NCAA) and the US Olympic Committee. Table 12.1 shows the different elements of this operational protocol, or in other words, the activities that need to be executed in sport licensing programs. The number of organisations (out of six) actually using the listed elements of the protocol are given.

Table 12.1 presents a good overview of the operational activities that need to be considered when managing a sport licensing program. Before a sporting organisation can start managing a program, however, it has to be put together.

Operational element of program	Number of sporting organisations using the element (out of 6)
Program governance and leadership	
Internal licensing authority	5
Full-time principal licensing assignment	5
Direct report to central administrator	5
Licensing policy committee assembled	3
Professional licensing agency assistance	1
Program protection and enforcement	
Legal specialist consultation	6
Majority of logos registered as trademarks	6
Licensee application and screening process	6
Licence issuance and renewal procedures	6
Non-exclusive basic agreement	1
Execution of joint-use agreements	5
Execution of international licences	5
Product sample required for quality control	6
'Licensed product' identification required	6
Counterfeit logo detection procedures	6
Counterfeit logo reduction procedures	6
Program promotions and public relations	
Proactive recruitment of licensees	5
Proactive recruitment of retailers	4
Licensee/retailer public relations program	6
Advertising used to promote products/program	5
Publicity used to promote products/program	6
Licensing program information published	6
Revenue management	
Advance payment required	6
Uniform royalty charged on all products	2
Written royalty exemption policy	6
Royalty verifications routinely conducted	5
Royalty verifications conducted by specialist	5
Written royalty distribution policy	6

TABLE 12.1

Use of elements of an operational protocol for sport licensing programs

Source: Adjusted from Irwin and Stotlar (1993, p. 9).

Key factors

Baghdikian (1996) has developed a model to assist the sport marketer in identifying the key factors when building a licensing program. The model is presented in Figure 12.1, and the different issues will briefly be described next.

Organisational objectives

Like the other marketing tools discussed in this text, licensing should serve the broader purpose of achieving the marketing goals of the organisation, which in turn, should support the achievement of overall strategic goals. In

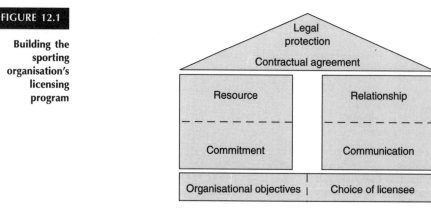

FIGURE 12.1

**Building the
sporting
organisation's
licensing
program**

Source: Baghdikian (1996, p. 39).

sport, licensing the organisation's trademark for merchandising purposes often aims to raise funds or to increase brand awareness. If these goals fit the marketing strategy, the organisation can pursue finding a licensee or licensees.

Choice of licensee

In the light of the functions of the trademark and the organisational objectives, it is important to find the right licensee. Pertaining to the functions of the trademark, the potential licensee should be capable of satisfying the quality control standards and should maintain the function of identifying the source of the products. From an organisational perspective it is important for the sporting organisation to find reputable partners with an ability to deliver quality on time with regular payments.

Commitment

Rather than leaving the work to the licensee and simply 'licensing' it to use the sporting organisation's trademark, the sporting organisation should commit itself to do the preliminary market research and financial analysis. Baghdikian (1996) states that:

> . . . the San Jose Sharks, during their first season, compiled the worst on-field record in the National Hockey League (NHL). However, due to the organisations *spending 13 months on consumer research, and planning a name and design that would create an exciting image in the market*, the Sharks outsold all other NHL team-licensed products. (p. 38)

Resource

In investigating sport and collegiate licensing programs, Irwin and Stotlar (1993) concluded that 'with nearly half of all colleges assigning program administrators less than 10% of their time to licensing, the complex administrative tasks associated with a licensing program cannot effectively be addressed' (p. 15). Although the resources invested in managing a sport licensing program might be high, the resulting benefits are likely to be proportionately higher than the investment.

Communication

Although the licensing agreement (including contractual agreements) should serve as the basis for business communication, regular and open channels of communication should be established. A clear understanding of both parties' goals, the early detection of problems and effective quality control are the results of open and frequent communication between licensor and licensee.

Relationship

The more formal business communication described above can be complemented with more informal communication (e.g. between the two chief executive officers). An afternoon on the golf course with the aim to foster personal relationships has often proved to be vital for the maintenance of business relationships.

Contractual agreement

The contract represents the written agreement that both the licensor and licensee are legally obliged to fulfil. Examples of areas, suggested by Sherman (1991), to be included in a contract were listed earlier in this chapter. The contract is the agreement that the licensor and licensee can turn to when they feel that one or the other party is not fulfilling the requirements of the agreement.

Legal protection

In Chapter 10, *ambush marketing* was described as the practice where a business markets its goods or services in a way that suggests that the business has a connection with a team, event or a competition, where there is in fact no connection. The practice of ambush marketing is of particular interest when considering the power of trademarks. Without the law and legal advisers, the sporting organisation has little to protect it from organisations ambushing its trademarks and other properties. The specialised nature of licensing in general, contracts, interpretations of law and the management of licensing programs requires the support and advice of legally qualified experts. Figure 12.1 illustrates this by picturing legal protection as the 'roof' of the program.

Issues that can arise

The second part of this chapter has first provided a range of activities to be executed by sport licensing program managers and then the different steps that need to be taken when building the organisation's licensing program. Before discussing branding in the context of the sport licensing process, Sportview 12.3 will give an insight into different issues that can arise when building a sport licensing program.

SPORTVIEW
12.3

MINOR LEAGUES TO GET MAJOR SUPPORT

'In the US, the marketing of minor league baseball in licensed merchandise is no longer as simple as putting product on the shelves. Insiders say that retail penetration and consumer familiarity have both reached a flattening point on the growth curves, and that means new challenges for this once burgeoning market. More active licensing bodies and in-store promotions may be what's needed to sustain some of the momentum minor leagues have built.

'"We're going to be much more pro-active," said Steven Roberts of Sony Signatures, which recently became the licensing agent for the International Hockey League after the league doubled its licensing revenues for three straight years while under Brain Hakan & Associates. "There will be set promotional programs where retailers can obtain point-of-sale materials, perhaps sweepstakes, and different vehicles which will help them build traffic in the stores." Roberts said an IHL theme shop will also debut shortly in Wal-Mart, and an authentics program with Bauer, CCM and Starter as its main licensees will hit sporting goods stores right after Super Show.

'Major League Baseball Properties (MLBP), licensing agent for the minor league circuit as well, is taking similar measures. "We're trying to take it to the next step by getting more involved with retail," said Jonathan Frank, minor league licensing director at MLBP. "We have created retail point-of-purchase, and we've developed minor league retail co-op programs."

'Several major chains including the Sports Authority, Champs and Herman's experimented with minor league baseball concepts shops last season, featuring merchandise from local clubs and teams with hot graphics or national reputations. While the minor leagues remain a heavily regional buy, new logos and colours are what generally drives the business, in both local markets and beyond.

'New Era, the official headwear supplier to minor league baseball, reports that the Norwich (CT) Navigators and Wisconsin Timber Rattlers were its top selling teams last year, both with new logos. The company forecasts that the Lancaster (PA) JetHawks will be among this year's leaders, along with Prince William (VA) Cannons and Lethbridge (Alberta) Black Diamonds, all of whom have never-before-seen marks.

'Poor attendance for some of the IHL's new expansion teams have hurt sales, but Sony reports that Orlando Solar Bear items are among its top sellers, and last season's expansion teams from Detroit, Chicago and Minnesota also remain strong at retail.

'The IHL's Grand Rapids Griffins, an expansion team for 1996–97, have already debuted their marks and the streets with merchandise, while over 30 minor league baseball teams have new looks in store this spring.'

Source: Reprinted from Bernstein (1996, p. 34).

BRANDING

The branding process

Chernatony and McDonald (1992) define a *successful brand* as:

> . . . an identifiable product, service, person or place augmented in such a way that the buyer or user perceives relevant unique added values which match their needs most closely. Furthermore its success results from being able to sustain these added values in the face of competition. (p. 18)

We can all associate with the practical application of the brand concept. Powerful brands are immediately associated with the product or service they represent. Coca-Cola is a softdrink, McDonald's sells hamburgers, Manchester United deals with soccer and the Indy 500 is about car racing. A brand represents the combination of the core product and the perceptions that consumers have *about* the product and its unique *added values*. Figure 12.2(a) shows what distinguishes a brand from the core product. In Figure 12.2(b) this is applied to a sport example.

Developing successful brands is important for organisations because the brand can be used as a means to communicate with consumers. Branding, as the process of developing and sustaining successful brands, has strategic relevance for the marketing function. In other words, the full marketing mix is used in the strategic branding process. The marketer tries to position the brand 'in the mind' of the consumer. Consumers start perceiving the brand as the *symbolic total* of the packaging, design, recall advertising, quality of product, price paid, and store or outlet where the product can be purchased. This total brand perception enables the marketer to link mental visions to the organisation's branded products, expressing, for example, a lifestyle, a personality or a feeling. Powerful brands differentiate themselves from similar products of competitors and provide the opportunity to build long-term relationships with consumers, developing brand-loyal buyers.

Table 12.2 describes eight different ways of using a brand in practice. Irrespective of which usage is chosen from this list, adding value, as perceived by the consumer, is the critical activity in the branding process. The marketer can use the brand as a symbol of, for example, prestige, status, lifestyle or personality and position the symbol in such a way that it expresses physical and psychological comfort for the target market.

If the sport marketer chooses to build the registered trademark into a brand, licensing in many ways can assist in achieving branding objectives. This is explained in the next section.

Branding and licensing

In the first part of this chapter the relationship between the trademark of an organisation and the licensing process was explained. Trademark licensing, as

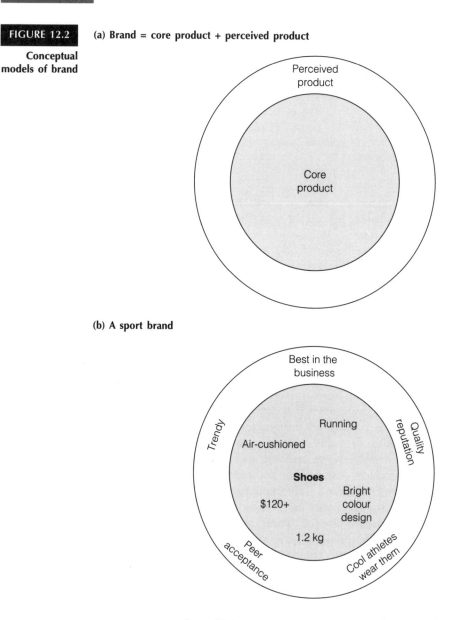

FIGURE 12.2

Conceptual models of brand

(a) Brand = core product + perceived product

Perceived product

Core product

(b) A sport brand

Best in the business

Trendy

Running

Air-cushioned

Quality reputation

Shoes

$120+

Bright colour design

1.2 kg

Peer acceptance

Cool athletes wear them

an arrangement by which one party consents to the use of its trademark in accordance with specified terms and conditions, makes sense only if the trademark in any way is valuable to the potential licensee. The trademark can have value as an established brand, making it a powerful means of communication. If the trademark has the potential value of becoming an established brand, it has future earning power, making it an interesting investment. Sporting organisations can capitalise on this potential value by using other organisations to raise their own brand awareness.

Usage of brand	Why use it in that way	
Brand as a sign of ownership	Buyer knows which organisation produced the product	**TABLE 12.2**
Brand as a differentiating device	Buyer knows the product is different from comparable products	**Different ways of using a brand in practice**
Brand as a functional device	Buyer knows why and how to use the product	
Brand as a symbolic device	Brand communicates something about the buyer	
Brand as a risk reducer	Brand communicates trust about the producer of the product	
Brand as a shorthand device	Brand is a means to recall sufficient brand information from memory at a later purchasing time	
Brand as a legal device	Trademark registration is legal protection from counterfeit production	
Brand as a strategic device	Brand positioning is a means of ensuring a long-term future for the organisation	

Source: Adjusted from Chernatony and McDonald (1992).

The potential power of sport brands

In Chapter 10 we discussed the advantages of sport sponsorship. These advantages also explain why sport brands, or sport trademarks, are potentially powerful tools to add value. The advantages, explaining the potential power of sport brands, may be summarised as follows:

- Sport consumers tend to identify themselves personally with the sport, which creates opportunities for increasing brand loyalty in products linked to the sport.
- Sport evokes personal attachment, and with this the licensee can be linked to the excitement, energy and emotion of the sporting contest. In other words, sport has the potential to deliver a clear message.
- Sport has universal appeal and pervades all elements of life (geographically, demographically and socioculturally). This characteristic presents the opportunity to cross difficult cultural and language borders in communication, enabling the licensee to talk to a global mass audience.
- The variety of sports available makes it possible to create distinct market segments with which to communicate separately.
- The universal appeal and high interest that sport has in society give sport a high media exposure, resulting in free publicity. Free publicity can make a licensing deal very cost effective.
- Because of the clear linkage of the licensee to the sporting organisation's trademark, the relationship stands out from the clutter, contrary to advertising, in which people are bombarded with hundreds of 'sender unknown' messages each day.

Earlier, this chapter presented some examples of how organisations use licensing and for which purposes. These purposes are repeated here in the context of the sport industry.

Using the sport brand to add value

Adding value, as the most important activity of creating powerful brands, can be done in many ways. It has been explained that branding is a strategic effort in that the marketer should use the whole marketing mix to build the brand. Using an established trademark or brand to add value to another brand is one means of applying the marketing mix. The Olympic TOP sponsors are licensed to link the Olympic rings to their products. A variety of consumer good licensees (e.g. Four'n'Twenty pies, Coca-Cola, McDonald's, Spalding) are licensed to use the AFL logo on their products. The nine licensees in the opening example of this chapter use the Sukom 98 logo, all to add value to already existing brands or general products.

More specifically, this added value is needed to fulfil one of the following purposes:

- using the established brand/trademark to sell new products;
- using the established brand/trademark to sell in new markets; or
- using the established brand/trademark to increase sales.

The major aim of the sporting organisation in this process is to use its established brand/trademark to raise funds for the organisation. An extra bonus is the widespread attention that is given to its brand name through the promotional efforts of licensees. This is why careful selection of licensees is important, because the established sport brand should not be associated with a wrong or inferior product or organisation.

The branding process in a sporting organisation can be enhanced by using licensing as a means of raising brand awareness.

Using licensing to add value to the sport brand

If the sport brand is not established yet, but careful preparation and commitment has been put into preparing an appropriate and attractive brand name and symbols, licensing can be used as one way of informing consumers about the brand. The San Jose Sharks, used as an example earlier, raised their brand awareness and raised funds by offering a potentially profitable trademark to a selection of merchandise licensees. Using the marketing mix elements to integrate pricing, distribution and promotion of the merchandise, they successfully established the San Jose Sharks brand.

More specifically, licensing is used to fulfil the following purpose:

- licensing the unknown trademark to build brand/trademark awareness and raise funds.

The previous examples have shown that licensing plays a vital role in adding value to either the licensor's, licensee's or both organisations' brands. The realisation that brands/trademarks are successful only if they add value to the product or the organisation, as perceived by the consumer, highlights the strategic importance of branding. Powerful brands can be developed only if the organisation views the branding process as integral to the marketing function, using all marketing mix elements to build powerful brands.

SUMMARY

This chapter discussed the licensing of the sporting organisation's intellectual property (name and/or logo registered in a trademark) to a third party. It was shown that promotional licensing in the sport industry basically serves two purposes: promotion of the sporting organisation, and promotion of a third party or its products through use of the sporting organisation's name or logo. In the latter case, the major benefit the sporting organisation derives is a royalty fee, often calculated as a percentage of sales of licensed products.

The importance of registering a trademark was shown by discussing the different functions of the trademark. Registration of the trademark is always important because trademarks can become valuable organisational assets, namely brands. Through careful management, trademarks linked to products can be built into powerful brands. This was discussed in the last part of this chapter. A powerful sport brand is a valuable organisational asset because it has the power to represent multiple consumer perceptions. Consumers perceive a brand as a symbolic total of the organisation's product—in sport's case the excitement, speed and action orientation of the core product and its star players. Sport brands therefore are capable of linking powerful messages to other products through licensing.

The second part of the chapter discussed the process of building a sporting organisation's licensing program. This process was summarised in Baghdikian's (1996) model, but three issues were highlighted as being of particular importance. Operational activities in managing the program were presented, the minimum contents of a licensing agreement (as identified by Sherman 1991) were briefly summarised, and the importance of legal support and protection was emphasised. Promotional licensing is an expanding area in sport marketing and offers many sporting organisations potential for future income or growth.

SETTING UP A SPORTING ORGANISATION'S LICENSING PROGRAM

This case study was originally written by Eddie Baghdikian and is purely fictional. The organisations and persons in the case are non-existent.

In June 1992, Juan Garcia, director of hockey development at the South American Hockey Federation (SAHF), was approached by ALEGG Interdomestic Pty Ltd with a proposal promising to generate substantial revenue for the SAHF with no financial outlay required. ALEGG was proposing a licensing agreement by which the SAHF logo would be used to brand a wide variety of merchandise and these products would be marketed to SAHF members.

The role of the SAHF, as the central administrative body, is to manage, coordinate and unify the diverse facets of the sport of hockey in South America. This includes overseeing the development of grassroots programs, managing competitions and tournaments, and promoting hockey at all levels. As the representative body of all affiliated clubs and associations throughout South America, the SAHF ensures the commercial viability of hockey and seeks out and encourages sponsorship for hockey events on a national level.

The core product of the SAHF is essentially the development of the game of hockey. Until the approach by ALEGG, the SAHF had never undertaken any product extension strategies. ALEGG's proposal to enter into a licensing arrangement with the SAHF promised to develop and market a range of hockey merchandise and accessories aimed at SAHF members.

ALEGG was formed in late 1991 for the purpose of entering into licensing agreements with organisations such as the World Soccer Federation (FIFA) and other sporting bodies. The combined experience of its two directors and its South American general manager boasted more than 30 years knowledge in the areas of manufacturing, importing, wholesaling, retailing and marketing in a very wide range of consumer items. At the time of the approach to the SAHF, ALEGG informed Juan Garcia that as of February 1992 the company had entered into a merchandise licensing agreement between themselves and FIFA.

Juan did not believe that there was much of a market for SAHF-logoed products. He felt that there was no particular attraction or brand equity in the registered trademark of the organisation. However, with no financial outlay required, Juan also felt that he had nothing to lose if ALEGG thought that it could make the idea work.

The concept of a licensing program that to Juan represented no risk and no responsibility held considerable appeal, and so he and the SAHF ventured into the world of licensing.

The basis for the relationship

The negotiations began. Over the next four months the SAHF and ALEGG discussed the basis for the relationship that would ultimately lead to drafting the licensing agreement.

ALEGG would develop a range of SAHF merchandise known as the SAHF Members Collection. The range of licensed products would be entirely up to the SAHF. ALEGG would source the selected product line through its 'worldwide' manufacturing and supplier network, which was predominantly concentrated in the South East Asia region. All sourced products would be 'branded' as well as displaying the SAHF name and logo. The list of products included tracksuits, pens, keyrings, cufflinks, playing cards, calendar posters, diaries, umbrellas, T-shirts, sports bags, calculators and hats.

ALEGG would be primarily responsible for the promotion and distribution of all agreed merchandise, including a SAHF Members Collection brochure and other advertising material such as posters for all clubhouses. Coinciding with the marketing campaign, ALEGG would also have the entire range of goods made available at all major South American hockey competitions and have a salesperson to service this area. The SAHF would not be responsible for holding and purchasing stock.

The SAHF agreed to assist in the promotion of the merchandise through:

- *South American Hockey News* (communications newsletter for members);
- advertising;
- exposure at all SAHF events;
- regular mailouts to all clubs;
- a list of club secretaries to be provided to ALEGG; and
- general promotions mutually agreed on.

So far, the negotiations for the SAHF's first licensing program were going along well. Estimating the projected income from the marketing program was not as important to Juan as the ability to make money out of something requiring no financial expenditure and with a minimal amount of resources required. In addition, the program would lift the profile of the organisation in the marketplace through the promotion of the SAHF name and logo. These were the broad objectives Juan set for the licensing program. In ALEGG's final proposal, Juan was also told that anticipated income figures in the first formative year would be exceeded significantly in subsequent years as the promotion programs gained momentum and the SAHF name and logo grew in recognition.

The licensing agreement

The 'exclusive licensing/marketing/manufacturing agreement' between the SAHF and ALEGG was drafted and arrived on Juan's desk. From this time onwards the normal printed ALEGG letterhead was no longer used and communications were now with ALEGG's international marketing director, and not the SAHF's usual ALEGG contact, the South American general manager— who seemed to have vanished.

ALEGG was to become the sole and exclusive producer, manufacturer, wholesaler and marketing representative of the SAHF. The agreement stated that the appointment of ALEGG was verbally formalised and agreed to on

Thursday 8 October 1992 in order to permit ALEGG to incur expenditure in time and money to set up the logistical, administrative, and initial manufacturing and marketing requirements of the project. However, the three-year term of the agreement was to officially start on 1 January 1993, with a three-year option commencing on 1 January 1996, the three-year option being automatically renewable except for either party cancelling the agreement.

Cancellation of the agreement could be done only during the 30-day period in the month prior to the expiration of any three-year term of the agreement by giving eighteen months notice in writing. Alternatively, cancellation could be effected, by the SAHF only, during the 30-day period in the month prior to the expiration of any three-year term of the agreement by giving 90 days notice in writing and purchasing and paying the freight-on-board (FOB) price for all goods and/or services and/or work in stock and/or in progress for and on behalf of ALEGG in relation to ALEGG fulfilling its obligations and undertakings as part of the agreement. Payment then would have to be made prior to the expiration of the 90-day notice period. In fact, whether the SAHF or ALEGG breached any of the conditions of the contract, and cancelled, the SAHF would still be obliged to pay the FOB price under the terms of the agreement.

Juan pondered over this legal document. He did not like it in its present state. Even with his non-legal background and inexperience with licensing programs he figured that there was no 'out' clause without a substantial penalty to pay. He read on that ALEGG would pay the SAHF a licensing fee equal to 15% of the manufactured cost, paid at the end of each calendar month. ALEGG would also conduct the reconciliation and monitoring of all royalty payments.

Although there was the issue of the termination terms and conditions to resolve, the SAHF still thought that there was some scope for the program to work. Consequently, ALEGG was encouraged by the SAHF to review the contract and keep working with the SAHF, even though an agreement was never signed.

Disjointed proceedings

The SAHF did not hear directly from ALEGG for some time. During the period up to May 1993, Juan heard that ALEGG had only made a few approaches at different SAHF-affiliated clubs. At this point Juan started to believe that the project had basically ended.

It was at this juncture that the SAHF changed its trading name to Hockey South America and embraced a new corporate logo. With the proliferation of initialled identities in the business world, the use of 'SAHF' was continuously being confused. The decision to adopt this new identity also brought the organisation in line with Hockey International, the controlling hockey body at the international level. Hockey South America, realising the importance of the role of marketing to its organisation and in line with the identity change, appointed a marketing and media officer in April 1993. This position, which reported to Juan, had as its primary objective the task of lifting the profile of the sport through the media and business world. Juan, who now was the director of development and marketing, decided to inform ALEGG of the changes.

On receiving the news, ALEGG advised Juan that it had more than $US400 000 of SAHF-logoed goods on order and approaching delivery, and further advised that the SAHF should consider not changing its name until 1994, to allow a stock rundown without financial loss to all parties concerned. In the same communication ALEGG conveyed that in the last few months it had been gearing for sales, through the 2931 affiliated clubs, to the 1 102 000 SAHF members.

The situation did not improve. The SAHF name change went ahead, and ALEGG kept struggling for credibility—without success. Juan rang FIFA to gauge the progress of FIFA's licensing agreement with ALEGG. He was told that FIFA was wanting to get out of the agreement. In September 1993, Juan wanted 'out' too. The last twelve months spent in attempting to develop a suitable merchandising relationship with ALEGG was sufficient time. Juan did not see evidence of any prospect for progress, now or in the future. Hockey South America informed ALEGG in writing that it wished to terminate the proposed agreement and would deal with ALEGG only on a non-exclusive basis, as required by Hockey South America, the exclusive nature of the agreement also being part of the reason to terminate.

ALEGG had other ideas. It wanted to continue with the exclusive manufacturing and marketing licensing arrangement. It was committed to the three-year agreement with SAHF/Hockey South America. The subsequent meetings with ALEGG worried Juan. Present at these meetings was a person taking the minutes in shorthand. Anticipating the worst from an agreement that was not actually signed, and with no in-house expertise on these types of contracts, Juan sought legal advice.

In the meantime, ALEGG argued that the SAHF proposed to change its name to Hockey South America in or around July 1993 with little or no prior notice given. As a result, more capital investment and greater time allowance were now required. ALEGG also debated that it had outlaid in excess of $1 200 000 in time and money, all with a view to completing at least the first three years of the program, with an intention to ensure success so that the relationship would go beyond this initial three-year period.

ALEGG was determined to represent itself as a dedicated organisation with the right intentions to implement the letter of the agreement, and to represent SAHF/Hockey South America as the main cause of the current state of the project, through its lack of cooperation, commitment and communication. Nevertheless, ALEGG continued to have dialogue with Hockey South America on the 'new' line of merchandise and the 'new' 1993/94 catalogue/brochure incorporating the Hockey South America logo. ALEGG also discussed new club member updates, marketing strategy, and looked forward to receiving Hockey South America's positive response and full support.

Essentially, the response from the solicitors advised Juan to adopt a 'wait and see' posture—meaning, to await further approaches from ALEGG, hoping that, as a result of the lack of enthusiasm and support from Juan, the relationship would simply wither away. The solicitors also pointed out, however, that although Juan had not signed the proposed agreement with ALEGG there could be an enforceable agreement based on negotiations and part performance of the agreement.

Questions

1   Discuss the risks and rewards to an organisation of licensing its brands.
2   How well does the strategy of product extension, through licensing, fit the corporate objectives of the SAHF?
3   Identify the reasons why the licensing agreement between the SAHF and ALEGG failed.
4   What factors should Juan Garcia have considered in making his decision on whether or not to enter into the licensing agreement?
5   Juan felt that the SAHF logo had no inherent appeal or value. On what criteria should the marketer judge the equity in a brand and its suitability for licensing?

REFERENCES

Australian Trade Marks Act 1995, s. 17.
Baghdikian, E. (1996). 'Building the sports organisation's merchandise licensing program: the appropriateness, significance, and considerations', *Sport Marketing Quarterly*, 5 (1), pp. 35–41.
Bernstein, A. (1996). 'Minor leagues to get major support', *Sporting Goods Business*, February, p. 34.
Chernatony, de L. and McDonald, M. H. B. (1992). *Creating Powerful Brands*, Butterworth/Heinemann, Oxford.
Irwin, R. L. and Stotlar, D. K. (1993). 'Operational protocol analysis of sport and collegiate licensing programs', *Sport Marketing Quarterly*, 2 (1), pp. 7–16.
Jayasankaran, S. (1996). 'The big leagues: Malaysians expect a Games windfall', *Far Eastern Economic Review*, 8 February, 50.
Lans, M. S. (1995). 'Sports team logos are big business', *Marketing News*, 29 (12), 5 June, p. 6.
Schaaf, P. (1995). *Sports Marketing: It's Not Just a Game Anymore*, Prometheus Books, Amherst, NY.
Sherman, A. J. (1991). *Franchising and Licensing: Two Ways to Build Your Business*, American Management Association, New York.
Wilkof, N. J. (1995). *Trade Mark Licensing*, Sweet & Maxwell, London.

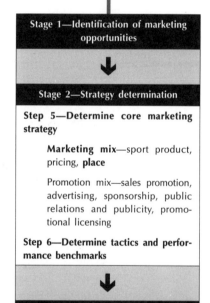

13

The place of the facility

Stage 1—Identification of marketing opportunities

Stage 2—Strategy determination

Step 5—Determine core marketing strategy

    Marketing mix—sport product, pricing, **place**

    Promotion mix—sales promotion, advertising, sponsorship, public relations and publicity, promotional licensing

Step 6—Determine tactics and performance benchmarks

Stage 3—Strategy implementation, evaluation and adjustment

CHAPTER OBJECTIVES Chapter 13 introduces the facility as the most important means by which sport services are distributed. Place as an element of the marketing mix is discussed in terms of preparing for and delivering quality service to visitors to the facility. Where to focus attention in relation to preparation for the sporting contest and actual delivery is a central concept discussed in this chapter. The concept of blueprinting is introduced to assist in this analysis. This chapter also examines different channels of distribution in sport.

After studying this chapter you should be able to:

1   Identify critical information needed to deliver quality service.
2   Identify and apply the four variable components of place.
3   Create a blueprint of how a sport product is delivered.
4   Identify the marketing channels through which sport products can be delivered.

HEADLINE STORY **VENUES FOR NOW AND THE FUTURE**

Sydney's Olympic Plan involves the development of world class sporting facilities in two primary Olympic locations—Sydney Olympic Park and the Sydney Harbour Zone. Sydney Olympic Park is a major new sports centre, forming part of the redevelopment of a 760 hectare site in the demographic centre of Sydney, 14 kilometres west of the central business district. The Sydney Harbour Zone incorporates existing venues on the immediate edge of the central business district. (Churches 1994, p. 10)

More than ten years before the actual Olympic Games, to be hosted by Sydney in the year 2000, the NSW government started the physical planning of venues, villages, media facilities, training facilities, transport services and security provisions, forming the technical infrastructure for the conduct of the Games. When in 1993 Sydney won the right to host the Games, the broad structure of what, and where to develop it (in terms of physical facilities), was already in place. Issues such as which sports to cater for, how many spectators to cater for, travel times to venues, maximised use of existing facilities, economically viable uses of all facilities after the Games, and the design of facilities to fit the environment and suit their use all needed to be considered.

In Chapter 1, *place* as an element of the marketing mix was described as distributing the product to the right place at the right time to allow ease of purchase. A unique characteristic of the sport distribution system was described in that sports generally do not physically distribute their product. Most sport products are simultaneously produced, delivered and consumed at the one location, at the one point in time. The exceptions are sporting goods and broadcast sport. Given this characteristic of the sport distribution system, the sport venue or facility becomes the most important element in the distribution strategy of the sporting organisation. In other words, the place variable in the marketing mix is the sport facility.

By manipulating the elements of the marketing mix into varying combinations, different marketing strategies can be created. For one group of customers, the sport marketer will use the place variable in a different way compared with another group of customers. To be able to do this, it is necessary to identify the variable components of the marketing mix element place, namely:

- facility planning,
- physical evidence,
- process,
- people.

These variable components are presented in Figure 13.1 and will be discussed in more detail in following sections of this chapter. The variables are presented in the sequence shown in Figure 13.1 because decisions made at a higher level (e.g. facility planning) dictate decisions at lower levels.

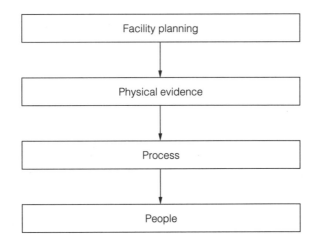

FIGURE 13.1

Variable components of place

After identifying the different variable components of place, bringing them together in an integrated fashion becomes the primary task of the sport marketer, which will be the topic of the next section. Where and when to interfere and influence can be mapped out in a blueprint, or overview of the sport service delivery system. The chapter will finish with a discussion of more traditional distribution systems, mainly used to distribute sporting goods but, as a conceptual model, also applicable to sport service products.

Sport as a service product was discussed in Chapter 5. The next section will expand on this information and explain how a quality service product can be delivered. Critical gaps exist between what service customers expect to receive and how they perceive actual service delivery. These gaps need to be managed by the sport marketer.

DELIVERING QUALITY SERVICE

Differences in perception

Simple market research like surveys or interviews can be conducted to gain an insight into customer perceptions about service quality. For the sport marketer, however, it is also important to know where differences in perception between the sport marketer and the customer occur, in order to optimise service quality before production and consumption. Figure 13.2 shows the service quality model developed by Parasuraman et al. (1985), identifying how customers' quality perceptions are influenced by four different gaps.

The model shows, as previously described in Figure 5.1, that the initial expectations of service quality depend on word-of-mouth communications, personal needs and past experience. The gaps between expected service and perceived service are created by lack of information to the sport marketer. *Gap 1* is the difference between customer expectations (e.g. an exciting game and comfortable seats) and management perceptions of customer expectations (e.g. a winning home team and a seat to sit on). *Gap 2* is the difference between management perceptions of customer expectations (a winning home team and a seat to sit on) and how they are formulated into service

FIGURE 13.2

Conceptual model of service quality

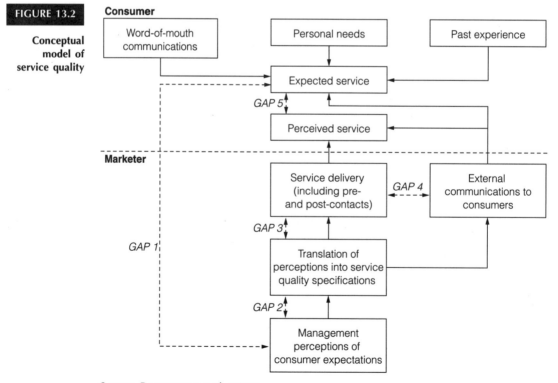

Source: Parasuraman et al. (1985).

specifications (e.g. we must field a winning team and provide something to sit on). *Gap 3* is the difference between the specifications (we must field a winning team and provide something to sit on) and actual service delivery (e.g. the team loses sometimes and some people cannot sit because too many tickets have been sold). *Gap 4* is the difference between actual service delivery (e.g. the team loses sometimes and some people cannot sit because too many tickets have been sold) and what the sport marketer communicates to be the actual service delivery (overstating or understating). The model shows that the accumulation of the four gaps leads to a level of perceived service quality by the customer. This enables the sport marketer to identify *Gap 5*—the difference between the service quality the customer expected to receive (an exciting game and comfortable seats) and how the customer perceived the actual service quality.

Dimensions of service quality

McDonald et al. (1995) use and adapt the service quality model shown in Figure 13.2 to measure service quality in professional team sport. Five dimensions of service quality were surveyed to identify the most important ones as perceived by the customer. The five dimensions are:

- *tangibles* (physical facilities, equipment, appearance of personnel);
- *reliability* (ability to perform the promised service dependably and accurately);
- *responsiveness* (willingness to help customers and provide prompt service);
- *assurance* (knowledge and courtesy of employees and their ability to inspire trust and confidence); and
- *empathy* (caring, individualised attention to customers).

Customers of a US professional basketball franchise perceived tangibles and reliability as the most important dimensions. In other words, appearance of equipment, personnel, materials and venue (tangibles) and how dependable and accurately services can be provided (reliability) are the most important variables to control in closing the gap between expected and perceived service quality.

In managing the delivery of quality service, the sport marketer should focus on tangibles and reliability issues but not ignore responsiveness, assurance and empathy issues. This will help the sport marketer in developing a service delivery system through which customer expectations can be met, or better, exceeded!

The example of the Sydney Olympic Games at the start of this chapter serves as an example of the first important consideration pertaining to planning the sports distribution system: facility planning.

FACILITY PLANNING

Planning of facilities for mega events like the Olympic Games, or facilities for a professional basketball club, or facilities for the local sport clubs, all should involve a long term perspective in terms of the prospective usage of the facility. With production and consumption of the sport products taking place in the facility, not only current provision but also future provision need to be taken into consideration. It is extremely costly to redevelop and redesign existing facilities.

The sport facility as it is highly determines opportunities and limitations for sport product provision. The Olympic Park soccer stadium in Melbourne, for example, due to its size and design is not able to host a cricket or Australian Rules football match. Soccer matches cannot be played at Olympic Park when, due to poor drainage, excessive rainfall floods the field. The Amsterdam Arena in the Netherlands, on the other hand, can host soccer matches at any time of the year. Opened in 1996, it is the world's first 'real grass' soccer stadium with a retractable roof. Excessive rainfall, in this case, is not a potential limitation.

Many sporting arenas around the world were originally developed and built to host sporting events and enable a certain number of spectators to watch the game. Few of the older arenas, however, were built to host guests in corporate boxes. With many sporting organisations dependent on corporate dollars, being left with an old stadium can turn into a severe competitive disadvantage. In other words, the ability to cater for a range of sport products is highly dependent on the planning and design of the sport facility. Sportview 13.1 further discusses the importance of the sport facility and its physical environment.

THE IMPORTANCE OF THE SERVICESCAPE FOR SPORT CONSUMERS

In the case of leisure services, it is more than just the perceived quality of the service rendered (e.g. whether a meal was delivered in a timely fashion) that influences whether consumers are satisfied with the service experience. For example, the purpose of going to an amusement park, a theatre, or a sporting event would seem to be for the excitement and stimulation of the experience. This kind of situation differs from a trip to the dry-cleaner, in which the customer is not likely to have any expectation of emotional arousal.

Because the sport product is generally purchased and consumed simultaneously, and typically requires direct human contact, customers and employees interact with each other within the organisation's physical facility. Ideally, therefore, the organisation's environment should support the needs and preferences of both service employees and customers simultaneously. Even before purchase, consumers commonly look for cues about the organisation's capabilities and quality. The physical environment is rich in such cues and may be very influential in communicating the organisation's image and purpose to its customers.

Bitner (1992) found that the facility itself, or the *servicescape*, may have a substantial effect on the customer's satisfaction with the service experience, and hence will play an important role in determining whether the customer will repatronise the service-providing sporting organisation. The important aspects of the servicescape are the spatial layout and functionality of the facility and the elements related to aesthetic appeal.

Wakefield and Blodgett (1994) tested the importance of the servicescape on Major League Baseball (MLB) consumers.

The effect of the servicescape has been gaining increased attention by owners of MLB teams, as rising attendance and increased fan satisfaction have accompanied new stadiums in Baltimore, Cleveland, Texas, Toronto and Chicago. MLB stadiums provide a good setting in which to explore both the layout and functionality aspects of the servicescape, as well as the aesthetic appeal. The ways in which seats, aisles, hallways and walkways, food service lines, restrooms, and entrances and exits are designed and arranged influence fan comfort, while the external environment, the architectural design, facility upkeep and cleanliness, use of decorative banners and signs, and personnel appearance all influence the ambience of the place.

Wakefield and Blodgett (1994) exposed potential customers to two different servicescapes: one old, low quality servicescape stadium and one new, high quality servicescape stadium. They found that the old stadium was being perceived as a significantly lower quality servicescape compared to the new one.

Respondents who perceived the servicescape to be of high quality reported higher levels of satisfaction with the servicescape, and hence were more willing to attend future games. Respondents who perceived the servicescape to be of high quality also experienced greater levels of excitement, and hence satisfaction with the servicescape. It was also found that respondents who felt crowded were less excited about the servicescape and perceived the servicescape to be of lower quality.

The results of the study may have direct implications for those who have investments in stadium projects. A return in increased gate receipts might be expected owing to new stadiums or renovations. Spectators are likely to be more excited and more satisfied when in a high quality stadium and therefore more likely to come back. Consistently fielding a winning team is increasingly expensive and difficult owing to uncontrollables such as player injuries and changes in competitors' performances. Thus another basic recommendation coming from this study is that owners/managers should be sure that the controllable aspects of the servicescape are properly managed to maximise stadium capacity.

Source: Adjusted from Bitner (1992, pp. 57–71) and Wakefield and Blodgett (1994, pp. 66–76).

Based on extensive market research, economic trend analysis and environmental scanning, the sport marketer can determine current demand and predict future customer needs. This should lead to market information on which specialists like the architect and the engineer can base their sport facility planning and construction. If the sport marketer can influence facility location, design and construction decisions, the place variable will be optimised in terms of facility opportunities. It should be noted that many sport marketers have to work with existing sport facilities. Identification of the service provision opportunities and limitations of the facility, however, remains a task to be performed by the sport marketer in order to move on to the next step: supplying physical evidence.

PHYSICAL EVIDENCE

As described in Chapter 1, the sport product itself is intangible and subjective, making it harder for the sport marketer to sell the sport product as a commodity, standardised in quality and physical shape. Legg and Baker (1987) identify three major areas of concern that customers face when purchasing services:

- understanding the service offering;
- identifying the evoked set of potential service providers; and
- evaluating the service before, during and after purchase.

Stated differently, it is hard for the customer to judge the quality of the product, and compare it with other products (providers) to arrive at a final purchase decision. If the sport marketer is able to make the sport product more tangible for the customer prior to purchase, the customer is more likely to buy it. The sport marketer has to give the sport product physical evidence.

Physical evidence should support the quality characteristics of the product because the majority of customers will judge the product on its quality. Physical evidence can be enhanced by optimising:

- sport facility design;
- promotion material and advertising; and
- service provision.

The third factor, service provision, will be discussed in the 'Process' section below.

The sport facility

The sport facility is the most tangible and visible physical evidence a sport marketer can have for their products. The name of the facility can be displayed and marketed as the place where exciting events take place. The FA Cup at Wembley, the Australian Football League (AFL) Grand Final at the Melbourne Cricket Ground and the National Basketball Association (NBA) playoffs at Madison Square Garden are all examples of events increasing in their perceived quality in combination with the respective venues. Who would get excited about the FA Cup at Queenstown football ground, the AFL Grand Final at Bendigo Football Oval or the NBA playoffs at Pinola basketball stadium?

High-tech scoreboards showing instant replays and the provision of sports trivia increase the tangibility of the event. In addition, banners, photographs or statues of sporting heroes can decorate the outside and inner walkways of the facility. All past Australian Open tennis champions decorate the inside walkways of Melbourne Park. Video or television screens and trophy exhibitions can show the famous moments of success of the teams playing in the facility. The museum at Barcelona Football Club's Nou Camp stadium in Spain has a continuous video display of Ronald Koeman's winning goal in the final of the 1992 European Club championships at Wembley football stadium. To add impact, the European Cup stands next to the video display.

Promotion

Because of the intangibility of the sport product, promotion is another way to add to the physical evidence. Adding this physical evidence is not specific to distribution through the facility, and examples are therefore not necessarily facility linked. Through either advertising or promotions, distributed among potential customers or distributed through direct mail to selected markets, the quality image and brand name of a sporting organisation can be enhanced. Legg and Baker (1987) suggest that advertisements should be vivid, using relevant tangible objects, concrete language and/or dramatisations. Photographs of past events, listings of services and explanations of different product offerings can visualise and materialise intangible services offered by the organisation. Media channels used are another important consideration. When satisfied customers are prepared to participate in these promotions, they can be used to endorse the different products, communicating their satisfaction. Celebrities, or even athlete celebrities, can also be used in this process as an influential and forceful communication channel. This type of promotion was explored in Chapter 10.

Irrespective of the media channel used, the sporting organisation should try to link pictorial (posters, merchandise, advertisements) and written (brochures, flyers, advertisements) physical evidence to the name of the organisation. Licensing strategies (team merchandise) used by the Chicago Bulls, the Australian Cricket Board (ACB) and Manchester United Football Club are excellent examples of sporting organisations adding to their physical evidence and making money with their marketing promotions. These organisations also show that the fit between the name of the organisation and physical evidence is very important when considering a licensing and merchandising strategy. This topic was discussed in Chapter 12.

PROCESS

So far only the variables that can be manipulated when preparing for the customer to come to the facility to purchase and consume the product have been discussed. Purchase and consumption involve the process by which the sporting organisation actually distributes the product to the customer. The sport marketer should be heavily involved in this sport service delivery process in order to influence and optimise the contacts between the customer and the sporting organisation. Shilbury (1994) notes that 'the facility is of paramount importance because it represents the convergence of the marketing and operations functions' (p. 31).

The marketing function

Grönroos (1990) distinguishes between the marketing department and the marketing function of an organisation. In traditional consumer goods marketing, the *marketing department* is the unit responsible for planning and implementing marketing activities. How to market a can of beans is almost the sole responsibility of the marketing department of the manufacturer; the retailer only has to put it on the shelf and sell it.

In an emerging service economy, however, marketing activities (delivering the service as opposed to selling the beans) cannot be taken care of solely by the marketing department. Contacts between the service provider (e.g. the basketball club) and the customer are so important in overall customer satisfaction that marketing activities have to be carried out by the whole organisation, not only the marketing department. Ushers and food and beverage sellers are producing and delivering parts of the overall service package and can be identified as 'part time marketers'. They belong to what Grönroos (1990) defines as the *marketing function*, 'including all resources and activities that have a direct or even indirect impact on the establishment, maintenance, and strengthening of customer relationships, irrespective of where in the organisation they are' (p. 177).

Sport servuction model

The process of how the overall package of services is planned, produced and delivered to the customer can best be explained with the help of the *sport servuction model* shown in Figure 13.3. This model will be further explained by using service delivery at a basketball match as an example. The term 'servuction' refers to the visible production and delivery of the service experience.

The sport servuction system model portrays the invisible and visible parts of the organisation. In the *invisible* part, facility management and the two basketball clubs' managements combine to organise and plan for game night. This can be classified as the traditional marketing department role. The *visible* part of the organisation consists of the facility itself, the inanimate environment (physical evidence) and the service providers (contact people). The importance of the inanimate environment was described earlier in this chapter. Contact people, like ticket sellers, ushers and food and beverage sellers, but also the basketball players, provide the different services to the customers. This accumulation of services represents the customer's overall perception of their interaction with other customers, facility staff and players.

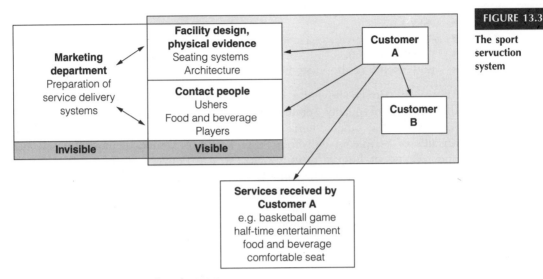

FIGURE 13.3

The sport
servuction
system

Source: Adjusted from Langeard et al. (1981).

It is in the invisible part of the organisation where managers put together the service delivery process. Questions like where do we locate merchandising stands, how many ticket sellers and ushers do we need, how do we want ticket sellers and ushers to approach customers, and how many food and beverage stands will be operated are asked and answered in order to optimise the service delivery process. Later in this chapter, the sport service delivery system will be blueprinted, based on the sport servuction system model. First, however, it is necessary to include people as the final variable component of place.

PEOPLE

Staff are responsible for the delivery of the product, and as a consequence they are the main distinguishing quality factor in the consumption process. The outcome of the basketball game cannot be guaranteed; therefore consistency in service delivery is of the utmost importance in determining the customer's overall perception of the quality of the sport product. In Chapter 5, ten criteria that customers use to evaluate service quality (Zeithaml et al. 1990) were introduced:

- tangibles,
- reliability,
- responsiveness,
- competence,
- courtesy,
- credibility,

- security,
- access,
- communication,
- understanding the customer.

These ten criteria show the importance of marketing function personnel in the delivery of quality service. Apart from tangibles (partly personnel) and security, all the other criteria are fully dependent on the training, skills and abilities of people in delivering high levels of service quality. The selection and training of human resources for service delivery in sport are a task in which the sport marketer should have strong involvement. The level of training, skills and abilities of potential employees of the sporting organisation become 'people variables' that will make the difference between mediocre and excellent service provision.

BLUEPRINTING THE SPORT SERVICE DELIVERY SYSTEM

Having identified the four variable components of the marketing mix element place, and knowing how one component can be varied independently from the other components, the sport marketer can start looking at how to combine the different components in an integrated fashion. By identifying operations (service preparation and service delivery) within the physical design of the sport facility, it is possible to make an overview or *blueprint* of the sport service delivery system. The blueprinted sport service delivery system will incorporate the four variable components of place. It now is up to the sport marketer to create the right mix of what is to be produced and consumed in the system.

Figure 13.4 displays a blueprint of the sport service delivery system for a basketball match. It follows the flow of customers through the facility and identifies different parts of the sport facility where interactions between the customer and facility personnel take place. The accumulation of these interactions contributes to the overall service experience of the customer.

Facility planning and physical evidence directly impact on all *visible* operations. The design of the facility determines how easy it is for customers to move between their seats, restrooms, and food and beverage stands. Physical evidence such as signage not only tells the customer where to go and what is going on in the facility during their visit, but can also be used to advertise or communicate upcoming events. Poster and video displays of past events can increase the customer's perception of being in a place where the product is basketball entertainment.

Facility planning has an equally important influence on *invisible* operations. How monitoring, maintenance and television operations take place is highly dependent on provisions made in the design and construction of the facility. Figure 13.3 showed that the planning and preparation of the service

Blueprint of the sport service delivery system of a basketball game FIGURE 13.4

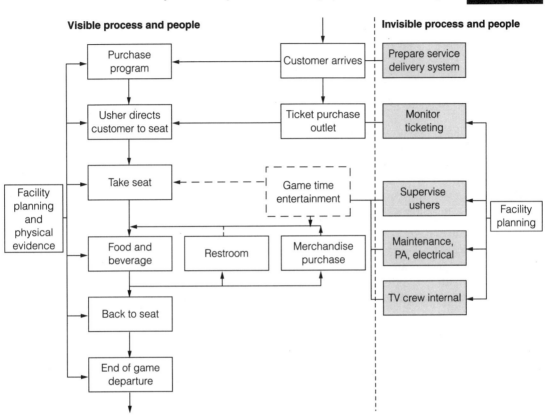

delivery system took place in the marketing department (invisible part of the organisation). This involved process and people issues such as how to approach customers, how to supply them with information or food, how many employees will be needed on game night and in which functions (ushers, food and beverage sellers, ticket sellers), and how often and when to clean restrooms. With larger crowds, parking issues and crowd flow to and from the facility become important.

The blueprint tracks the customer from entering the facility to exiting the facility and maps all possible interactions with the sporting organisation and its personnel. The blueprint identifies where the sport marketer can influence and vary the different components of place. A blueprint therefore is a vital instrument for the sport marketer in order to optimise the service experience. It is, however, only a start. As described at the beginning of this chapter, the actual delivery of service is the key to success.

In the final section of this chapter, traditional marketing channels will be discussed. The basketball example will be used again to relate these channels to the distribution of sport products.

MARKETING CHANNELS FOR SPORTING GOODS AND SERVICES

Earlier in this chapter it was noted that most sport service providers deliver the sport product to the customer directly. The organisations involved in the process of making the product available for consumption or use are jointly called a *marketing channel*. The marketing channel performs different functions in order to enable producer and customer to exchange goods or services. Boyd et al. (1995) identify the following functions of marketing channels:

- transportation and storage,
- communication of information via advertising,
- personal selling,
- sales promotion,
- feedback (marketing research),
- financing, and
- services such as installation and repair.

A trade-off between costs and benefits will decide whether channel *intermediaries* are necessary to perform some of these channel functions. Figure 13.5 shows different marketing channels for sport products.

Channels A and B are the most important marketing channels for sport products. The majority of sport service products will be delivered through those channels, as discussed earlier in this chapter. Channel A shows the delivery of the sport product through the sport facility. Because the facility usually is owned and operated by a third party, the facility provider is the channel intermediary. Channel B shows the distribution of televised sport and distribution through a facility provider. Both the television station and the facility owner are channel intermediaries at the same level in the channel. They depend on each other to get the product to the consumer.

Channels C and D are more applicable to sporting goods. Manufacturers of sporting goods will often use wholesale organisations or even *agents* (persons selling to wholesale organisations) to channel their product from the manufacturing plant to the retailer and ultimately to the final consumer. Manufacturing organisations use other organisations in the marketing channel to concentrate on what they do best, namely, manufacturing. Overall costs will become too big for the manufacturing organisation if it has to fulfil all marketing channel functions (e.g. marketing and sales to the final consumers of the product). The manufacturing organisation therefore hires other organisations to perform those functions.

The longer a marketing channel, the less control an organisation has over delivery of the product to the final consumer. Because actual service delivery is critical to consumer satisfaction, sport service organisations should aim to keep their marketing channels as short as possible, as shown in Channels A and B.

In this chapter's opening example, the organising committee of the Sydney Olympic Games will probably use all described marketing channels to

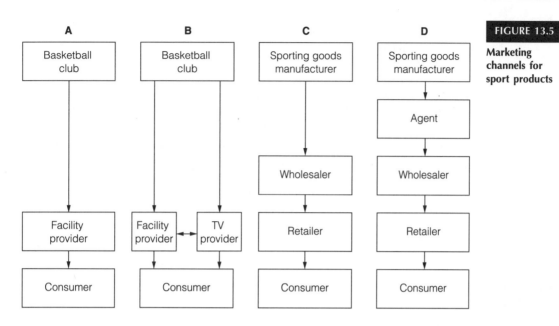

FIGURE 13.5

Marketing channels for sport products

distribute the variety of sport products. Olympic sport events will be distributed through newly built facilities or existing/renovated government-owned facilities. Some events will not be shown on television (Channel A). The majority of events, however, will be broadcast throughout the world on television (Channel B). Huge amounts of Sydney 2000 Olympics licensed merchandise will be produced by many different manufacturers around the world, using Channel C or D as their means of distribution. After the Games, ownership of the facilities and actual users will largely be separated, and the distribution of sport products will predominantly take place through Channels A and B. Both before and during the distribution process, facility planning, physical evidence, process and people are all place variables to consider in the short and long term. Quality service delivery both during and after the Games will be of the utmost importance to ensure that the Sydney Games are remembered as the best of the twenty-first century.

SUMMARY

This chapter described and explained the unique characteristics of the sport distribution system. Identifying sport products primarily as service products, it was explained how a quality service product can be delivered. Critical gaps exist between what service customers expect to receive and how they perceive actual service delivery. A conceptual model of service quality shows that these gaps are created by lack of information to the sport marketer. Research in the sport industry has shown that the appearance of equipment, personnel, materials and venue (tangibles) and how dependable and accurately services can be provided (reliability) are the most important variables to control in closing the gap between expected and perceived service quality.

The chapter also discussed the four variables of place: facility planning, physical evidence, process and people. Sport product delivery can be enhanced by planning and designing the facility to suit customer and management needs. Providing physical evidence to the intangible sport service product can enhance distribution of the sport product and the actual service delivery process, and the people involved in this process are crucial for the success of the sporting organisation. Where and when to intervene, and how to influence the service delivery process, were highlighted by introducing the blueprint, or an overview of the sport service delivery system. The chapter finished with a discussion of distribution systems or marketing channels, used to distribute sport products.

CASE STUDY

GAME, SET AND MATCH

'The facilities at Melbourne Park (formerly known as Flinders Park) were built to satisfy two quite different needs. The first was for a tennis facility of the very best international standard to ensure the Australian Open Tennis Championships retained its status as one of the four Grand Slam Tournaments. The second was for a high quality, mass entertainment indoor facility in Melbourne—a city of some 3.7 million people. A revolutionary design solution—the world renowned moveable roof—enabled these requirements to be satisfied within the one facility.

'Planning of Melbourne Park began in earnest just over a decade ago. A joint initiative by the Lawn Tennis Association of Australia—Tennis Australia—and the State Government of Victoria saw the completion of feasibility and site selection studies together with an environmental impact statement. The decision to construct was made in June, 1985. Controversy raged over the selection of the site on the banks of the Yarra River within walking distance of the heart of Melbourne as the site chosen was six hectares of public parkland. Construction work commenced in March, 1986, and was completed utilising a fast track design and construct method in time for the Ford Australian Open in January, 1988. The ringing endorsements at the time of the opening are probably best summed up by Tim Colebatch's commentary in the Melbourne Age newspaper which, in laconic Australian fashion, read;

'"We are a race of knockers. When our government proposes anything as ambitious as the Tennis Centre by the Yarra, vested interests quickly rise up to fling all the mud they can reach at it. But this time lets admit it, the government got it right—and the knockers got it wrong. The National Tennis Centre is a triumph. Its first day of business yesterday left the spectators, officials and observers of the tennis world wandering through in a state of wonder at the scale, beauty and excellence of the facilities."

'The accolades continued when Melbourne Park won twelve major international and national design and construction awards. They also won the prestigious IAKS gold medal for both outstanding design and operational performance. Detailed analysis by an international consulting group has confirmed that Melbourne Park is the bench mark by which multi purpose facilities are judged in Australia. Since opening in 1988, Melbourne Park has consistently out-performed other Australian facilities in terms of market penetration and in key areas such as catering. It has regularly out-performed other facilities (including Sydney with its larger population) in absolute terms in the key areas.

'The Ford Australian Open is the major event conducted at Melbourne Park each year, producing approximately 75% of the revenue generated by the facility as well as up to $60 million a year to the benefit of the State economy. The first event in 1988 attracted some 245,000 patrons, up from the 140,000 patrons who attended the last event at Kooyong the previous year. In each of the last 5 years the event has attracted more than 300,000 patrons with a world-wide television audience of over 500 million.'

(Spangler 1994)

'Many of the over 312,000 patrons visiting the 1995 Ford Australian Open not only came to enjoy the tennis. A variety of services were offered at Melbourne Park and the combined quality of the facility and services offered ensure patrons come back to Melbourne Park, home of the Australian Open. A report on the 1995 Open by the National Institute of Economic and Industry Research provides an overview of the opinions and expenditure on several Melbourne Park services.

'In terms of food and refreshments:

- A majority, 78%, of visitors indicated that they spent less than $50 during their visit to the 1995 Ford Australian Open.
- A larger proportion of overseas visitors (53%) had an expenditure greater than $50 compared to Victorian (15%) and interstate visitors (37%).
- 29% of males and 19% of females indicated an expenditure level above $50.
- 73% of visitors were satisfied with food and refreshments on offer.
- Visitors were pleased with the variety, but unhappy with the price.

'Of the merchandise on sale:

- 84% of visitors indicated that they spent less than $50 on merchandise.
- Similar to food and refreshment expenditures, a larger proportion of overseas visitors spent more than $50 on merchandise compared to Victorian and interstate visitors.
- 19% of males and 15% of females spent more than $50 on merchandise.
- 87% of the visitors were satisfied with the merchandise on offer.
- In general, visitors were pleased with the quality of the merchandise, but at the same time were unhappy with the price.

'In relation to parking facilities:

- 44% of visitors drove to the Ford Australian Open. Not surprisingly, the proportion was significantly higher for Victorian visitors than for interstate and overseas visitors (55%, 12% and 8% respectively).
- A large majority were satisfied with the parking facilities (90%).
- Accessibility was the main area of concern both for visitors who were satisfied and those who were not satisfied with the parking facilities.

'In terms of staff:

- 96% of visitors indicated that they were satisfied with the staff.
- A large proportion of visitors found the staff to be friendly (83%), efficient and helpful (58%).

'In terms of ticketing:

- The majority of interstate and overseas visitors purchased their Ford Australian Open tickets from BASS Victoria (46%), while the proportion of overseas visitors obtaining tickets from travel agents or "other" sources was larger compared to Victorian visitors.
- 87% of interstate and overseas visitors did not experience difficulty in obtaining their Ford Australian Open tickets.
- Of those who did experience difficulty, many were displeased with the service provided by BASS Victoria staff, and with ticket purchase selection.'

(National Institute of Economic and Industry Research 1995)

'Besides the Ford Australian Open, an extraordinary diversity of other events like rock concerts, sport events, conventions and other spectaculars are presented each year at Melbourne Park. Specialist staff are responsible for managing the facility including event administration, marketing, building, court hire and coaching services. There is also a small team under separate management dedicated to the preparations for the Ford Australian Open each year. These core staff number less than 40, with catering, cleaning, security, ticketing and many of the building maintenance services undertaken by contractors. The number of people involved in presenting a major event varies from several hundred to almost 3,000 for the Ford Australian Open.

'The recently completed stage two development, including 10 new match courts and a new function area will ensure Melbourne Park's competitive position in relation to the other 3 Grand Slam facilities which have either completed or are undertaking major expansion programs. Melbourne Park combines planning for the future with delivering excellent services now in order to win the game, set and match!'

(Spangler 1994)

Source: Excerpts from Spangler (1994) and National Institute of Economic and Industry Research (1995).

Questions

1   Comment on how the variables 'facility planning' and 'physical evidence' were/are (not) used in the case of Melbourne Park.
2   Comment on how the variables 'process' and 'people' were/are (not) used in the case of Melbourne Park.
3   Create a blueprinted sport service delivery system for the Ford Australian Open.
4   With the 3000 part time staff, which problems in service delivery are management likely to encounter during the Ford Australian Open?
5   Given the list of Melbourne Park services and the related marketing information, where would you as the sport marketer focus your attention for further improvement? Why?

REFERENCES

Bitner, M. J. (1992). 'Servicescapes: the impact of physical surrounding on customers and employees', *Journal of Marketing*, 56 (2), pp. 57–71.

Boyd, H. W., Walker, O. C. and Larréché, J. C. (1995). *Marketing Management*, Irwin, Sydney.

Churches, D. (1994). 'Sydney 2000', *Panstadia International*, 2 (2), pp. 10–14.

Grönroos, C. (1990). *Service Management and Marketing*, Lexington Books, Mass./Toronto.

Langeard, E., Bateson, J., Lovelock, C. and Eiglier, P. (1981). *Services Marketing: New Insights from Consumers and Managers*, Report No. 81–104, Marketing Science Institute, Cambridge, Mass.

Legg, D. and Baker, J. (1987). In *Add Value to Your Service*, ed. C. Surprenant, American Marketing Association, Chicago, pp. 163–8.

McDonald, M. A., Sutton, W. A. and Milne, G. R. (1995). 'TEAMQUAL: measuring service quality in professional team sports', *Sport Marketing Quarterly*, 4 (2), pp. 9–15.

National Institute of Economic and Industry Research (1995). 'An economic impact study', in *Survey and Analysis of the 1995 Ford Australian Open*, prepared for Tennis Australia, Melbourne/Clifton Hill.

Parasuraman, A., Zeithaml, V. A. and Berry, L. L. (1985). 'A conceptual model of service quality and its implications for future research', *Journal of Marketing*, 49, Fall, pp. 41–50.

Shilbury, D. (1994). 'Delivering quality service in professional sport', *Sport Marketing Quarterly*, 3 (1), pp. 29–35.

Spangler, I. (1994). 'Game, set and match', *Panstadia International*, 2 (2), pp. 24–8.

Wakefield, K. L. and Blodgett, J. G. (1994). 'The importance of servicescapes in leisure service settings', *Journal of Services Marketing*, 8 (3), pp. 66–76.

Zeithaml, V. A., Parasuraman, A. and Berry, L. L. (1990). *Delivering Quality Service*, Free Press, New York.

PART III

Strategy implementation, evaluation and adjustment

14

Coordinating and controlling marketing strategy

CHAPTER OUTLINE

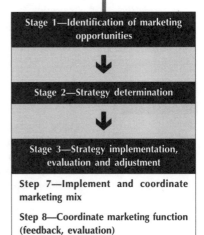

Stage 1—Identification of marketing
opportunities

Stage 2—Strategy determination

Stage 3—Strategy implementation,
evaluation and adjustment

Step 7—Implement and coordinate
marketing mix

Step 8—Coordinate marketing function
(feedback, evaluation)

Chapter 14 summarises the important concepts introduced throughout this book. It does so by reviewing the role of the control function in coordinating and implementing the selected marketing strategies. Three forms of control are introduced: feed forward, concurrent and feedback, and their role is discussed in relation to the key measures used to determine the success of the sport-marketing program. A short section reviewing careers in sport marketing is also included in this chapter.

After studying this chapter you should be able to:

1 Understand the importance of control in the marketing function.
2 Identify the three types of control.
3 Identify the primary measures of success.
4 Comprehend the relationship between measures of success and the control process.
5 Recognise the importance of coordinating and implementing marketing strategies.
6 Identify possible career options in sport marketing.

VOLLEYBALL DIGS IN

Spikes, digs and kills will be rampant throughout the country 17 June to 25. Thanks to the week-long 'Volley across America,' volleyball enthusiasts will have the opportunity to participate in a wide-reaching grassroots promotion, designed to help increase the interest in the game and build participation . . . As part of the year-long celebration of the sport's centennial birthday, spearheaded by the SGMA Volleyball Council, 'Volley across America' will open with a range of participatory activities to be held on The Mall in Washington DC. It will include the set-up of volleyball courts on the city's grassy expanse, and free clinics featuring some of the country's top volleyball players. (Pesky 1995, p. 22)

Volleyball's need to 'dig in' brings us to the last theme of this book: coordinating and implementing marketing strategies. This book has considered the marketing mix and as a consequence all the variables that the sport marketer can manipulate to ensure that a sport is able to identify and sustain a competitive advantage. Volleyball's decision to implement a year-long promotion campaign in association with its centennial birthday is an example of a range of marketing and promotion mix variables combining to form a marketing strategy. How these strategies are implemented is part of the management aspect of marketing.

This chapter reviews the range of functions necessary to implement strategies. It examines some of the control mechanisms available to the marketer to ensure that performance targets are met, and considers some of the more relevant measures used to gauge success in sport. Inherent in these measures is the question of game design and its contribution to the marketing process.

Also, the place and importance of sponsorship are discussed in the context of overall strategy determination. Finally, the chapter revisits the question of sport marketing planning, noting the importance of integrating all the components of the marketing mix in one overall strategy. Given that the strategy determination process is the job of the sport marketer, it is important to review their role in sporting organisations. As part of this analysis, careers in sport marketing will be examined.

CONTROLLING THE SPORT MARKETING FUNCTION

Boyd and Walker (1990) note that the *control* process 'consists essentially of setting standards, specifying and obtaining feedback data, evaluating it, and taking corrective action' (p. 865). Setting standards is part of the marketing planning process discussed in Chapter 2. Marketing objectives established during this process will have identified the standards to be achieved. In sporting organisations these objectives and standards differ from those of organisations solely concerned with profit and providing dividends to shareholders.

Sport is unique in this regard as there are often broader goals than simply maximising profits, as was discussed in Chapter 6. For example, in the dispute between the Australian Rugby League (ARL) and Superleague, the judge noted that the ARL board 'were motivated in large part by considerations other than the pursuit of profit. It is concerned with the preservation and enhancement of the traditions of the game' (Burchett 1996, p. 65).

Recognition of these broader considerations does not in any way lessen the importance of marketing sport. In fact it is quite the opposite, as sport, like most non-profit entities, often does not have access to financial resources to the same extent as for-profit entities. Sporting organisations rely on the ability of marketing programs to raise the revenue required to run the club, association or league. Several consistent themes have emerged during this book alluding to the main measures of success in sporting organisations. Most of them are directly aligned to elements of the marketing mix. Establishing and benchmarking performance standards are the first step to controlling the marketing program.

Types of control

There are three types of organisational control:

- feed forward,
- concurrent, and
- feedback.

Feed forward control takes place before production and operations begin and commences during the strategic sport-marketing planning process (SSMPP).

FIGURE 14.1   The control process and measures of success

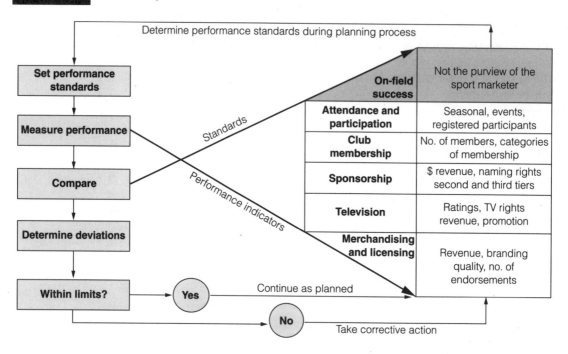

Determining the operating procedures and setting standards for the operation of a facility prior to a season commencing are examples of feed forward control. As part of this review of operational procedures, appropriate staff training will be provided consistent with service quality policies. This form of control is designed to ensure that all inputs are of the highest quality to ensure optimum spectator enjoyment.

Concurrent control occurs during the sporting fixture, or in other words, while the plans are being carried out. Often in sport this will be a major event or the weekly fixtures in a season. In the sport facility, monitoring the quality of service delivery exemplifies concurrent control. Supervisors will be responsible for checking that staff carry out their jobs in a manner consistent with the organisation's policy. In some cases it is possible to fine-tune the activity as it occurs or to rectify problems immediately. Where this is possible it is an example of concurrent control. Concurrent control can also occur during a major event or a season when monitoring attendances. If these are lower than expected, advertising may need to be intensified, or altered, or sales promotions implemented to return the organisation to a satisfactory level of performance. Determining acceptable levels of performance requires the identification of appropriate measures during the strategic sport-marketing planning process.

Feedback control focuses on the final performance measured against the standards or targets foreordained. As a consequence of this feedback, the marketing plan can be reviewed and modified where necessary to ensure that the defined performance standards can be achieved during the next season or event.

Figure 14.1 displays the link between the stages of the control process and the measures typically used to ascertain success in a sporting organisation.

MEASURES OF SUCCESS

On-field success

On-field success is typically the most obvious and visible measure of success by which to assess the performance of sporting organisations. It is, however, as indicated in Chapter 1, an area over which the sport marketer has little control. Unlike most products, where the marketer has some input into design and packaging, the sport marketer has no control over the quality of the team selected. The selection and development of players are not the purview of the sport marketer. The sport marketer, however, is responsible for promoting the team based on the quality of the team and its star athletes. Elements of this marketing effort will be seen in ticketing and games promotions, advertising, public relations and sponsorship strategies, all discussed in earlier chapters of this book.

It has been stressed in this book that the sport marketer needs to ensure that overpromising is not a feature of the promotion mix. It could be argued, for example, that the head coach of the Australian swimming team at the 1996 Olympic Games overpromised in relation to the success of his athletes. Ultimately, the Australian swimming team performed well, but expectations were so high that the actual performance (in terms of medals) was seen to be relatively poor. What could have been a perfect situation on which to build future marketing strategies turned into an exercise in managing negative public relations.

On-field success, then, is an organisation-wide measure not specific to the efforts of marketing personnel. The derivates, however, of on-field or off-field success *are* the purview of the sport marketer. These will now be discussed.

Attendance and participation

Attendance and participation are two key measures of marketing performance. They are linked, as elite athletes serve as role models for those participating at lower levels of sporting competition. Known as the 'Norman factor', the effect that Greg Norman has on golf participation and attendance when he visits Australia to play in major golf tournaments is undisputed. Typically, attendances at the event and interest in golf both rise, as was evident in the 1996 South Australian Open. Increased participation in a sport has the added benefit of contributing to increased attendances, as people's affinity with a sport increases via participation and they are therefore more likely to watch it, either live or on television.

Sporting organisations are therefore concerned with increasing the number of registered participants. Strategies designed to ensure participation have been discussed in this book. The introduction of modified rules for juniors has been the main strategy designed to attract juniors to play sport. These modified rules programs become integral parts of marketing strategy as all sports strive to capture a finite group of participants. Registration numbers are important measures of success, in particular of the success of marketing programs.

Attendance also is a frequently cited measure of success for an association, club or league. Elements of the promotion mix, pricing policies, service quality and facility management have been important factors discussed in this book contributing to the likely success of maximising attendances.

Club membership

Club membership is another important measure. As discussed in Chapter 7, club members represent heavy attendance on the frequency attendance escalator and as a consequence are an important source of revenue. More importantly, this revenue often comes well before the season, providing much-needed income during a period when no games are conducted to generate weekly revenues. Chapter 7 also highlighted the importance of ensuring loyalty for long-term members. Marketing programs should be designed to reward longevity and minimise defection, or season ticket holders 'falling off' the frequency attendance escalator.

Sponsorship

Sponsorship is another key measure of success in the marketing program. In fact, sponsorship has been considered so important that many sports have developed unidimensional marketing programs aimed at attracting sponsorship revenue. In the long term, this myopic view is detrimental to the sporting organisation for two reasons:

- It negates the extent to which the sporting organisation can devise a full range of marketing-related benefits that can be provided to the sponsor.
- It concentrates the success of the marketing program on one objective.

Concentration on any one objective is potentially poor strategy. Sporting organisations need to diversify their range of marketing strategies to ensure that there is not an over-reliance on any one area. For example, if sponsorship income falls well below anticipated projections, the overall success of the organisation will be threatened because no effort has been made to raise revenues by ensuring attendance, attracting members and selling merchandise. As Chapter 10 noted, sponsorship myopia is caused by the capacity of sport to attract sponsors seeking a relatively inexpensive way to promote their products. As some sporting organisations have the capacity to fulfil sponsor objectives easily, this adds to the potential to concentrate solely on sponsorship income at the expense of developing a broad-based marketing program including all elements of the marketing mix.

Television

The importance of television to the marketing effort has been stressed throughout this book. Television has the capacity to provide significant streams of revenue as well as to act as an important promotion vehicle for sports, even if no television revenue is forthcoming. Therefore television as a measure of success is very important.

Sport marketers must carefully determine the role of television in their marketing plans. Questions to be answered in relation to setting marketing objectives include: Is the sport capable of attracting television rights revenue? If so, how much? If not, can some coverage be obtained to help promote the sport? Answers to these questions determine the marketing objectives set in relation to television, and as a consequence the measures used to assess performance. Chapter 9 conveyed in detail the range of measures used to assess the success of sport programming and the subsequent advertising revenue that these programs can attract. Successful sport marketers need to have an intimate knowledge of the way in which the television business operates to ensure that television revenues or promotions are successfully implemented in the overall marketing strategy.

Television's impact on sport is an important strategic issue for sport marketers. To what extent are sports required to modify their game to make it more attractive to television? The opening to Chapter 1 of this book highlighted this issue using soccer as an example. Sportview 14.1 provides another example, this time in Taekwondo. Television exposure is so critical in the overall promotion mix that tensions often exist between the marketing perspective of what is good for a sport and the sport operation's view as to what is best for the sport's development. The scheduling of major events also can be subject to the influence of television. Sportview 14.1 indicates that this is a common problem worldwide. Taekwondo's dilemma also shows the range of issues confronting a sport wishing to expand its participation base and reposition itself in a wider market. Being accepted as a medal sport at the Sydney 2000 Olympic Games affords Taekwondo the opportunity to reposition and market itself accordingly. The next four years represent the ideal period in which to formulate a new strategy for the sport, some of which is already reflected in the need to become more appealing to television audiences.

Although the need to appease television can be a potential problem, in some instances it has also forced sports to modernise and therefore present a more attractive product. Cricket, as discussed in this book, has been better off for the World Series Cricket revolution in 1977. The introduction of the one-day game, with a variety of new rules better suited to television, has brought an added dimension to playing standards through improved fielding, more creative batting and an array of tactics not seen previously. It is not the purpose of this book to take one view as to whether television's impact on sport in relation to changing the game is either good or bad. Clearly, there are examples where such changes have benefited sport and others where they have been to the detriment of the sport. This is an important issue, and rather than adopt an extreme position either way sport marketers should carefully think through the implications of change. The sport marketer should conduct research, consult past and current players and trial changes, in just the same way as marketers do when preparing to introduce new products.

NEW KICKS FROM KOREA

'Taekwondo specialists are head-over-heels—with joy. Korea's venerable martial art, famous for its acrobatic kicks and flying punches, has been accepted as a full Olympic sport for the summer games at Sydney in 2000. For the first time taekwondo black-belts will fight each other for the top range of Olympic medals on a par with gentler types such as high jumpers and hurdlers. The Koreans who supervise the sport of taekwondo campaigned hard for Olympic recognition, which became official on September 4th, and, if worldwide numbers are any test, their victory was overdue. In the 30 years since taekwondo was codified into a modern sport its popularity has soared. There were no more than 35,000 black-belt holders in the world in 1970. Now there are more than 3 million, with perhaps another 50 million practitioners at lower levels of skill. Well-known taekwondoists include King Juan Carlos of Spain, action-movie heroes Chuck Norris and Steven Seagal, not to mention two dozen or so American congressmen. In South Korea it was recently reported with pride that President Bill Clinton has a taekwondo teacher whom he respectfully addresses as "Grand Master".

'But international recognition does not come free. To complete its transformation from a relatively minor martial art into a genuinely popular pastime-cum-spectator sport, taekwondo has to become more exciting to watch. And if taekwondo continues its spread across the world, exclusive control of the sport is likely to slip from South Korean hands. Despite its flashy reputation, only exhibition taekwondo is visually exciting. In match bouts the present way of scoring encourages cautious, unspectacular sparring. Easy blows, such as the straight punch to the chest, win as many points as crowd-pleasing—and much harder—airborne assaults such as the flying kick to the head.

'This is a shame. Taekwondo is distinguished from the Japanese martial art of karate mainly by the variety and elegance of the kicks its practitioners inflict on one another. An afternoon spent watching one of the better Korean junior high school exhibition teams is likely to convince even the most martial-arts-weary observer that taekwondo, properly adapted, could be a winner on television. Petite nine-year-old girls in pigtails leap up and smash with their insteps blocks of wood held high above their heads. A twelve-year-old soars over a classmate's head, twists in mid-air and kicks a cola can into the next world. Fifteen-year-olds shatter three shoulder-high targets, one to the north, one to the east and one to the west, without either foot touching the ground.

'Competitive taekwondo could become equally enthralling if changes to the rules now under discussion were put into effect. It is proposed, for example, that combatants get one point for a punch, two for a standing kick, and three for a jumping kick. Some diehards object to changing an ancient martial art to please television viewers. But they are in the minority. And they may even be wrong about taekwondo's traditions. Rewarding kicks more than punches would in a sense be a return to taekwondo's roots. Before protective helmets became compulsory, it was easier to flatten an opponent with a kick to the temples than with a punch to the midriff.

'As worrisome for the more conservative members of taekwondo's governing body, which is based in South Korea's capital, Seoul, is the fact that taekwondo cannot forever be kept a Korean preserve. At present South Koreans outkick the world in taekwondo. This is no surprise. For South Koreans anxious about their communist North Korean neighbour taekwondo is a mixture of national sport and military duty. Almost all young men in South Korea must do time in the armed forces, where taekwondo is obligatory. The sport, it is believed, helps recruits withstand the ordeal of military life, with its brutal exercises and frequent beatings. South Korea has the world's most dangerous (unarmed) bar brawls—and a vast pool of potential medal winners.

'One sign of change is the growing share of non-South Korean prize winners in international games. Another is a likely loosening of South Korea's grip on the system of promotion. In order to rise beyond first-degree black-belt under the current system, a taekwondoist needs the recommendation of an extremely high ranking instructor. Such instructors are rare outside Korea and America. So it is unreasonably hard for a Ghanaian or a Turk to rise through the taekwondo ranks, a wrong that non-Koreans want righted.

'The South Koreans, for all that, seem readier to open up their sport to the world than is Japan's Sumo Association, to take a notorious example of xenophobia. Taekwondo has no top-ranking bigots on a par with Kojima Noboru, a sumo kingpin. He argued in 1992 that quarter-tonne foreign wrestlers should be barred from sumo's highest grade because they lacked the uniquely Japanese quality of hinkaku—a term hard to translate but which means something like dignity, self-knowledge and self-control. In South Korea, unlike other Asian countries, the sporting authorities tend to play down the spiritual side of their nation's martial art. Like it or not, they say, modern taekwondo is a sport, not a devotional rite. According to an American taekwondo expert, the Zen approach to taekwondo as a path to enlightenment probably appeals now more to foreigners than to Koreans. Perhaps Zen is less help in bars.'

Source: Reprinted from *The Economist* (1994, p. 121).

Merchandising and licensing

Merchandising and licensing are important marketing objectives. Promotional licensing was the subject of Chapter 12, where it was shown that sporting organisations license their logos and trademarks for two reasons:

- to create awareness of the sport, club or league, and
- to endorse product lines outside of sport as a means to generate additional revenue.

Revenue from licensing income becomes the main measure in determining the success of such a program. Clearly, this revenue can be easily measured.

Service quality

Another important, but less tangible, measure is service quality, which has been developed as an ongoing theme through this book. It has been discussed in Chapters 5 and 13 as providing the basis for establishing a competitive advantage. It also indirectly affects everything that is concerned with attracting spectators, members and sponsors, contributing to the likelihood of repeat purchase. Strategically, it is significant because it has the capacity to even out the fluctuations in enjoyment governed by winning or losing. An enjoyable night at the basketball, for example, may to some extent offset the disappointment of losing.

This raises the critical question in relation to this intangible area of assessing how much participants and spectators enjoy the sport experience. Equally, this question relates to winning. Clubs, associations and leagues are increasingly realising that their marketing programs should be designed to build loyalty—loyalty that has the capacity to withstand periods of poor on-field performance. The reality of most sporting competitions is that it is in their own interests to ensure that winning is shared by all, and therefore mechanisms will be put in place to even out the competition. Clubs will experience periods during which they are successful and periods when they perform poorly. Success on the field does not guarantee success off the field, but poor on-field performance almost certainly guarantees poor off-field success based on the measures previously discussed in this section. Reducing the impact of these periods of poor on-field performance enhances the likelihood of achieving financial stability.

Financial stability

Despite an earlier statement in this chapter that profit is not the sole goal of sporting organisations, it has increased in importance during the last decade. Many sporting organisations typified the extreme position where debt could be freely incurred without considering the consequences. Fortunately, this culture is changing, reinforcing the importance of control in the implementation of marketing activities. Modern sporting organisations more readily understand the balance between on-field success and sound off-field success.

Most of the measures of success discussed in this section contribute to the income-generating potential of the organisation. The ability to reign in costs is the subject of broader texts in the management domain covering the issue of control in more detail.

COORDINATING AND IMPLEMENTING MARKETING STRATEGY

The framework for determining marketing strategy was discussed in Chapter 2. Coordination and implementation of this strategy are primarily the responsibility of the marketing department. Kotler et al. (1989) define *marketing implementation* as 'the process that turns marketing strategies and plans into marketing actions in order to accomplish strategic marketing objectives' (p. 635). Coordination cannot occur, however, without the support of the entire organisation. Marketing staff are often reliant, for example, on sport operations staff to allow star players to become involved in promotion activities. Typically, these star players are in high demand for such promotion activities, often conflicting with training and playing schedules.

Implementation is primarily about staff management and in essence deals with the *who, what, where* and *when* of the marketing plan. The who, what, where and when activities are the result of the strategies determined, otherwise referred to as the *what* and *why*. Implementation is often difficult, more difficult than determining the strategies. It is easy to dream up a range of interesting and creative strategies; however, when it comes to actual implementation it may be found that they are totally unrealistic or impractical. When setting SMART objectives, as discussed in Chapter 2, the 'R' for realistic is of paramount importance. Ultimately, it is the staff and their expertise that determine the ability of the organisation to coordinate the marketing strategy.

Added to the difficulties of coordinating marketing strategies is the relatively recent introduction of marketing personnel, even marketing departments, in sporting organisations. In fact, in some sporting organisations in Australia, a national development officer or state development officer is responsible for the marketing program, based on their responsibility for promoting and encouraging participation. In some sports, specialist sport-marketing staff are now being employed. The Australian Cricket Board (ACB), for example, now employs a marketing manager, marketing assistant, licensing assistant and marketing service manager. Careers in sport marketing are beginning to flourish.

Careers in sport marketing

The ACB is indicative of the range of career options emerging in this field. Professional sports in particular offer the greatest range of career options.

Marketing staff employed in Australian Football League (AFL) clubs have increased markedly during the 1990s. The Carlton Football Club, for example, employed seven staff in its marketing division in 1995. These included a marketing manager, corporate marketing manager responsible for sponsorship, Optus marketing executive, marketing service manager, marketing executive, marketing administration assistant and marketing assistant. All seven staff were responsible for the implementation and coordination of all the club's marketing activities. Also, their employment is indicative of the breadth and range of activities undertaken by the club. Sponsorship, coordinating the ground sponsorship deal with Optus, managing club and social club memberships, fundraising events, licensing and merchandising, and servicing game day functions cover the gamut of marketing mix variables discussed in this book.

Most large sporting organisations now incorporate media relations in their marketing department. Tennis Australia is one such organisation, with a marketing and media department. The importance of public relations has been stressed throughout this book as a vital function within the marketing mix, and as a consequence it should be integrated into the activities of the marketing department. Table 14.1 illustrates some of the employment and career prospects emerging in the field in Australia. The jobs shown in Table 14.1 were advertised during 1995 and 1996 in *The Age* and *Weekend Australian.*

Slowly, there is evidence that marketing personnel are being employed in a greater variety of sporting organisations. The biggest hurdle to overcome in expanding an organisation's staff expertise has been the view that sport promotes itself and therefore does not require marketing staff. This complacency has been responsible for the slow pace at which sport has embraced the need for marketing expertise. Clearly, there is evidence of this changing. Interestingly, the pace of change has become more urgent as sporting organisations realise the capacity of a skilled marketing team's potential to contribute to the full range of revenue-earning possibilities via marketing programs. It is true that in some instances it is necessary to spend money

TABLE 14.1	Job	Organisation
Careers in sport marketing	Marketing and membership manager	South Australian Cricket Association
	Marketing assistant sport sponsorship	Australian Institute of Sport
	Promotions and marketing executive	Victorian Soccer Federation
	Marketing assistant	Brisbane Broncos
	Marketing manager	Port Adelaide Football Club
	Membership coordinator	Hawthorn Football Club
	Marketing manager	NSW Cricket Association
	Marketing and promotions executive	Basketball Australia
	Marketing manager	Tennis Australia
	Membership services director	Gymnastics Australia
	Sponsorship sales executive	Victoria Racing Club
	Marketing manager	WA Cricket Association
	Public relations and media manager	Australian Institute of Sport

up front to ensure that revenue-earning potential is maximised. Advertising, public relations launches and staff training in terms of service delivery are examples of this. However, they are also the means of communicating with a public that is increasingly subject to an attractive range of recreation and leisure pursuits capable of detracting from interest in sport. The last decade in particular has seen a rapidly intensifying range of competitive forces within the recreation and leisure industry. In many ways this has been good for sport, as sports have been forced to professionalise their operations and modernise the way they deliver the overall sport package. The overall sport package remains the domain of all staff and board members associated with various sports, but the sport marketer's input to the package is rapidly increasing.

SPORT-MARKETING PLANNING REVISITED

Central to this book has been the role of strategic marketing planning in sporting organisations. Figure 2.1 showed the steps involved in the process. Sport marketers should follow the steps shown until they become familiar with the process. It is possible to vary the steps at times, but in general the process remains unchanged for the variety of different sporting organisations. What does change is the emphasis placed on the importance of various steps in the process. A summary of the strategic sport-marketing plan (SSMP) is shown in Figure 14.2. Sport marketers required to develop an SSMP should use this framework to prepare their plan. This book has provided the added detail in the respective chapters to assist the sport marketer to consider all necessary issues at each stage of the marketing plan.

Stage 1, 'Identification of marketing opportunities', should remain fairly constant. As each organisation prepares to enter a new three- to five-year plan, a renewed analysis of the environment and review of the organisation's capabilities should be undertaken. Importantly, this review should recognise the changing forces driving competition in the sport and recreation industry. This book has already noted changes in the competitive forces confronted by sporting organisations during the last ten to fifteen years. Decisions taken in regard to the overall analysis of the organisation filter down to the marketing mission and objectives set, to allow marketing activities to contribute to broader organisational goals. Most of these decisions are based on the market research and data available to accurately assess buying patterns and consumer behaviour in general. Understanding consumer behaviour in sport and market research and segmentation were covered in Part I of this book. In general, these stages remain constant components of the SSMPP.

Stage 2, 'Strategy determination', represents the greatest detail provided in this book. This is because it is at this stage of determining the core marketing strategy that the range of marketing mix variables can be varied to suit the circumstances confronting an organisation. The reason for selecting

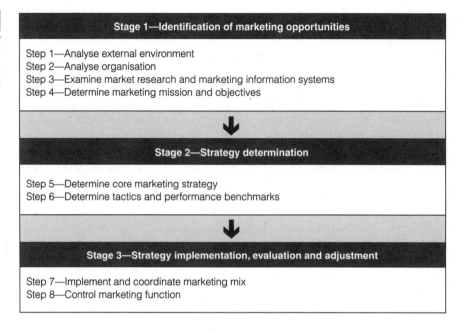

FIGURE 14.2

**Summary of
the strategic
sport-marketing
planning
process**

Stage 1—Identification of marketing opportunities

Step 1—Analyse external environment
Step 2—Analyse organisation
Step 3—Examine market research and marketing information systems
Step 4—Determine marketing mission and objectives

Stage 2—Strategy determination

Step 5—Determine core marketing strategy
Step 6—Determine tactics and performance benchmarks

Stage 3—Strategy implementation, evaluation and adjustment

Step 7—Implement and coordinate marketing mix
Step 8—Control marketing function

the mix of variables also changes, depending on whether a repositioning exercise is required, such as that described for the NSW Rugby League (NSWRL) during this book, or the development of product offerings aimed at specific market segments. Stage 2 also represents the greatest unknown in terms of 'Have we chosen the right core marketing strategy?' There is no correct answer to the question. It can only be answered over time, and even this is subject to the ability of staff to implement marketing plans.

Stage 3, 'Strategy implementation', consists of measuring performance based on standards determined earlier in the process and, where necessary, modifying or altering the way in which the core marketing strategy is implemented. Control, implementation and coordination, as discussed in this last chapter, are crucial to the overall success of the marketing strategy. Implementation, like strategy determination, is an ongoing process. As one season or event rolls into the next, it becomes important for marketing personnel to step back every so often to assess progress and to ensure that strategies are not subject to rapid change based on short-term success. In particular, for seasonal sports it is important that week-by-week winning or losing does not unduly interfere with strategic marketing plans, usually prepared for three to five years. This is one of sport's greatest pitfalls: reacting to short-term poor on-field performance. It also represents the main difficulty confronted by the sport marketer: to market a product over which there is little control.

Implementation is also guided by the assumptions made during the planning process. Because all strategies and action plans are based on these assumptions about the future they are subject to considerable risk. It is necessary for marketing managers to assess continually the assumption on which strategies were based. It is here that the beginning and end of the planning process meet. In fact, there is never an end, as the cycle continues in a feedback loop that sometimes blurs beginning and end. To some extent this is a good sign. It indicates that once the plan and associated strategies are formulated they are not simply put on the shelf. Plans put into action are subject to contingency planning to correct assumptions that do not prove to be true. Therefore the SSMPP is dynamic, rarely stagnant and laden with challenges to ensure that the full potential of marketing's contribution to the overall functioning of a sporting organisation is optimised. We wish you well with this challenge.

THE MELBOURNE CRICKET CLUB—A CASE FOR MARKETING STRATEGY

This case study was originally prepared by Julie McLoughlin, as part of her studies towards the Graduate Diploma of Sport Management at Deakin University in 1994.

Introduction

The Melbourne Cricket Club (MCC), ground manager of the Melbourne Cricket Ground, had its inaugural meeting in 1838 and is argued to have been the first Club established in Melbourne. The Club's first site was in William Street, the current site of the mint. After two temporary relocations the Club found its home in Yarra Park on Crown Land in 1853, which subsequently became the land on which the Melbourne Cricket Ground (MCG) was located. The first grandstand was built on the MCG in 1861 and football was first played in 1858. Prior to this time cricket was the sole sport played at the ground. The Club was incorporated in 1974 by an Act of Parliament and has existed as a legal entity ever since.

The Melbourne Cricket Club

The mission of the Club in regard to the management of the MCG was perhaps best stated in the 1986–87 Annual Report by the then President, Donald Cordner, '. . . The Club's long standing policy of providing the most comfortable, spacious viewing facility in a secure environment.' He also mentioned in the 1989–90 Annual Report, in reference to the Club's mission, '. . . a private club with public responsibilities'.

By 1995, the MCC did not have a formal mission statement. It was being formulated and early drafts suggest that the MCC's mission is;

1 To provide quality service and valuable opportunities to Club members and to fulfil the desire of large numbers of people to become and remain members;
2 To provide a world class venue (the MCG) capable of housing various events including sporting and other entertainment activities; a high quality

administrative service for promoters and associated organisations, and event day service for MCC and AFL members, corporate clients and general public;

3 To provide a world class sports museum in honour of Australia's sporting heritage, which will attract both local and international visitors to the ground seven days a week.

Membership

There are currently 55,000 members.

> All nominations are accepted and admission to membership is based entirely on chronological order of enrolment. Currently the waiting list for membership is 100,000 and nominations are received at the rate of about 11,000 annually. (Lill 1994, p. 29)

This statement from the 1984–85 Annual Report regarding membership, supports the notion that its strength has led to the success of the MCC. 'No other controlling bodies of sport world-wide can take such comfort from a tailor-made future audience of this dimension' (see figure 14.3).

Percentage increase over ten years:

- No of Members   63%
- Waiting List   65%

Membership primarily offers a reserve to view sporting events at the MCG; the Club also offers playing memberships. The sporting sections of the Club are, tennis, lawn bowls, shooting, cricket, hockey, squash, baseball, football and lacrosse. Though public perception of the Club and its involvement with the ground has not always been positive, the members of the Club have helped to finance a large amount of the improvements at the ground over the years.

MCC membership

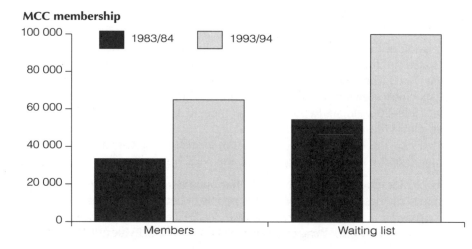

In fact, members paid almost the entire cost of the Olympic Stand for the 1956 Olympics. In the 1984–85 Annual Report, in relation to the members voting overwhelmingly to increase subscriptions to pay for stadium development, the then President, Bernard Callinan wrote

> I convey my personal gratitude for . . . a demonstration of the loyalty that always has enabled the Club to fulfil its Charter in relation to progressive stadium development.

The venue

According to research completed in 1992 by the Strategic Management Group, most facilities are under utilised and are unused 90% of the time. This statement may have had limited validity in 1992, however things have changed drastically since the building of the new Southern Stand. The current capacity of the MCG is 102,000 and the average crowd (not including Interstate cricket) close to 50,000. The ground is used as a venue on 25% of the 365 days in the year. Due to maintenance of the cricket pitch and the arena in general, utilisation of the ground is limited, and current usage is close to its maximum for sport. Also, long-term agreements with the AFL and the VCA leave little space in the calendar for other events to take place.

In 1994, the MCG hosted 51 AFL games (including the Grand Final), 1 Rugby League State-of-Origin match, 9 days of International cricket, 22 days of Interstate cricket, and numerous product launches, conferences and luncheons. A concert was not scheduled for 1994; however, 1993 saw seven major concerts at the MCG and 6 more are possible in early 1995. Major events at the MCG attracted around three million patrons to the ground in 1994.

MCG attendance 1983–1994

Year	No. event days	Total attendance	Average
1983/84	55	1 333 781	24 251
1984/85	68	1 564 937	23 014
1985/86	67	1 331 712	21 106
1986/87	57	1 503 312	26 374
1987/88	68	1 291 158	18 988
1988/89	68	1 446 533	21 272
1989/90	58	1 409 970	24 309
1990/91	50	1 575 900	31 518
1991/92	60	1 144 595	19 073
1992/93	70	2 239 100	31 987
1993/94	90	2 636 592	29 295

The MCC and the Trust have always been dedicated to improving the facilities at the venue, and have attempted to keep up with technological and social change when implementing improvements: e.g., scoreboards, floodlights and corporate areas. In support of this statement and referring to corporate areas taking up seats, the President, Donald Cordner, wrote in the 1986–87

Annual Report, 'The reduced capacity is a reflection of the expectations of modern sporting audiences for increased comfort'.

Prior to 1989 the MCC had no leasehold over the MCG, and as stated by the President, Bernard Callinan, in the 1984/85 report,

> It has been my continuing concern as President that the MCC, which for 147 years had done more to promote sport than any Club in Australia, cannot be master of its own destiny under existing legislation. The Club manages Australia's number one stadium, yet has no leasehold and can be dismissed at the behest of any government.

In 1990, the MCG Trust finally granted the MCC a 27 year lease on the Ground and a 52 year agreement for the Club to act as ground manager, subject to compliance with provisions of the agreement.

The Australian Gallery of Sport (AGOS)

The AGOS was opened in 1986. Operation of the AGOS is the responsibility of the MCG Trust though management is handled by the Club. In 1993–94 the AGOS attracted 61,000 people to tour the gallery and MCG. Volunteer guides carry out the tours, and due to increased demand, the number of guides has increased from 17 to 100 since its opening. According to the 1992/93 Trust Annual Report, the expenditure attributed to AGOS was $930,269 while the income was only $622,251. AGOS was established for the public interest and to foster interest in Australia's sporting history. As supported by the President, it was not intended to be profit generating:

> The Club is responsible for the very considerable expense associated with the operations and maintenance of the Gallery and I would like to emphasise that this is another example of the discharge of our responsibility to the general public. (D Cordner, 1986–87 Annual Report).

Organisational structure

The MCC has been a traditional Club run by a general committee and is currently staffed by a General Manager and 50 full time employees. The Events Department employs around 800 casual employees on event days and the Maintenance Department employs numerous casuals for cleaning and maintenance work around the stadium.

The MCG is on crown land, with ultimate authority resting with the Victorian Government.

> The MCG is administered by a government appointed trust which delegates day-to-day management responsibility for the ground to the MCC—a situation that has stood the test of time since 1861. The MCC is a private organisation with 55,000 members with public responsibilities which traditionally have centred around the erection and maintenance of grandstands and other facilities for the sports followers of Melbourne. (Lill 1994, p. 29)

There has been a recent move for the Club to become more business-like. The organisation has become a lot more structured in its staffing and the need for a marketing department has been recognised and the department has been formed. The Trust consists of 21 members and is responsible to the public. They vacate their position only if: they die; reside outside the State of Victoria; resign; become incapable of acting as a trustee; or if they were appointed after the MCG Act of 1983, they reach the age of 72 years.

For legislative and lease purposes, certain incomes and expenditures of the MCC are handled through bank accounts in the name of the MCG Trust, but all of these monies are handled by Melbourne Cricket Club employees. This mainly relates to monies received and expended through the operations of the stadium and the AGOS.

Leadership

The MCC and the MCG Trust have both been led by prominent and successful business professionals throughout history. Due to the popularity and reputation of the Club and Ground, the pinnacle of politically prominent and professionally successful people have been more than willing to serve time on the Committee and or Trust. The appointment of Dr John Lill for the past decade, as General Manager, has also provided strong leadership for the Club's management team. His unique leadership ability has been noted in many of the Club's Annual Reports over the past decade. In interviews with management, low absenteeism and low turnover of staff were reported.

Financial situation

The MCC's 1993–94 financial report shows net assets of $13,198,350 and a net surplus of $262,944. The financial situation is strong, however there are $160,183,284 worth of non-current liabilities which must be repaid. The MCC is a multi-million dollar enterprise with assets of over $150 million generating more than $35 million annually.

Internal strengths and weaknesses

The MCG is a unique venue summed up by Lill in the following comment, 'It will always draw people to it, winter and summer, like no other sporting magnet in the world' (1994, p. 30). The following quotations from the 1983–84 Financial Report speaking of tourists at the ground, also support this sentiment:

> It is as though they regard the MCG as the very heart of our city . . . the predominant theme is worldwide affection for the MCG . . . I think it safe to say that the MCG meant something special to them as it does to me. (1984, p. 6)

In the same Report regarding Hans Ebling (ex MCC President), 'He saw the Club . . . as an institution of tremendous value and significance to Victoria and Australia' (1984, p. 7). Then in the following Annual Report, 'More than ever before, the MCG under lights is an international focus as a mighty symbol of Australia and its sporting heritage' (1985, p. 1).

According to 'The Strategic Planning Group' who were commissioned by the Club to advise on strategic planning in 1992, the following strengths of the MCG were identified:

- Unique
- Mythical status
- Home to two elite sports and other sports
- Historical associations
- Size, presence, stature
- Common enthusiasm for the MCG
- Location: parkland, proximity to city and other stadia
- Embarrassment of riches with unique and fascinating attractions
- Exclusiveness and prestige of the MCC
- Members goodwill, hospitality and pride
- Public affection

One of the major weaknesses mentioned was 'complex and potentially conflicting management structure: Amateur Club ↔ Professional Business (The Ground). It was also mentioned that the internal focus was on the sporting calendar, and that there was an indifference, even antipathy, to non-match activities. Another weakness revealed was the lack of financial and market data available/accessible, and the lack of a marketing focus. A marketing department has since been formed; the major focus being the development of Corporate Packages and the leasing of Corporate Suites.

Strategies

The MCC has not been focussed on formalised strategic planning. There have been several consultants employed by the Club over the years to examine and report on the strategies and structure of the Club, the most recent being the Strategic Planning Group in 1992. Currently, one of the main goals of the Club is to formalise a mission statement, objectives and a long term strategic plan.

THE MCC'S COMPETITIVE ENVIRONMENT

The **AFL** (football) and the **VCA** (cricket) are the main promoters of events. A valid weakness of the Club, as illustrated by the Strategic Planning Group Report in 1992, is 'Reputation disproportionately controlled by others, e.g., AFL, VCA, BASS (ticketing agency), Melbourne City Council'. As the events held at the MCG are under control of the promoter, the Cricket Club often receives the blame for decisions made which are out of its control. For example the AFL, as promoters of football, sets the prices and the Cricket Club's casual staff sell the tickets. The AFL insists that the ticket sellers check two identifications for all concession entries, which often causes customer aggravation aimed at the Cricket Club.

In 1989, the MCC secured an agreement with the AFL to ensure the MCG was the 'home' of football for the next forty years, this includes guaranteed events at the ground in addition to the AFL's lease of the Southern Stand offices and members' reservation. The Club also has a ten year agreement with the VCA, ensuring continued cricket matches.

Five Tenant Football Clubs (Melbourne, Richmond, North Melbourne, Essendon and Collingwood) play the majority of their home games at the Ground. This enhances ground utilisation, but causes difficulties in entry, ticketing and reservation variations for different matches, and consistency/'ownership' problems for their Club members.

Yarra Park, the MCG car park, is run by the **Melbourne City Council.** The Club has little control over how it is managed although it is part of the overall facility and as a consequence the total service experience for spectators. **Victoria Police** have an interest in public safety at the MCG and the event must pay for whatever number of Police are deemed necessary, regardless of the security personnel the Club may employ as they cannot direct the Police to carry out specific activities.

The **State Government** has major influence over the MCG. The Club is answerable to the MCG Trust which consists of delegates from government, VCA, AFL and the MCC. The Trust represents the government and the people of Melbourne and keeps a close eye on pricing structures. The State Government actively encourages major events at the MCG realising the associated tourist influx benefits for the State; even to the extent that pressure may be put on the Club to hold an event that may not be desired by management due to technical difficulties, e.g., damage to the arena surface and insufficient time to repair for upcoming cricket or football matches.

The Media influences the public perception of the MCC. Patron 'lock outs', are often reported on the news, management is often criticised by the media for a variety of reasons, articles are written which would be of little interest if not connected to the MCG. Due to this, management must consider the impact of decisions from a media perspective. This interest has also affected the MCC's position with unions, 'The MCG, with its high profile, had traditionally been an industrial target' (Lill & Wilkinson 1994, p. 3). The building of the Northern Stand for the 1956 Olympics was so plagued with industrial unrest that IOC President, Avery Brundage, threatened to transfer the Games. The media interest can also be used to the advantage of the Club, as unlike other sporting clubs, gaining media coverage when required is relatively easy.

BASS Victoria is the sole ticketing agency serving the MCG. The tickets currently produced are inferior to the high technology systems available in the United States and Europe. The limited ticket variation makes them difficult to read causing problems for both the patrons and the staff at the ground, e.g., one patron attempted to gain entry to the Ground for a concert by presenting a Bass Olympic Park car park ticket, the MCG staff on refusing entry, discovered that the patron had gained admission to the car park on presentation of his concert ticket!

Spotless Catering are the long-term contracted caterers for the MCG. The Cricket Club is ultimately responsible for the quality and quantity of their produce, and need to keep a close eye on their performance. MCC managers meet with Spotless Management on a monthly basis formally, and a weekly basis informally, to discuss any problems along with enhancing relationships and communication.

In general terms, the MCC needs to maintain close and harmonious relationships with all of the above mentioned bodies to ensure the best possible quality of service for the patrons of the MCG.

Competitors 'Whilst superficially the MCG may not appear to be operating in a competitive environment, the reality is very different' (Strategic Planning Group 1992). Competitors mentioned were: alternative Saturday afternoon activities; business conference, training and entertainment venues; tourism and entertainment providers. It competes with other Melbourne locations and events to be the landmark of the city for sponsorship and advertising dollars.

The primary **customers** are the promoters of events, currently the AFL, the VCA and various concert promoters, along with MCC members and Corporate clients. The secondary customers mainly consist of the 3 million Melburnians, along with people from all over Australia and the world. J C Lill (1994, p. 29) stated,

> Melbourne's reputation as one of the world's great sporting cities is well-deserved. In 1994 there will be three million visitors to the MCG in a city of three million people!

The macro environment

The Cricket Club is in both the entertainment and tourism industry, so changes in these areas indirectly affect the Club. The Strategic Planning Group 1992 report noted the following as influences on the Club's macro environment:

- a shift northward of commerce, industry and tourism populations;
- an ageing population, fewer youngsters;
- the success of video as easy, cheap entertainment as a new competitor;
- the growth of Victorian tourism. (In 1990/91 Victoria accommodated 12.8 million tourists; with only 0.08% of those visiting the MCG, this suggested a large potential market.)

On an international basis, the Club is influenced by **economies**, people's financial ability to travel, International Sporting Bodies; decisions of event venues (if a large international event is to occur in Melbourne it is very likely that the MCG will be a selected venue), decisions of 'mega performers' to tour Australia (if they believe they can attract over 100,000 spectators in Melbourne, chances are they would prefer to play at the MCG).

Technological advancements have had direct influences on the MCC. Major technological advances have allowed the introduction of floodlights in 1984, new scoreboards constructed in 1986 and 1994 respectively, and the successful rebuilding of the Southern Stand in 1991.

Social opinion trends have influenced decisions made by the Club. A notable example of this was the introduction of full membership for ladies in 1984. Also the decision to introduce 'smoke-free areas' at the ground which was initiated in 1991.

THE PRODUCTS

The MCC products, are not so much the sport itself, but the other parts of the package. As reported by Lill (1994, p. 30) the breakdown of income for the MCC is as follows:

Membership Subscriptions	40%
Corporate Facilities	35%
Catering Commission	12%
Share of Gate Receipts	8%
Other Income (Advertising, etc)	5%

With this in mind the products/services of the Club are defined as follows.

Primary products

■ **Membership of the Club** which avails purchasers of unlimited attendance to a prestigious and well catered for members' reserve and pavilion area, to spectate with their guests at a variety of sporting and other events. The sporting sections of the Club also offer active sport participation.

■ **Reserved area** including dining facilities for AFL members, for all AFL football and VCA cricket events.

■ **Corporate facilities** including 133 private suites available for long-term lease and numerous dining rooms for one-off usage, and seasonal packages: an exclusive and privileged alternative to view the events.

■ **Seating and standing areas for the public** to view the events held at the MCG. This can be sold as general admission, reserved seating, and in various price ranges depending on the event promoter's requirements.

■ The Club also provides the opportunity for tourists, academics, general and sport historians to view and tour **the library, the museum and Gallery of Sport.**

■ The Club also offers facilities for **meetings, dining, conferences, product launches, advertising and filming backdrops.**

Secondary products

Through the contracted caterers, a range of **food and drink** for all patrons of the MCG.

Through the promoters of events, the MCC provides a venue for **live entertainment** to foster the interests of the various patrons of the MCG.

On event days, **ancillary services** are also made available through various organisations depending on the event, e.g. programs/records, souvenirs, merchandise, various Club membership information, car parking and public transport.

THE CONSUMERS

The consumers of the MCC's products can be divided into two distinct types: Primary and Secondary. The *primary consumers* are those who have direct relationships with the MCC/MCG, that is the consumption is primarily motivated by the **desire to utilise the venue,** with less emphasis on what event is taking place. The *secondary consumers* are those who attend or use the MCG to view a particular **event or series of events** with less emphasis on where the event is taking place.

Primary consumers

- The AFL—as tenants and promoters of football
- The VCA—as promoters of cricket
- Concert promoters
- Corporate suite holders
- MCC members
- Tourists and educational groups
- MCG based football clubs—as tenants when playing as home team

Secondary consumers

- AFL members
- Public patrons
- Football club members

The secondary consumers at the MCG are generally sports fans and as stated by J. C. Lill (1994, p. 5) 'As more amenities are provided to satisfy the **sophisticated needs of the modern sports fan,** so the total capacity of the ground must be reduced'.

SUMMARY

The Melbourne Cricket Club for many years has been a product of its environment. In the sporting industry, planning and formulating marketing strategies have not been prevalent. As the MCC is a sporting club, albeit a special type of club, it too has neglected to formulate and implement strategies to ensure its future strength. It could be argued that the perceived strengths of the club led to a level of complacency. By the 1990s, however, this began to change. The MCC must develop an integrated marketing strategy. Perhaps you can suggest a process which the MCC should follow to develop an adequate marketing strategy.

Source: Reprinted from McLoughlin (1994).

Questions

1   Which mission statement do you think best reflects the MCC's reason for existence? You may like to write your own if those contained in the case study are not considered satisfactory.

2   What advantages would a club such as the MCC gain from undertaking the strategic sport-marketing planning process (SSMPP)?
3   Is there evidence of marketing strategy in terms of the club's operations? Why or why not?
4   Describe why the public relations component of the sport promotion mix will be critical in the club's marketing strategy.
5   What other marketing mix variables may be important? Why? Discuss the relative importance of each, and also examine possible ways in which these variables could be used to develop a marketing strategy.

REFERENCES

Boyd, H. W. and Walker, O. C. (1990). *Marketing Management: a Strategic Approach*, Irwin, Homewood, Ill.

Burchett, J. (1996). *News Limited v Australian Rugby League Limited and Others, NG 197 of 1995*, Federal Court of Australia, Sydney.

Kotler, P., Chandler, P., Gibbs, R. and McColl, R. (1989). *Marketing in Australia*, 2nd edn, Prentice-Hall, Englewood Cliffs, NJ.

Lill, J. C. (1994). 'The modern coliseum', *Panstadia International*, 2 (2), 28–30.

Lill, J. C. and Wilkinson, D. K. (1994). 'The Great Southern Stand at the Melbourne Cricket Ground: anatomy of an effective project delivery system', *The MCC News*, Melbourne Cricket Club, pp. 1–4.

McLoughlin, J. (1994). 'The Melbourne Cricket Club—a case for marketing strategy', unpublished, Deakin University, Melbourne.

Pesky, G. (1995). 'SGMA council serves up week long volley across America', *Sporting Goods Business*, 28 (4), p. 22.

Strategic Planning Group (1992). *Interim Report on Building a Strategic Vision for the MCG*, Melbourne.

The Economist (1994). 'New kicks from Korea', 333 (7889), p. 121.

Credits

The authors gratefully acknowledge material which has been reprinted in *Strategic Sport Marketing* from other sources. Every attempt has been made to contact the copyright holders of this material.

Figure 2.3 Forces driving industry competition. Reprinted with the permission of The Free Press, a Division of Simon & Schuster, from *Competitive Advantage: Creating and Sustaining Superior Performance*, by Michael E. Porter. Copyright © 1985 by Michael E. Porter.

Sportview 2.1 AFL goes for the gap. From Case, B. (1996). 'AFL goes for the gap', *The Bulletin*, 27 February, pp. 92–3. Reprinted with the permission of *The Bulletin*.

Sportview 2.2 Footscray kicks back. From McMinn, I. (1992). 'Footscray kicks back', *The Bulletin*, 31 March, pp. 46–8. Reprinted with the permission of *The Bulletin*.

Chapter 2 case study. From Massey, M. (1995). 'Cricket creates its own playing field', *Business Review Weekly*, 20 November, pp. 87–9. Reprinted with the permission of *Business Review Weekly*.

Figure 4.3 The sport industry segment model. From Pitts, B., Fielding, L. and Miller, L. (1994). 'Industry segmentation and the sport industry: developing a sport industry segment model', *Sport Marketing Quarterly*, 3 (1), p. 18.

Chapter 4 case study. From Stanton, W., Miller, K. and Layton, R. (1995). *Fundamentals of Marketing*, 3rd edn, McGraw-Hill, Sydney. Reprinted with the permission of McGraw-Hill.

Sportview 5.1 A winning game plan. From Macnow, G. (1990). 'A winning game plan', *Nation's Business*, March, pp. 82–4. Reprinted by permission, *Nation's Business*, March 1990. Copyright © 1990, US Chamber of Commerce.

Table 5.1 Understanding the nature of the service act. From Lovelock, C. H. (1991). *Services Marketing*, 2nd edn, Prentice-Hall, Englewood Cliffs, NJ, p. 26. Reprinted with the permission of Prentice-Hall, Inc., Upper Saddle River, NJ.

Figure 5.1 Customer assessment of service quality. Reprinted with the permission of The Free Press, a Division of Simon & Schuster, from *Delivering Service Quality: Balancing Customer Perceptions and Expectations*, by Valarie A. Zeithaml, A. Parasuraman and Leonard L. Berry. Copyright © 1990 by The Free Press.

Chapter 5 case study. From Gladman, M. and Cross, D., 'The tradition continues—the Australian Masters', completed as part of studies towards the authors' Graduate Diploma of Sport Management at Deakin University. Reprinted with the permission of the authors.

Sportview 6.1 AFL kicks a goal on marketing strategy. From Henderson, I. (1996). 'AFL kicks a goal on marketing strategy', *The Australian*, 23 July, p. 5. Copyright © *The Australian*. Ian Henderson is Economics Correspondent at *The Australian*. Reprinted with the permission of *The Australian* and the author.

Chapter 6 case study. From Cockerill, M. (1996). 'The high price of being there', *Sydney Morning Herald*, 5 April, p. 32. Reprinted with the permission of the author.

Figure 7.1 Promotion strategy. From Cravens, D. W. (1994). *Strategic Marketing*, 4th edn, Irwin, Ill.

Sportview 7.1 Nabisco blankets Canada with card promotion. From *Team Marketing Report* (1992). 'Nabisco blankets Canada with card promotion', 5 (1), October, pp. 3–4.

Figure 7.3 The frequency escalator for sport attendance and participation. From Mullin, B. (1985) 'Internal marketing—a more effective way to sell sport', in *Successful Sport Management*, eds G. Lewis and H. Appenzellar, Michie Co., Charlottesville, Va., p. 163. Reprinted with the permission of Michie, Charlottesville, Va., in conjunction with LEXIS-NEXIS.

Chapter 7 case study. From White, J. and Grant, C. H. B. (1985). 'Report on NCAA record crowd', University of Iowa, Women's Athletic Program, Athletic Department Publication. Reprinted with the permission of the authors.

Figure 8.1 The advertising management process. From O'Hara, B. and Weese, W. J., (1994). "Advertising theory applied to the intramural—recreation sports environment', *Sport Marketing* Quarterly, 3 (1), p. 11.

Table 9.2 Sunday night NSWRL ratings 1992 and *Figure 9.2 Wide World of Sports Telecast Guide for the Australian Formula 1 Grand Prix, Adelaide 1993.* From GTV Nine (1993). *Wide World of Sports Telecast Guide*, Melbourne.

Chapter 9 case study. From Mandese, J. (1994). 'Murdoch adds football to list of global ambitions', *Advertising Age*, 65 (25), p. 13. Reprinted with the permission of *Advertising Age* © 1994, Crain Communications Inc.

Figure 10.1 Areas of sponsorship expenditure (US) in 1984 and 1992. From Lyall, S. (1995). 'Cause and effect', *Sponsorship and Events News*, May, p. 24.

Sportview 10.1 Marketing Michael. From Hay, D. (1996). 'Jordan plays the money game', *Sunday Age*, 26 May, p. 18; and Naughton, J. (1992). 'Marketing Michael: the making of a commercial superstar', *Washington Post Magazine*, 9 February, pp. 11—29.

Sportview 10.2 Ambush marketing at the Olympics. From Sandler, D. M. and Shani, D. (1989). 'Olympic sponsorship vs. "Ambush" marketing: who gets the gold?', *Journal of Advertising Research*, August/September, pp. 9–14. Reprinted with the permission of *Journal of Advertising Research*, © 1989 by the Advertising Research Foundation.

Sportview 11.1 The Great Dunlop squash racquet. From Greener, T. (1990). *The Secrets of Successful Public Relations and Image-making*, Butterworth/Heinemann, Oxford. Reprinted with the permission of the publisher.

Sportview 11.2 Riley facing drugs ban. From Jeffery, N. (1996). 'Riley facing drugs ban', *The Australian*, 13 February, p. 24, © *The Australian*; and Magnay, J. (1996). 'IOC steps in over Riley ban', *The Age*, 14 February, p. B12.

Sportview 11.3 Shane Kelly press release. From Woodhouse Management (1996). 'Cyclist Shane Kelly launches five year sponsorship deal', Press release, 9 August. Reprinted with the permission of Woodhouse Management.

Chapter 11 case study. From Oakley, R. (1996). 'Racism: new rule', *Football Record*, Round 13, 30 June – 2 July, pp. 3/9. Reprinted with the permission of the publisher.

Sportview 12.1 The rugby union 'All Blacks/Wallabies/Springboks' video game. From Schaaf, P. (1995). *Sports Marketing: It's Not Just a Game Anymore*, Prometheus Books, Amherst, NY. Copyright © 1995. Reprinted with the permission of the publisher.

Sportview 12.2 Sport team logos are big business. From Lans, M. S. (1995). 'Sports team logos are big business', *Marketing News*, 29 (12), 5 June, p. 6. Reprinted with the permission of the American Marketing Association.

Table 12.1 Use of elements of an operational protocol for sport licensing programs. From Irwin, R. L. and Stotlar, D. K. (1993). 'Operational protocol analysis of sport and collegiate licensing programs', *Sport Marketing Quarterly*, 2 (1), pp. 7–16. Reprinted with the permission of the publisher.

Figure 12.1 Building the sporting organisation's licensing program. From Baghdikian, E. (1996). 'Building the sporting organisation's merchandise licensing program: the appropriateness, significance, and considerations', *Sport Marketing Quarterly*, 5 (1), pp. 35–41. Reprinted with the permission of the publisher.

Sportview 12.3 Minor leagues get major support. From Bernstein, A. (1996). 'Minor leagues get major support', *Sporting Goods Business*, February, p. 34. Reprinted with the permission of the author.

Chapter 12 case study. Written by E. Baghdikian and not previously published. Printed with the permission of the author.

Figure 13.2 Conceptual model of service quality. From Parasuraman, A., Zeithaml, V. A. and Berry, L. L. (1985). 'A conceptual model of service quality and its implications for future research', *Journal of Marketing*, 49, Fall, pp. 41–50. Reprinted with the permission of the American Marketing Association.

Sportview 13.1 The importance of the servicescape for sport consumers. From Bitner, M. 0J. (1992). 'Servicescapes: the impact of physical surrounding on customers and employees', *Journal of Marketing*, 56 (2), pp. 57–71, reprinted with the permission of the American Marketing Association; and Wakefield, K. L. and Blodgett, J. G. (1994). 'The importance of servicescapes in leisure service settings', *Journal of Services Marketing*, 8 (3), pp. 66–76, reprinted with the permission of the publisher.

Figure 13.3 The sport servuction system. From Langerd, E., Bateson, J., Lovelock, C. and Eiglier, P. (1981). *Services Marketing: New Insights from Consumers and Managers*, Report 81–104, Marketing Science Institute, Cambridge, Mass. Reprinted with the permission of the publisher.

Chapter 13 case study. From Spangler, I. (1994). 'Game, set and match', *Panstandia International*, 2 (2), pp. 24–8; and National Institute of Economic and Industry Research (1995). 'An economic impact study', in *Survey and Analysis of the 1995 Ford Australian Open*, prepared for Tennis Australia, Melbourne/Clifton Hill.

Sportview 14.1 New kicks from Korea. From *The Economist* (1994). 'New kicks from Korea', 333 (7889), p. 121. Reprinted with the permission of the publisher.

Chapter 14 case study. McLoughlin, J. (1994). 'The Melbourne Cricket Club—a case for marketing strategy', unpublished, Deakin University, Melbourne.

Index

Page numbers in **bold** indicate the definition of term.